OUT OF THE TIGER'S MOUTH

Out of the Tiger's Mouth

The autobiography of
Malcolm Phipps 7th Dan

eMPi Publishing
Hemel Hempstead
Hertfordshire
England

First Edition
Copyright © 2009 Malcolm Phipps

Printed by:

Direct Print On Demand Ltd
Saxon Fields
Old Harborough Road
Brixworth
Northamptonshire NN6 9BX
www.direct-pod.com

British Library Cataloguing-in-Publication Data.
A Catalogue record for this book is available from the British Library.

ISBN 978-0-9519835-2-2

Acknowledgements

The author and eMPi Publishing are grateful to the following people for their excellent help in the publication of this book:

Dave Hazard for the wonderful *Foreword* but more importantly his friendship.

Stephanie Farrer for all her hard work in editing and putting the book together.

Jim Stouffer of *Stouffer's Photography* for the brilliant cover photographs.

Ron Shelley and Emma Rowe at *Rainbow Printing Services Limited*.

Steve Hudson at *Deadline Reprographic and Printing Services*.

Dale Burgess at *Direct Print on Demand* for the printing of this masterpiece.

To Winter,

This book is number   158

of a Limited First Edition of 250 signed copies.

Best wishes.

Malcolm Phipps

Dedicated to my Lord, without whom my life and
therefore this book would not have taken place.

Foreword

I met Malcolm Phipps many years ago through our shared love of martial arts and in a world where martial arts instructors often have egos far larger than their ability. Malcolm epitomises the meaning of that saying: 'The more you know, the less you need to show'.

Malcolm's ability as a karate exponent commands respect from his peers and his students alike and he is a teacher of the highest calibre. His exceptional teaching talent has produced an outstanding group of karate students and instructors. His integrity and dedication shine through his karate as they do his life. He doesn't shout about his ability or success and is a great example of an unpretentious man, in strength of mind, body and spirit, which all who know him admire. He has the qualities that we all aspire to. Add to this a great sense of humour and an open and honest heart and all in all you have a pretty special human being.

Life throws all of us some bad stuff from time to time and Malcolm has had his share. It is those difficult times that reveal the character within and Malcolm has faced his own hurdles head-on and with his usual quiet fortitude.

As with his previous books, Malcolm's easy style of writing makes for a wonderful read. Having shared many meals, drinks, laughs, good and bad times with him over the years, I am sure, like me, you will enjoy reading more about this wonderful man's rich and adventurous life.

Malcolm is a true gentleman and I am proud to call him my friend.

Dave Hazard 7th Dan
Chief Instructor to the Academy of Shotokan Karate.
August 2009

Introduction

I was going to originally name this book, *In Nakayama's Nightmares*, in a similar vein to my first instructor's autobiography, John Van Weenen's, *In Funakoshi's Footsteps* but thought this might look a little bit like copying, so now we have, *Out of the Tiger's Mouth*. I thought this was an appropriate title, as the tiger is a symbol of Shotokan karate worldwide and I thought the cover photograph was excellent. Also I couldn't think of a suitable cover photograph for the book's original title, *In Nakayama's Nightmares*, especially as Nakayama sensei is one of my karate heroes and I wouldn't like to be disrespectful to his memory in any way, shape or form.

So here we have it, my life's story. Sometimes comical, sometimes boring, sometimes very sad but I hope reasonably entertaining. I have done things I am not proud of and things that I am proud of but please do not judge me on the past, as what you have now, is the real me. I hope I have not upset anybody by writing this book but have told the truth, as I remember it. There are bits of my life that I could easily have left out but what's the point in writing an autobiography if you're not going to tell the truth and only leave the good bits in?

I hope you enjoy it and thank you for taking the time to read it.

Malcolm Phipps

In the Beginning!

Birth

It was a damp and cold mid December night as the pregnant woman arrived at the Inn, only to be informed that there were no vacancies. (No womb at the Inn)! She was about to give birth and panic had started to set in. What should she do? Where could she find shelter for the night? Perhaps a stable! But no, as luck had it a kind and generous couple let her stay for the night in their nursing home.I knew nothing of the above as I was ensconced in the warmth and safety of my mother's womb.Later, on the very next day she gave birth to the infant baby, MALCOLM who was clothed in swaddling clothes and lying in a manger! People sang special anthems and lights were put up in windows and on the outside of houses. Trees were beautifully decorated and everyone bought presents for each other. Sadly, this had absolutely nothing to do with the birth of the infant baby Malcolm but heralded a baby boy born nearly two thousand years before and one that I would come to know more personally much later in my life.

No, it was not Bethlehem but Torquay on the so-called English Riviera. The year was not Zero AD but 1942 AD and my mum, Hilda had been evacuated (thanks to dear Adolf) to a nursing home in Torre, Torquay to give birth to her first son, yours truly, the infant baby, Malcolm Richard Moran/Dorey/Phipps (I will explain the three surnames thing a little later).It was not the birth of a child that would change the face of the world but of a child that would be the scourge of the seven seas, the Hertfordshire town of Hemel Hempstead and karate dojos throughout the world and just about roughly in that order!

I didn't know much about the next few months as most of my time was taken up by filling nappies, being fed and watered, and trying to mouth the word, mama. I am told I grinned a lot, ate and drank a lot, tried to talk and mumble a lot of unintelligible rubbish and crapped and pissed a lot. Nothing much has really changed!

And so a new life had begun. But where and who was Daddy? I found out much, much later, approximately a couple of weeks before joining the Royal Navy to

My earliest photocall!
With my mum at 2 weeks old!

11

be exact. My mum had decided it was time to spill the beans before her first born, now fifteen and a half years of age, became a real man and sailed around the world on the Grey Funnel Line. It turned out that my blood father was a certain Thomas Moran, an Irish Guardsman stationed in London during the earlier part of the war. Mum had had a wartime romance with him and nine months later who should pop along but yours truly. The only sad part to this wonderful romance was that he was already married and had a family in Kilkenny in Ireland, unbeknown to mum at the time, and to which he hastily beat a quick retreat.

What a bastard! Sadly, the only person who was a real bastard was me!

Wealdstone (1943-1953)

After the first few months of my life in Torquay, we returned to live with mum's parents, my nan and grandad, Joseph and Gertrude Dorey in the Middlesex town of Wealdstone (part of Harrow if you're posh)! And so my first name was to be Malcolm Dorey but later in life I quite fancied Mal Moran as it sounded much more like a professional footballer, or an actor or pop star of great repute. My first recollections of life at, 37 Talbot Road in Wealdstone, were of a man in an army uniform who carried a huge gun, which I was forbidden to touch and which I was told many years later was a .303 rifle. Indeed this is the first thing I can honestly remember in my whole life. It was 1945 and the war was just coming to an end. I liked the man in the khaki uniform immensely as he brought with him wonderful gifts. My favourite of these was a small wooden train that was beautifully handmade in Germany, where I was told this man had spent the last few weeks with the conquering British army. The

The man in the khaki uniform - my wonderful dad to be!

man was, George Henry Phipps, an ex-miner from Stonebroom in Derbyshire and a gunner in the Royal Artillery, who had spent a lot of the war in Burma and finally in Germany. He was my mum's new sweetheart and it wasn't hard to see why. He was immensely strong for his small size and wonderfully kind. I loved him to bits and as luck had it he was to become the man I knew for the rest of my life as dad.

Unbeknown to my good self, my mum had married this wonderful man at a registry office wedding, and on the 17th April 1945, at Wealdstone Petty Sessions Court, I was fully adopted by George Henry Phipps for the princely sum of sixteen shillings. And so, Malcolm Richard Phipps came to be. Later in my life my mum told me that my dad cried as we came out of the Petty Sessions Court and picked me up and said, 'You are all mine now'. So, I could've been called Malcolm Richard Moran, was definitely called Malcolm Richard Dorey for a while and was now Malcolm

Richard Phipps. So what's in a name? I seemed to have more aliases than bloody Jack the Ripper. Not bad for just over two years on the planet!

A few years later I found out to my utter joy that my new dad was an excellent footballer, and before the war had started in 1939, had played for Matlock Town FC and was on Derby County's books as an excellent right winger. Sadly, with a young wife and family to look after and now six years older, the war had taken its toll, and dad playing serious football became a thing of the past. He played a couple of times for the local London Transport team but that was it. His passion for football remained with him for the rest of his life and he fervently supported Sheffield United and Wolverhampton Wanderers, and most definitely in that order.

Still looking good at 17 months!

Life was wonderful at Wealdstone. My nan and grandad absolutely idolised me and I them in return. As there was an apparent lack of coalfaces and mines in Middlesex, dad had gained a job as a bus conductor with London Transport and worked out of the Watford Garage for London Country Buses, (the green ones). This was exciting for a young boy, as Wealdstone and the surrounding districts only ever witnessed the red double-decker buses and my dad only ever worked on the wonderful green ones and this fact made him even more special. Over the next few years dad would take me out on his bus every once in a while and this was the greatest experience in the world for a young lad. He would let me ring the bell for the bus to restart after stopping at a bus stop. When it wasn't too busy he would let me walk round with him and punch the ticket machine hanging around his neck that made a hole in the ticket at the appropriate place and gave out a wonderful dinging sound as you pressed the little silver lever. Joy of joys! I can still hear his

37 Talbot Rd. Wealdstone,
with grandad's white Rolls Royce van outside!

My lovely nan and grandad,
much later in life in Hemel Hempstead

voice shouting such delights as, 'Any more fares please?' and 'Plenty of room on top'. My favourite trips were the 355 bus to Windsor, where I used to look in awe at the wonderful castle and the River Thames, with my second favourite the 347 route to Hemel Hempstead (which of course would later be our home). He had a wonderful driver called Stan, who was a large man and who I thought was brilliant and made the bus go very fast when he knew I was looking through the window which separated him from the passengers.

Grandad in turn, was one of the top car mechanics at the Rolls-Royce factory in Willesden, North London and although he didn't come home in anything so grand, on a couple of days a week his little white van could be seen outside our house in Talbot Road. In the main though, he would commute on the train from Harrow and Wealdstone to Willesden Junction as the van was the property of Rolls-Royce and he was only allowed to bring it home twice a week. Every once in a while he would take me to work in it and I sat proudly on two occasions in the actual Rolls-Royce of King George VI. He would sit me in the back of the car amongst all the cut glass decanters and glasses, plush leather seats and purple ermine surrounds and then send the car up on to the ramp. I surveyed all my subjects and gave them a royal wave from my lofty perch and had all the workers at the factory in fits. My dad and my grandad were my early heroes.

Grandad's shed in the back garden was an absolute treasure chest of little boy's delights. He had a German bayonet in there, a trophy from the First World War, which he used for levering off paint pot lids! Of course I was not allowed to play with this, even though it was now rusty and blunt it could still cause some serious harm. There was a selection of gas masks in case of gas attack from Hitler's friends, the Luftwaffe. My one was in the shape of Mickey Mouse but every time I put it on the lenses would annoyingly mist up and many was the time I used to fall over or bump into things with this dreaded contraption on my head. I looked like a sad reject from the Walt Disney studios.

My first love in sport was when my grandad and dad took me to watch my first ever football match.It was at the Lower Mead football ground, (sadly, the last I heard it was a Tesco's supermarket – what sacrilege) and was the home ground for the Athenian League team of Wealdstone FC. It was Boxing Day and they played Hendon FC, their local rivals. We walked from our house in Wealdstone to the Lower Mead ground, over the Harrow and Wealdstone railway bridge and where Wealdstone joined up with

Anyone for cricket!
Forever the sportsman!

Wealdstone FC versus Hendon FC (my first football match as a spectator)!

Harrow. (A bridge incidentally, that came crashing down on 8th October 1952 in one of the worst train disasters of the 20th century in England. Two express passenger trains crashed into a commuter train at the station and as a result 112 died and 150 were seriously injured. My grandad, who should've been at the actual station, waiting for his train to Willesden Junction at the very time of the crash, was late out of bed that morning and arrived at the station around fifteen minutes after the horrendous disaster had taken place. I think someone from above was looking after him).

We mixed with the rushing crowd and eventually made our way through the turnstiles, where grandad and dad both bought a programme (one of which I still own today). What a wonderful sight! I think I stood on the terraces with my mouth open for the whole ninety minutes only to change in to chewing mode when my grandad handed me the odd toffee. At half-time we queued at the small café in the ground and drank piping hot Bovril and devoured a small packet of Smith's crisps each, gossiping about the antics of the first forty-five minutes and eagerly awaiting the second half.

What a wonderful experience, especially as Wealdstone FC won the match and this fuelled my love for this brilliant game of football. I already knew at such a tender age what I wanted to be when I grew up. I now attended most of the home games against many teams from the same division and of course the wonderful cup games. Magical names for me in those early days. Teams such as, Hendon FC, Tooting & Mitcham, Pegasus FC, Corinthian Casuals, Edgware Town, Wembley, Finchley, Walthamstow Avenue, Sutton United, Walton & Hersham and Southall. My dreams eventually came true when in the 1950/1 season and to my utter joy we won the Athenian League. Much later in 1966, the only year that England won the coveted World Cup, another momentous occasion happened in the footballing world. We beat our fierce rivals Hendon FC in the Amateur Cup Final at Wembley 3-1 but by this historic date I had been in the Royal Navy for quite a few years.

1954 though was the highlight of my young footballing experiences. Wolves were the champions of England for the 1953/4 season and my grandad took me to my first match at Wembley. It was the Amateur Cup Final

Standing proud in my Wealdstone FC kit - Eat your heart out Ronaldo!

15

and although it didn't feature Wealdstone FC, it was an unforgettable experience. The match was on April 10th, 1954 and was between Bishop Auckland, the favourites, and Crook Town, two clubs from the north- east of England. I immediately took to Crook Town, as guess what? They played in yellow and black similar to my beloved Wolves. The score was 2-2 and it was a brilliant experience and eventually Crook Town won the replay 1-0 a week or two later.

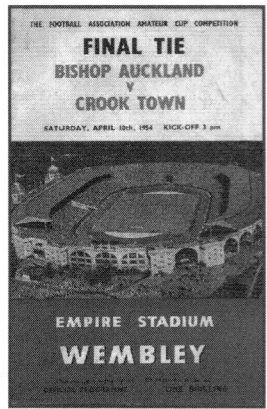

THE FOOTBALL ASSOCIATION AMATEUR CUP COMPETITION

FINAL TIE

BISHOP AUCKLAND

v

CROOK TOWN

SATURDAY, APRIL 10th, 1954   KICK-OFF 3 pm

Wolves also played what were to be named the Floodlight Friendlies. England had just been hammered by Hungary 6-3 and was their first ever defeat at Wembley but Wolves regained English pride by beating Honved of Hungary at Molineux 3-2. Honved hosted nearly all of the top Hungarian players including the wonderful captain of

EMPIRE STADIUM

WEMBLEY

My first trip to Wembley Stadium

Hungary, Ferenc Puskas. Wolves went on to beat the likes of Moscow Dynamo, Moscow Spartak, Real Madrid and Red Banner of Hungary. Wonderful matches watched by my dad and me on our little black and white television.

Going back a little and when I was five years of age another earth-shaking occasion took place. On the 30th of December 1947, my little brother, Martin was born. I had wondered for months why mum was getting fatter and was told many times that she was carrying a baby in her tummy but at the tender age of nearly five I hadn't a clue what these grown-ups were talking about. Two things I vividly remember about Martin John Phipps and that was that he cried a lot and for some unknown reason was very prone to severe nosebleeds. They would just start for no apparent reason and would scare the living daylights out of me. I had never

seen so much blood and each time I thought he was about to die. But as he grew older he became a great companion and to my utter joy, (and of course his) the dreaded nosebleeds ceased. We had our differences of course and the ancient art of brotherly love showed itself on many occasions. Two of the biggest differences between us were, he hated football with a passion and he had straight hair as opposed to my curly mop. But no matter what, (for I couldn't understand for the life of me how anyone couldn't like soccer) I loved him dearly. Much later in life I found out the reason for the differing hairstyles.

When Martin was old enough we used to play Cowboys and Indians in the garden and in the allotment at the back, with Martin as Roy Rogers and me as the fearsome Apache Indian, Geronimo. It was on one of

Me and Martin with nan in my Geronimo days!

these games that I actually shot my brother in the forehead with a homemade bow and arrow whilst playing in the allotment. I panicked as I thought I had killed him with the arrow, which just missed his eyes. Needless to say, my parents and grandparents were not amused and snapped the offending bow and arrows in front of me before sending me to my room for the rest of the day. This was my first real telling-off in life and I have to say, I didn't like it one bit. Luckily enough no real damage had been done and it was just a flesh wound. My brother didn't hold me accountable and proclaimed that it was just an accident, which was admirable but my days as Geronimo had sadly come to an end. From that moment on I became Billy the Kid! A bit of a come down from scalping to gun-fights! At least the six-gun on my hip didn't fire any real missiles, unless of course, I actually threw it at my brother!

Christmas was another occasion to behold in Wealdstone and indeed is one of my most cherished memories of my childhood. On Christmas day every year I would religiously awake at the ridiculous time of 4am after an extremely restless night waiting for a large, bearded, and jolly man in a big red suit to appear, only to be told to go back to bed for another hour at least. Martin slept in my mum and dad's room all the time we lived at Wealdstone, firstly in a cot and then in a small bed in a far corner of their room. After an hour of torment and at 5am on the dot I would race headlong into nan and grandad's bedroom, where the whole family gathered every Christmas morning at this unheard of hour. The small gas fire was lit and dad would go off and make the tea. On his arrival with tray in hand we got down to the serious business of the opening of the magical presents, spread out on nan and grandad's bed. I was by now a staunch Wolverhampton Wanderers and Wealdstone FC supporter. I had made the choice of Wolves over Sheffield United as I liked the colours of old gold and black much better than the red and white stripes of Sheffield United (or The Blades as my dad constantly called them). Anyway, Wolves was a much cooler nickname than The Blades! Of course, Wolves being the best team in England and probably Europe at that time had no bearing on the matter whatsoever! It was destined to be one of the two teams that my dear dad supported, as with the kids of today, they are suitably but nicely brainwashed by their dads into who they WILL support. Luckily enough with my dad though, I had a choice.

Every year I received the wonderful Football Diary with pictures and statistics of all the famous players and teams of the day. One Christmas I received a Wolves bobble hat, kindly knitted for me by my dear mum and was my pride and joy and was taken just about every where with me (including the loo but sadly not the bath). Each year and without fail I would receive football kit of various kinds and one year even a shirt of my beloved amateur heroes, Wealdstone FC. Another year a full-sized football, along with the pump and adaptor to inflate it awaited me and I remember hurriedly ripping off the paper, hoping and praying that it wasn't a huge bloody orange. Hanging at the bottom of the bed was the Christmas stocking and this was filled with small goodies, which were mainly of the confectionery variety

Easy Rider! My first ever bike.

and right down the very bottom of the stocking there lay the inevitable tangerine. (I remember thinking that it had probably taken it all night to struggle to the bottom of the stocking, for without fail and every single year, there it was – Christmas stocking ballast!) I remember on one of these magical Christmas days receiving my first bike. I think I was about four or five years old and it was a black three-wheeled affair and was my pride and joy for the next two or three years. I felt like a king.

When I was five years old I started school. The school was Belmont First School in Hibbert Road, Wealdstone and I loved those early years with the kind old lady teachers, learning how to draw and paint and do up your shoelaces. It was here in the juniors that I was to meet the first love of my life and by far the prettiest girl in the school. Her name was Carol Thorne and she lived at 19 Weston Drive in Wealdstone (a stone's throw from Belmont Circle and shops). She was an extremely beautiful nine year old blonde and I had my first playground fight over her and still remember the fight vividly. It was against a boy in my class, Malcolm King and to my utter surprise I won. Very few punches were thrown and certainly no kicks. It just involved a lot of wrestling about on the playground tarmac but eventually I made him submit. I remember walking in to the classroom after the playtime period was over and was clapped and cheered by the whole class. After the playground fight another girl in my class now fancied sharing her lunches with me and asked me round to her parent's house in Mountbel Road to see her postage stamp collection. Her name was Anne Pragnell and I would play one off against the other in a sadistic sort of way of making them both like me even more. I thought this fighting skylark was definitely the business until my next skirmish, where I was suitably battered and this changed my mind very quickly and I promptly chose Carol as she was much prettier. The boys used to play football in the playground at every conceivable opportunity. Two coats were placed on the floor either end of the playground and so the matches began. I still remember a couple of their names all these many years ahead. Derek Eddy and Barry Cotton were the two stars and along with my good self made up the school's top players in this playground arena.

Another boy in my class was Eddie Smith and a few years later he amazingly appeared in my class in Adeyfield Secondary Modern School in Hemel Hempstead. Quite a coincidence for a young boy but with Hemel Hempstead new town being built as an overflow town for Greater London, then I suppose it was no great surprise.

I absolutely adored my time at Wealdstone but sadly, at ten years of age and on 3rd September 1953 we moved to the new town of Hemel Hempstead in Hertfordshire.

Hemel Hempstead (1953 – 1958)

Leaving behind me all that I held dear in life was a huge wrench for a boy of only ten years. I had to make a whole new set of friends at a new school and get to know our neighbours and their children. I had to say goodbye to my childhood sweetheart, Carol and farewell to my beloved Wealdstone FC.

Hemel Hempstead FC weren't bad but not in the same league (literally) as Wealdstone FC. At my new school, Maylands Junior School in Adeyfield, I made friends and enemies relatively quickly. I wasn't a bad little footballer and after a couple of practice matches found myself in the school team. This was great for me but not for the boy whose place I had taken. He took an instant dislike to me and if he could humiliate me in anyway he would certainly try. But this died a natural death quite quickly as being ten years and ten months old it was nearly time to change schools and take the dreaded eleven plus examination. This is where he got his own back as he was certainly brighter than me. He passed his exams easily and was enrolled at Hemel Hempstead Grammar School. I failed my exams with honours and found myself enrolled at Adeyfield Secondary Modern. This wasn't too bad really as this school was situated at the end of the road that we lived in, Windmill Road, and I could walk there in five minutes. Also, most of my mates in the football team also were found academically wanting and joined me at good old Adeyfield Sec. Mod.

One small thrill was to meet my dad just over the road from the school where Windmill Road joined Longlands. This was where the green, double-decker, number 302 Routemaster bus terminated in Hemel Hempstead and turned round before making the journey back the other way to Watford Heath. The crew would have a small break before taking the bus to its other destination. My dad and his new driver, Bob Goss were often on this route and on my way to school I would sometimes meet them and join them on the downstairs backseats, sharing the odd boiled sweet or toffee with them and talking mainly about football. Like my good self with the change of schools, dad had had to change garages and now worked out of Two Waters Bus Garage in Hemel Hempstead, hence the new driver, Bob.Sadly, dad's first driver Stan from Watford passed away with a heart attack a few years later, a sad loss as he was a lovely man.

My dad was well known in London Transport circles and especially in the Hemel Hempstead and Watford areas. He had won, on many occasions the overall London Transport snooker and billiards titles. One year the prize was a beautiful cutlery set and the chance to play a frame against the then current world snooker champion, John Pulman. This match took place at the Hammersmith Odeon in front of a packed house but needless to say John Pulman defeated my dad relatively easily and this was after giving him a fifty point lead! My dad was a brilliant player, so how good must've John Pulman been! Well of course he was the best in the world but I was even luckier, I had the best dad in the world. Dad then went on to win, year after year, these titles at his local garage and indeed the darts

Dad (centre) London Transport champion!

title as well. He used to joke that it was the sign of a misspent youth. He also played darts for local pub teams each week, first for the 'Patch' (Post Office Arms) in Boxmoor and then later for the 'Boot' and the 'Albion' pub teams. Mum, on the other hand worked as a hospital receptionist for many years at the then West Herts Hospital in Hillfield Road in Hemel Hempstead and then at a doctor's surgery in the neighbouring town of Berkhamsted.

Before this though, mum and dad took in lodgers from the Addressograph – Multigraph Corporation factory in the Industrial Estate in Hemel Hempstead. These chaps would come from all over the world for a six week refresher course and would stay in local lodgings for this period. We had some real characters staying with us at 84 Windmill Road. Some were fun and some were boring but in the main they were a good laugh. One or two were football freaks and used to take me to top matches on Saturdays. We visited White Hart Lane and Highbury on regular occasions and I was in seventh heaven when Spurs or Arsenal played my beloved Wolves. We had one chap called Ken who had actually been on the books at Wolves for a while but hadn't quite made it. I used to go up the park daily and play football with him and my mates but he was in a different class to us. For six weeks he was my hero as he talked about the famous players he used to see at Molineux. England internationals such as, Billy Wright the captain of England, Ron Flowers soon to become the captain of England, Bert Williams, Johnny Hancocks, Bill Slater, Jimmy Mullen, Peter Broadbent and Dennis Wilshaw all of whom played for England at one time or another. Not bad, to say the least, eight England internationals all in one team and not one foreign player. Well, there was one South African but that was all. A little different from today's game, with the import of so many foreign players and the gigantic wage differences. These guys in the mid-fifties wouldn't earn a year what some players now get per week. And remember, at this time Wolves were the best in the country and probably in Europe as well. How times have changed.

It was when these refresher courses at Addressograph – Multigraph Corp. seemed to dry up that my mum became one of the receptionists at the local hospital. I was very lucky as they were absolutely wonderful parents and worked all their adult lives to give a good home to my brother Martin and me.

School though, was average. I cannot say that I enjoyed my school years at all and in all truthfulness couldn't wait to escape the daily boredom of Maths, History and Geography etc. The only two subjects that I really enjoyed was PE of any kind, mainly football of course, as I was playing for the school team, and strangely enough English. The main reason for these two particular subjects coming to the fore was that both subjects had brilliant teachers. The PE teacher was a Mr. Taylor, who actually played for Hemel Hempstead FC and the English teacher was a Mr. Webb. Both made the lessons really interesting and this was a lesson I would hopefully take into my teaching skills in my karate life many, many years later. The only other subject that I used to receive an 'A' for on my school report was RI or religious instruction. Someone up there must've been looking out for me, as this along with PE and English were the only subjects that I didn't get the usual, 'Must try harder', on the dreaded annual school report.

It is amazing though in hindsight, that the subjects that had really great teachers and that I enjoyed so much would take up a huge part of my life and make me what I am today. First it was football but then even more importantly karate, which let's be honest is most definitely a physical pursuit and I have also been lucky enough to have had half a dozen books published. Again, much later in my life I would become a Christian, so perhaps the plans and the map of my life were well and truly laid in my school years. But nevertheless, I still didn't enjoy school!

I had, probably, like a lot of lads my age started to mix with what my mum termed, rightly or wrongly, as the wrong crowd. And so it was that when I was very nearly fourteen years of age I had started to smoke and drink. My mum and dad both smoked at the time and they must've smelt the smell of tobacco on my clothes and in my hair, as I would return from school. Unbeknown to me at the time my mum had asked my dad to actually catch me at it. And so it was, on one fated day after school, my friends and I made for our little smoking club, which was just opposite the school bike shed and across the road and into a small wooded area. We would hide behind a bush and smoke our Player's Weights and Will's Woodbines, coughing and spluttering as we went. All of a sudden there was a hell of a commotion as the kids all scattered and there stood my dad, staring at me with my cigarette half way to my lips. 'Right, get home now son', he screamed and kicked me up the backside all the way home. I was immediately sent to bed for the rest of the evening without any tea or supper. Then, later that evening mum went off to play her weekly game of badminton at the local church. The worst thing though, in this sad story, is that it was Tuesday, 11th December 1956 and my heroes Wolves were playing Red Banner from Hungary that evening in a floodlit friendly at Molineux and it was live on TV. This was punishment indeed. I was bloody choked to say the least. Then all of a sudden my bedroom door flew open and there stood my dad. 'Well, do you want to watch the match or not?' he asked. I thought this might've been a trick question so I just nodded my head slowly in the affirmative. 'Well, what are you waiting for?' again he asked and again I wasn't too sure. 'It kicks off in five minutes. Get yourself down them bloody stairs'. I couldn't believe my ears and dived down the stairs about three at a time and sat on the floor in front of our little black and white TV. My thanks and joy knew no bounds. The game was a brilliant one with the match a draw 1-1. Again, this Hungarian team had many internationals playing for it, including one who had helped destroy England at Wembley two or three years previous, Nandor Hidegkuti. The comical thing was though at halftime, dad made a pot of tea for us both and then unbelievably offered me a cigarette. Once again I thought this might be a subtle trick and so I declined the offer. 'Go on, your mum's not here and I won't tell her.' He offered me the packet again and this time I slowly but surely removed a cigarette. He stood up and I was expecting a clip round the ear but he took out his lighter and lit it for me.

'I smoked when I was younger than you,' he said, 'it was your mum's idea that I should catch you and clip you round the ear.' We smiled at each other as he carried on, 'but as soon as the match is over, it's back to bed and not a word to your mum, okay?'

'Okay dad'. My smile must've lit up my whole face. Then right out of the blue he burst into uncontrollable laughter. 'What's so funny, dad?'

'It was like a scene right out of the bloody bible,' he spluttered.

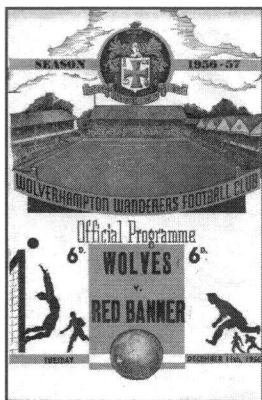

The match I watched with my dad, unbeknown to mum!

'What was?'

'You and your mates bloody smoking. All I could see was smoke erupting from behind the bush and it just reminded me of Moses!'

The penny dropped and I could now see the funny side of this and started to join him in his mirth. What a man! That night a huge bond was made between a boy and his wonderful dad.

Drinking though was even more pathetic. The gang of lads I mixed with would all chip together and buy a bottle of Bulmer's Woodpecker Cider. At that age, half a dozen gulps from yours truly was well enough. The world started to float and my speech became slurred. I laughed a lot but also tripped over a lot. This, I didn't like too much and so never really got caught up in serious drinking. Well, not at this age anyway. This pursuit was put on hold until my naval days.

Another funny episode around the same time and involving the whole family happened whilst dad was at work. We lived in a three bedroom terraced house and my mum and dad obviously had the main bedroom, my brother Martin and I shared the next large bedroom with two single beds along each wall and the third bedroom was kept spic and span for the Addressograph-Multigraph lodgers. Outside of our bedroom window there was a ledge which was over the front door. Martin and I were into our practical jokes stage and decided to play a prank on mum. It was around 9pm on a cold and dark December night, as I jumped out of the window and on to the ledge armed only with a cotton reel full of black cotton, which we had borrowed from mum's sewing kit. I lowered myself on to the floor and quickly tied the cotton around the door's knocker. I clambered back up the wall thanks to the dustbin and a lot of youthful dexterity, slowly letting the cotton off of the reel. Eventually Martin helped me back in to our bedroom. We pulled the curtains shut and turned off the light. I pulled the cotton reel. Knock, knock, knock! We heard mum go to the front door and open it. Nobody was there. Martin and I started to giggle. She shut the door and said nothing. Knock, knock, knock! We heard mum open the door again and this time she muttered something about bloody kids. We chanced our arm at least two or three more times and mum was getting more and more irate. Eventually the joke had ceased to have any more effect on Martin and me, as mum had actually refused to answer the door on the last occasion and so we hit the sack and fell sleep. A couple of hours later and we were abruptly woken by shouts outside the bedroom window. 'Bloody hell!' Whoops, it was dad.Next, we heard the front door open and footsteps bounding up the stairs. We pretended to be asleep. Our bedroom door was flung open and the light switched on. Martin and I pretended to have just come out of a deep slumber and rubbed our eyes. After getting us to eventually own up to the prank and noticing the guilty cotton reel dangling from my bedpost, dad could see the funny side of what had happened. Mum was now in the room with him and she was in tears of laughter. Dad explained. He had walked headlong into the cotton which was still taut as I had tied our end to my bedpost. Dad wore glasses and the cotton had whipped off his glasses and they proceeded to slowly move through the night in mid-air towards the front door. This must've been a spooky apparition and indeed made my dad jump and think seriously about things that went bump in the night! But eventually he cottoned on, (no pun intended) to what had happened and luckily enough for us he could see the funny side of it and so no punishment was dished out. Martin and I never spoke about it again in front of my dad but we told just about everybody else in the universe and mum still found it hilarious. Of course they both forbid us to try out such an exercise again and of course we obeyed. But there would be other pranks.

They would find all kinds of rubber spiders in their bed. Many times you could hear mum scream out, 'George!' This was usually followed by a series of bangs, as dad battered another rubber arachnid into submission with his trusty slipper. Another time was when I delicately placed some heavy books above my bedroom door and then called my dad in. Crash, bang, wallop! This was not the sound of the books hitting my dad on the head but the sound of his hand as he clipped me round the ear for being so bloody stupid. This was not one of my better ideas!

This, of course, was also the time of the birth of Rock and Roll. To my mum and dad's horror I started to really like this loud, new music and started to spend my pocket money from my paper round on collecting records of, Elvis Presley, Bill Haley and the Comets, Little Richard, Eddie Cochran, Gene Vincent and my hero of those days, Buddy Holly. We used to go down to the town on a Saturday morning and into the large Cooperative store, which became Quality House a few years later, and listen to the latest music, either on earphones that were situated on a long wall or in the little cubicles that were set aside for this purpose, in the hope that you might actually purchase something! Wonderful times, wonderful music.

I eventually left school at Christmas in 1957 and got a job in the following January at John Dickinsons in Apsley, which was the huge paper mill and printing firm that stretched for miles it seemed along the old A41 between Hemel Hempstead and King's Langley. I was called an apprentice printer but this was utter bollocks! I was an apprentice bloody dogsbody and general sweeper up! I hated my immediate boss, who of course, in turn hated me. He was heavily into politics and many, many years later he actually became the mayor of our local Borough! To this very day I've never trusted bloody politicians!

Anything that went wrong was my fault and I just couldn't stand being locked in with all the windows closed. These had to be constantly closed so as the stacks of paper and card didn't decide to hurtle around throughout the factory floor. I remember well, waiting by the huge gates of the factory at lunchtime and at going home time in the evening. There were bloody hoards of workers all trying to get to the front waiting for the gates to be opened and at the sound of a siren ran like bloody ants out of the gates in a frenzy to get home. You were not allowed to smoke in the factory for obvious reasons and so hundreds upon hundreds of workers had their cigarettes at the ready and immediately lit them once through the gates. I found all this absolutely pathetic and so the factory life obviously and most definitely wasn't for me. And so to the despair of my mum and dad and only after about four months, I left. Well more to the truth I was asked to leave. Mum and dad were quite strict on the subject of getting a job and rightly so. They were not going to have me dossing around idly doing nothing for the unforeseeable future and so I answered an advert for a shop assistant at Milletts, the high street store, which in those days was situated in Bridge Street, Hemel Hempstead. I loved it there and had a good boss and really got on with the senior staff. But this couldn't last, as my family and I all eventually and somewhat sadly, arrived at the same conclusion that this could not be for life. And so after six weeks as a very happy shop assistant, and on the pretence of a trip to London for my brother Martin to see a model railway exhibition, I found myself in the Royal Naval recruiting office in Charing Cross Road. Later my parents told me the truth that the real reason for going to London was for exactly that purpose, to get yours truly into Her Majesty's Royal Navy!

Royal Navy (1958 - 1968)

HMS Ganges (10th June 1958 – 19th Nov. 1959)

On 10th June 1958 and at the princely age of fifteen and a half years, I joined Her Majesty's Royal Navy as a boy sailor. I had got in with the wrong crowd at home (so I was told) and certainly as explained earlier, wasn't having much luck on the job front, and so here I was at the Royal Naval Recruiting Office in Charing Cross Road.

There I met a chubby and friendly Chief Petty Officer who told me that I had to take various tests to actually serve in the illustrious RN. I was informed that I could take the general knowledge paper test immediately but would have to come back a couple of weeks later for the medical. And so I sat the test. It was embarrassing to say the least. The first question was: Which of the following tools would you use to knock a nail into a piece of wood? There were then three pictures, one of a saw, one of a screwdriver and one of a hammer. I was very tempted to put the bloody saw. And so the paper continued in a rather similar fashion. Eventually, after waiting in the adjoining room for about ten minutes I was told that I had passed the test with flying colours. I had managed 96%. I was going to ask on what questions had I fallen down on but thought better of it. Perhaps I'd put the wrong date! The next big decision was what branch of the RN would be best for me. I had done a stint in the Boy Scouts a few years previous and had learned the semaphore code and a little bit of the Morse code (well I knew that three dits, followed by three dahs, followed by three dits was SOS). That seemed more than enough and so that was it, decision made. I was to serve in the communications branch and was informed that this was the cream of the RN. My giddy aunt, I thought, if I was to be the cream I'd hate to see what the bloody rest would turn out like! The medical was just as easy. Two legs, two arms, two ears, two eyes, one nose, two bollocks and cough! You'll do! In those days you signed on the dotted line for nine years from the age of eighteen, which of course in my case was going to be closer to twelve years including the time I would serve as a boy. This seemed like an eternity, and indeed was, but as I'd come this far there seemed no turning back.

And so, on the 10th June 1958, I met with many other lads my own age on a platform at Liverpool Street Station in London. My mum accompanied me on this trip as dad was working and my brother was at school. This early part of the journey was distinctly taking on a faint similarity to that of a prisoner on death row. There were many tears as we hugged on the platform and finally I waved my final goodbye hanging out of the train window. With the final farewells now over, the carriage load of young boys sat back and took in the view as the steam train huffed and puffed its way slowly towards East Anglia. We made new friends and shared a few cigarettes, as we progressed on this train to the town of Ipswich and then by RN coach to the village of Shotley and the infamous HMS Ganges.

HMS Ganges Annexe Class (Who is that good looking fellow on the very right of the front line?)

Our home, for the next six weeks was the Annexe. This was apart from the main buildings where you learnt how to become something that resembled a sailor. The Annexe was divided into two mess decks, Jellicoe 1 and Jellicoe 2. I was situated in Jellicoe 1. On the actual day that we all arrived at the Annexe, I made my first cock-up. We were sat down in the dining hall and treated to a fish and chip dinner, which was accompanied by a large enamel mug of tea. On the table in front of us was a large bowl full of white sugar. I spooned three or four heaped spoonfuls into my brew and stirred briskly. There were giggles around the table. I took my first large mouthful and immediately cringed as I spat the contents quickly back into the mug. Everyone rolled around laughing as the bloody white stuff was sodding salt. I quickly made comments that mummy and daddy had things called salt and pepper pots at home and not fucking buckets of salt on the dining room table. This somewhat alleviated my embarrassment a little and I soon learned to laugh at my own misgivings.

That first night was a nightmare, as the mess deck full of young lads tried to get their first night's sleep in the RN. There was a lot of incessant snoring, whimpering, and quite a bit of crying, as some of the young lads already felt quite homesick. Every now and then, the odd cute Victorian catchphrase would be heard, telling everyone to belt up or receive a fucking smack in the mouth. And so, this was it. Our start to becoming the seafaring guardians of England!

It was at the Annexe we learned to march, sew, wash and iron our own clothes and clean and polish the mess deck and general surroundings. The next humiliating thing on the agenda was the dreaded haircut. Some lads had Elvis like locks and many had Teddy boy type hairdos. I just had a curly mop. But no matter what you supported on your cranium it only took about three minutes for us all to look alike. The barber himself would've made Sweeney Todd look like he had just stepped out of children's television and the more you actually goaded him the worse you got treated. 'Just a little off the top, my man,' would land up with absolutely sod all on top. I had heard of a short back and sides but this went one better. It was a short back, sides and bloody top. I think this is where the saying, hair today, gone tomorrow might've come from.

This embarrassing performance was followed immediately by the mortifying kitting-out of our naval uniforms. We lined-up and gave our measurements to a miserable bastard that stood behind a large wooden counter. Behind this there were shelves galore full of naval items. This was a messy affair with rarely a satisfied customer. The giving of your measurements was a total waste of time as everybody landed up with kit that was at least two sizes too big for them, under the premise that we would grow into it. The only things that seemed to fit were the hat and footwear.One comedian stated that he would never make the Christian Dior line-up this year dressed in this crap. We all fell about laughing but the cretin behind the counter soon put a stop to this. In answer to this, the comedian again piped up that he had seen more humour in a bucket of funnel web spiders. This was the last straw for Mr. Happy behind the counter and so this time we doubled round the parade ground for fifteen minutes non-stop and what a sight it must've been to an outsider. Many of us had only been half kitted-out and so the motley crew that trudged around the small parade ground looked a rare sight indeed. There were

Babyface!

lads with drainpipe trousers that disappeared into great big black boots. Some had hats on that were at least two sizes two big as they were interrupted before receiving the correct size. Some had shirts flapping open and one poor bastard was dressed only in naval boots and underpants!

After the fun-run it was back to business. We had our names made up with small blocks of wood with letters of the alphabet on them and had to stamp our names into every single article of clothing, including socks and underpants. If the article was navy blue then the stamping was in white and if the article were a lighter colour then the stamping would be in black ink. Then to our utmost horror and over these neatly inked names, we had to sew our names into every article of clothing we owned in red cotton, using a stitch called the chain stitch. This took forever and if we didn't do it to the satisfaction of our designated Chief Petty Officer, a man called Nobby Clarke in our case, we had to undo it and start again. This was where you wanted a name like B. Cox or D. Lee and there were many young lads who cursed their parentage for having the name of E. W. K. Etherington or P. F. S. Wilkinson. Some poor sods even had hyphenated names! So all in all, M. R. Phipps wasn't too bad. We had one guy of Greek origin that had the name of Y. F. D. Maratheftis, who decided that the RN was victimising him alone and the very next night went over the wall, vowing to join the Greek Cypriot underground movement.

The shining of the boots and shoes was next, where we spat and polished for hours bringing up the front of the footwear to look like a mirror with our little yellow dusters. One trick was to set fire to the boot polish and make the stuff like molten lava. This made the polish easier to use and seemed to get rid of the little pimples on the toes of the footwear that little bit quicker. This exercise seemed to have only one problem as the lad in the next bed to me found out. His tin of polish seemed to have a mind of its own and was engulfed in flames and well out of control. He knocked the offending tin to the floor, jumped out of the way and screamed, 'Shit!' A so called helpful cretin two beds away, grabbed hold of a fire extinguisher and tried to turn the fucking mess deck into an Olympic-sized swimming pool. All it needed was someone to put a foot on the small tin of Cherry Blossom or smother it with someone you didn't like, but neither seemed to appeal to this new found idiot and we spent the next few hours mopping up and polishing the floor.

We also had to box, whether we liked it or not. We wore boxing gloves that were about ten bloody sizes too big and looked like Rocky Marciano's rejects. Typically, I had to fight a lad from Yorkshire that I had become quite friendly with and whose last name was Barrett. We very rarely used first names in those days, as everyone was eventually designated a nickname. His was Yorky due to the county of his birth and mine became Flip, a play on Phipps I guess. In the actual match neither of us wanted to fight and it was a pathetic performance by both of us. Eventually, after much yawning by the Physical Training Instructors who were refereeing, my friend was given the bout. I think he probably threw one extra punch than me but neither of us got hit in the head once but there was certainly a lot of hitting on the arms. Consequently, he went through to the next round and fought a small Scots lad named Willie Irvine. Willie was extremely wiry and was one of the lads who thought it bloody hilarious when I first took my sip of salted, naval tea. And so, at the back of my mind was, right you bastard I hope you get bloody hammered. But unbeknown to me and indeed Yorky Barrett, Willie had boxed for Glasgow boys and my friend was no match for his uncanny, subtle way of fighting. Willie was as hard as nails and poor old Yorky got well and truly battered. After that though and for the rest of our six-week stay in the Annexe we both became good friends with Willie Irvine. I think it's called grovelling. It was the first time I had come across the saying - size does not matter! A sentiment I would experience on more than one occasion with a certain person nicknamed, Grimble, and an individual who would appear later in my naval career and become the star character in my novel, *Wild Oats*.

The parade ground was also a scene of much amusement and bloody hard work for the next few weeks. It became a tarmac hell. Many couldn't figure out their left from their rights. We would march to the sound of the Gunnery Petty Officer, 'Eft, Oit, Eft, Oit, Eft, Oit, squaaaaad, 'eft wheel.' This was usually followed by such wonderful poetic prose as, 'Try the other left Phipps. You're marching like a fucking pregnant earwig!' This would cause much giggling in the ranks, which was usually followed by another marathon around the parade ground for ten minutes. I could never figure out what was wrong with, left, right, left, right and casually wondered why all these geezers in charge decided on, eft and oit. Parade ground dyslexia I guess!

Anyway, after six weeks of this humiliating hell we were to join the other two thousand boys in the main buildings of HMS Ganges. We were all designated our new mess decks and were put into groups of our chosen subjects, communications, seamen, stokers, electricians etc. My mess deck was to be Blake 8 Mess, 235 Class for boy signalmen in what was called the long-covered way. We made new friends and proceeded to learn our new and chosen professions. Mine was the visual signalling branch and we learnt the Morse code, semaphore, typing and flag hoisting and all their different meanings. The man in charge of our class was a Chief Yeoman Andresen, who was a nice guy and a very good teacher.

We seemed to double-march just about everywhere, as we frantically went about our everyday duties. We polished absolutely everything. There was a saying at HMS Ganges that had been handed down over the years, 'If it moved, salute it. If it didn't, fucking polish it!'

Another great cause for concern was the food. I suppose cooking for two thousand would have its problems but it wasn't the food itself that was the problem it was what sometimes appeared in it. The main dilemma was the infamous cockroach. They got bloody everywhere. You truthfully had to check your chips to see if any of them had legs. Also your porridge could have the extra vitamin in it, as a little black lump with legs would appear on your spoon. Of course they were well and truly dead but getting a kamikaze cockroach on your spoon or fork that had decided to commit hara-kiri in the chip fryer or vat of porridge left a little to be desired to say the least.

One thing you did need to be able to do reasonably well and that was to swim. Made sense really as this was the navy after all but sadly one of the many things I was crap at was bloody swimming. I had managed one width of our local Hemel Hempstead outdoor pool doing a stroke that would've graced a pregnant poodle! At HMS Ganges though, you had to pass a pretty tough swimming test before you could graduate. If you couldn't actually pass this test you were demoted to the Backward Swimmer's Class, which believe me had nothing at all to do with swimming backwards! You had to rise very early each morning, three quarters of an hour before everyone else and report to the swimming pool.This was bloody early to say the least, as Reveille or wakey, wakey for the rest of the two thousand boys was at 6.20am. You wouldn't dare miss a class, as punishment at HMS Ganges could be very harsh indeed. The Physical Training Instructors or PTI's as they were better known, showed absolutely no remorse for us pathetic bunch, as they had to be up even earlier than us to open up the indoor pool. The first degrading thing was that we had to practice totally in the nude. No flash swimming trunks here and even if you owned such an article you were not allowed to wear them. Scrotums would swing in the wind as we were told to jump into the middle of the pool, which was around the five-foot mark. We were then told to make a circle and start to do the breaststroke and go

The dreaded swimming pool!

round in a clockwise rotation. If you were seen to be not trying you were screamed at by the on duty PTI. For the life of me I couldn't keep this up and didn't particularly want to get a bollocking from the angry PTI. So, I had devised a method which looked and felt good to me and that was to keep lowering my left leg and keep pushing off the bottom of the pool with my left foot. This gave me the push required to complete a couple of strokes. I would repeat this action endlessly circling the designated area like an Olympic champion. Sadly, I was caught by the angry PTI and told in no uncertain fashion to get out of the pool.

'You, you curly headed cretin, out of the pool, now'.

I made a pathetic gesture and pointed to myself.

'Yes you. Get out of the pool, NOW!'

I quickly scrambled up the ladder and reported to the angry blue and white vested man that awaited me. A little earlier he had pulled two other unfortunates out of the pool for differing reasons and I was to be the third and last it seemed.

'You know why I have asked you to join me at the pool side don't you?'

'No, not really, sir.' We had to call anyone, Sir, who taught in any capacity at HMS Ganges, Petty Officers and Chief Petty Officers alike.

'You were cheating weren't you?' I looked as though butter wouldn't melt in my mouth and gave a short shake of the head. 'You were prancing round the pool on one leg like a fucking stork, weren't you?' Again I gave him a gormless look that said 'Me?' 'Right you three, up on to the top diving board.' I personally thought he was only trying to scare us and it was obvious that we couldn't argue and so we made our way slowly up the ladder to the top board. The pool at HMS Ganges seemed massive and the diving boards were getting on for Olympic height. We eventually arrived at our lofty destination and looked down. The pool looked like a blue postage stamp. 'Right you.' The PTI pointed to one of the other lads. 'Walk to the end and jump.' This lad was a lot braver than my compatriot and me and blatantly walked up to the end and jumped. A huge splash quickly followed and then he resurfaced and nonchalantly swam to the side.The PTI now pointed to the other lad who was now actually crying. This poor boy was cringing at the back of the board and refused to move. The PTI then grabbed a large wooden pole with a net on the end that was used for rescuing drowning idiots and cleaning the pool and made his way up on to the middle board. He then proceeded to poke the boy with the pole until he reached the end of the board. He then gave one last poke and pushed the boy off. Another gigantic splash as the PTI ran down the ladder with his trusty pole and rescued the surfacing boy. The lad grabbed hold of the pole with a death-like grip as he was pulled to the side and to safety. I now panicked like I had never panicked before. It was my turn. Perhaps if I tried to hide he would forget me. So I shuffled to a place on the board where I hoped he couldn't see me but to no avail. 'Next!' I didn't want to go through the performance with the pole and so I slowly made my way to the tip of the board. It felt like walking the plank. I hovered for quite a while. 'Come on, jump. We haven't got all bloody day.' I took one last look at the small blue square below me, closed my eyes and jumped. On the way down and for no apparent reason, I screamed 'Geronimo!' Just before I hit the water I made the gigantic mistake of opening my legs. My testicles hit the water at a million miles an hour and I had a vision of a huge pink scrotum leaping up from my groin area and covering my whole body with flaccid skin. After I had made my unceremonious splashdown all I could remember doing is flapping my arms and legs wildly in a blind panic. I think my right hand shot to my throat to see if three Adam's Apples had appeared but this is only conjecture. My eyes were still firmly shut tight as the wooden pole smacked me on the top of the head. I grabbed wildly at this wooden lifeline and eventually took a strong hold on the pole with both hands. I was pulled so violently to the edge of the pool by the PTI that I banged my lip on the side of the pool and started to bleed. It looked a lot worse than it was, due to the blood spreading in the water but it still bloody hurt.

'Come on, out! You're contaminating the whole bloody pool. You're about as much use as a fucking ashtray on a motorbike!' Merciless bastard, I thought but kept my mouth firmly shut. I was now safely on dry land, holding my bleeding lip. The PTI gave me a stern look, 'You okay?'

What a nice man I thought and nodded in the affirmative.

'Good. Up you go again!' He nodded in the direction of the top diving board. My mouth opened and my head shook in disbelief as I uttered, 'Why, sir?'

'I want to see if you know any more fucking Indian chiefs!' I was dumbfounded but he meant what he was saying as he pointed to the top board again and screamed, 'Now!' I went through the whole rigmarole once more but this time kept my mouth and indeed legs firmly shut. Through my mind went Sitting Bull and Crazy Horse but not even a whisper left my lips. I am absolutely sure he made me flounder for a little longer in the pool on this occasion but eventually he pulled me to safety and this time without smashing my lip on the side of the pool.

After many weeks of this early morning hell, I eventually passed the test. The test itself was to swim two lengths of the pool and float in the deep end for two minutes. This may sound easy but you had to perform the test wearing what was comically termed as a duck suit. This so-called suit was a bit like a pair of overalls with sleeves and was made of a thick and heavy canvas material. The texture was similar to that of a wet judo suit. The only stroke you could successfully achieve was the breaststroke and although not the fastest is by far the safest. If you tried the front crawl, butterfly or backstroke, the arms of the duck suit would fill up with every stroke and it wasn't long before you became very tired. We were told this would be no good if you were trying to escape from a sinking ship, as the suction of the ship actually sinking would take you down with it. So safety was paramount. I was so elated when I eventually passed this test but even to this very day, I am not what you would call a good swimmer and always jump in the pool with my legs and mouth most definitely shut! I often pondered on the thought that if I'd decided to join the RAF would I have had to learn how to fucking fly!

The next thing we had to master was our fear of heights. HMS Ganges had a massive white mast, which stood exactly 142ft proud at one end of the parade ground and could be seen for miles around. Although HMS Ganges no longer exists (it finally closed on 28th October 1976, when the white ensign was hauled

HMS Ganges mast (I am definitely not the one on the bloody top!)

down for the very last time) the mast has been preserved as a national monument. On special days, such as the Queen's birthday or parent's visiting days, it was manned by boys who climbed, stepping one step at a time, to either the steady beat of a lone drummer or to a tune by the Royal Marine Band or the HMS Ganges bugle band. It was an awesome sight, especially the young boy who had volunteered to be the button boy. This was the lad who would proudly stand on the very top of the mast and salute with only a lightning conductor held between his knees for balance. The size of the button was about the size of a large dinner platter, so you could see why this was a voluntary act. After the playing of the national anthem and at a specific signal the boys would all man the ropes and speed down them to the safety of the ground below. The button boy was then presented with a prestigious silver crown by the Captain for his bravery and was the toast and hero of all the other two thousand lads at the camp. A million pounds would not have been enough for yours truly to volunteer for this task. It was said that on a windy day the top of the mast could sway a few feet either way. On a windy day I want my bloody feet well and truly planted on terra firma and if I have to sway a few feet either way it will be through alcohol and not high bloody winds standing on a sodding dinner plate 142ft in the air!

But everyone had to do what was called mast class. This is where you had to climb to the second level on one side of the mast and come down the other side. The only trouble with this was that the first level contained what was aptly named as the Devil's Elbow. This was where you comfortably climbed toward the first large platform, but to actually get on to this platform and relative safety, you had to scramble over the rigging and on to the ledge with your back to the ground. This was not easy to say the least and many boys froze at this moment in time and came back down. But, like the swimming test it was something you had to achieve before you left Ganges. Coming back down was even worse as you had to dangle precariously off the first platform, searching hopefully for the rigging with your dangling feet. Then it was very slowly, hand after hand around this dreaded elbow and back down to safety, where you had to run over to your instructor and salute and inform him, 'JTO Phipps, P/J 979447. Reporting from aloft, sir!' JTO stood for Junior Tactical Operator which was a posh name for boy signalman and the number was our official naval number designated to us for the rest of our time in the RN. There was a huge rope safety net around the bottom of the mast but to this very day I'm not sure it would have worked to be truthful. When you were safely on the first platform you could look out and see for miles around. Harwich harbour was just over the water and in the distance you could see Felixstowe. As you looked down you could see HMS Ganges sprawled out over the beautiful Suffolk countryside. Directly below were the short-covered-way, where many of the divisions of boy's mess decks were housed and also the parcel office. We all noticed it had a part of its roof renewed with a new set of tiles shaped oddly like that of a human being. When we asked our Chief Petty Officer what this was all about, he told us the story of a young lad who had fallen from the first yardarm, on to the safety net and bounced straight through the parcel office roof. Heck of a way to post a parcel! Only one fatality was recorded on the mast and that was a suicide where a young rating couldn't stand any more and literally threw himself off the first yardarm on to the parade ground. If you want to actually see the Ganges mast being manned by the boys, log-on to www.youtube.com on the Internet and type in HMS Ganges Mast!

The rifle range was the next atrocity to rear its ugly head. We were shown the basics, such as which way to point the bloody thing and how to load the rifle. One poor soul, who went by the name of, O'Connell and was the class idiot, dared to call it a gun. He spent the next half an hour running around the huge parade ground with the so-called gun above his head. At no cost were we to call it a gun – it was a .303 rifle. These were reasonably old rifles and I'm pretty damned sure that bloody Sir Michael Caine had used mine in Zulu! Eventually we were allowed to fire the things at a target at the other end of the rifle range. 'Hold the rifle tight into your shoulder and slowly squeeze the trigger', the Gunnery Instructor informed us. Bang! I shrieked as I thought I had broken my bloody shoulder blade as the rifle had the kick of a mule. I was only one of a few who had let out a piercing scream on their first attempt. And I only had another five shots to go! By the time the sixth and last shot was fired all of us were rubbing our extremely bruised shoulders only to be called, wimps by the grinning GI. If I had met an enemy that I had to shoot with this damned instrument, I personally think I would've done more actual harm to myself than to them. But, as with most things we slowly started to get the hang of it and in all truthfulness became quite good shots. Each time after our first pathetic attempt we used to place a couple of shoe dusters inside our shirts to pad out our shoulders and then it wasn't too bad.

We seemed to spend endless time doing some very ridiculous things like polishing the dustbins and huge silver coloured ashtray type things called spitkids, until you could shave in them. A spitkid was a large round aluminium ashtray-cum-rubbish bin. In the old days of wooden ships and the likes of Nelson etc. a spitkid was usually a bucket or used shellcase in which sailors would spit into whilst chewing a plug of tobacco. It was a punishable offence to spit anywhere else other than the

My mess deck at HMS Ganges (what about that for a dustbin and a couple of large ashtrays!)

dreaded spitkid. (See photo of mess deck. The spitkids are either side of the dustbin). Likewise the wooden mess deck floor had to look like a bloody mirror. If the class had been sloppy in any one day we had to spend one hour in the evening on our hands and knees polishing the wooden floor with one of our boot brushes! We had to fold our blankets in a special way every morning and if they weren't good enough they were then ruffled up again by the duty Petty Officer and we had to fold them all over again. (Again see photo of mess deck). There were three sets of very long concrete steps near the Communication School that led to the foreshore. They went by the wonderful name of, Faith, Hope and Charity. These dreaded steps were used as a punishment for any class not pulling its weight and we used to double march up and down these infamous steps until we dropped. Also at the back of our mess decks was the, also just as infamous, Laundry Hill. This hill had the back of the mess decks on one side and the laundry and a few other buildings on the other side. It had quite a slope on it and was used for individuals and indeed whole classes on jankers, which was the naval word for punishment. We used to be fully kitted-out and used to run up and down this horrible hill mercilessly for the best part of an hour. We were given small breaks to get our breath back and then off we went again. The rest periods had been introduced many years before, when a rating actually died of exhaustion from this terrible ordeal. But this hill and the dreaded steps of, Faith, Hope and Charity usually had the desired effect of bringing ratings back into line.

It was at HMS Ganges that I actually fainted and thankfully glad to say the only time to date. It was on Sunday divisions with all the boys lined up in their respective classes and dressed in their very heavy blue serge, naval uniforms. The stiff brims of our hats were very tight on our heads and could give you a headache on a very hot day. This was one such day in the height of summer. I was staring at the wall of Nelson Hall in front of me on the parade ground, when all the bricks seemed to start moving. I also experienced a sort of tunnel vision. I remember the Gunnery Officer on his podium shouting, 'Parade, parade, 'shun!' At this moment in time two thousand boys came briskly to attention and the Royal Marine band's drummers started their intro into one of the countries famous marches. As the boys came to

HMS Ganges Sunday divisions (7th down the line and not too long before the fainting episode!)

attention, I joined them and then everything went black. I remembered hearing the band's first couple of notes and that was all. The next thing I remembered was coming round, which was like coming out of a heavy dream. I found myself lying on some sort of bench surrounded by worried looking Petty Officers. I was now inside Nelson Hall and as I started to rise one of the Petty Officers told me to stay where I was and relax. He held a hand to my chin and I gingerly asked what had happened? It turned out that as we came to attention, yours truly decided to faint and come to attention on the bloody parade ground floor. He then removed his hand from my chin and I saw that he was holding a pad of bandages and they were drenched and red with my blood. I asked him what the damage was and this time as I spoke I could feel bits of teeth circulating in my mouth. I had obviously fainted due to the immense heat of the day and gone straight down on my chin. I had then been literally dragged by two of my classmates into Nelson Hall where I slowly came back to life. I was then transferred to the sickbay where I had five stitches in my chin. This was followed by a trip to the dentist where two of my back teeth had to be repaired after being badly chipped from the fall. To my utter dismay my wonderful spit and polished, shiny boots were now very badly scratched on the toes, where I had been unceremoniously dragged into Nelson Hall by my colleagues. Of course this turned out to be my bloody fault and I had to buy a new pair and go through the routine of getting them all nice and shining again.

The one thing I was good at though and that was anything to do with the actual signalling side of things. I loved reading the flashing light as it spelt out its hidden Morse code messages and I had already learnt how to read Semaphore in the Boy Scouts which I had attended for a while in my early teens. Also I found the flag hoisting and all their diverse meanings exciting. The hardest thing in the Communication School was learning how to type. We had to learn to touch-type and all the keys on the old typewriter were covered with little white plastic covers so we couldn't look down and find the key you wanted. If

My class at HMS Ganges (front line again, second right!)

you were caught looking at the keyboard you used to receive a rap across the knuckles with a wooden ruler for your troubles. We had to be able to type at thirty words per minute and with 94% accuracy. This may seem pathetic to a top secretary but to a fifteen or sixteen year old lad with fingers like sodding cucumbers this was no mean feat. Of course, much later in life this became a blessing with the invention of the home computer. We used to have VS (visual signalling) tests every six weeks and I came top of the class in all but one exam. I was chuffed to bits and so were my parents as I used to send home the exam results, especially as this was the first thing I had excelled in other than football. On the passing out parade I was presented with the HMS Ganges VS Efficiency Medal of which I was so proud, as only a very few boys ever received this in any one intake. I had been basically crap at school although always in the 'A' stream but had only really enjoyed two subjects, English and PE as I have explained earlier in this book. Later in life I came to realise that this was because these two teachers were excellent and gave encouragement instead of bollocking you all the time. They made lessons exciting and you always wanted to be at their classes. You never forget the names of good teachers and my two were Mr Webb for English and Mr Taylor for PE. I have tried very hard to take this example into my karate teaching much later in my life and hopefully people will remember my name for all the right reasons and not for the wrong ones!

We seemed to double-march everywhere and were probably as fit as fiddles except for the one bad habit and that was that nearly everyone smoked. The cancer scare hadn't really hit home in 1958/9 and therefore it was amazing the clout that a packet of cigarettes had. You were everyone's best friend!

Anyone with a higher rank than you were called, 'Sir' and anyone lower were called a 'Ganges Nozzer', a term aimed at lower ranks at Ganges. Seniority was everything!

On leaving, my last view of HMS Ganges (the entrance gate!)

Eventually, and seventeen demanding months later it was all over. We had passed all our tests and exams and it was time to be let out into the Royal Navy proper. We were sat in a classroom and on the blackboard were the names of many ships. I was one of the very first to be able to pick my first ship, as I had done so well at the visual signalling exams. I liked the look of HMS Dunkirk, a Battle Class Destroyer that had been launched in 1945. This sounded very grand to me and so this was the choice I made. Sadly, it was the wrong bloody choice but more of that later. I left HMS Ganges on the 19th of November 1959. On my official record sheet was the following: Character – VG, Efficiency – SAT. (JTO1). JTO(1) was my ranking, the highest I could achieve at HMS Ganges but sadly SAT did not stand for Saturday, it stood for Satisfactory. Huh! What did they know?

Below is a wonderful poem by author and ex-Ganges boy, John Douglas. John has written two very successful books on HMS Ganges and made one excellent video after the shore establishment had been closed down and was falling into dismal and depressing decay. Sadly, John passed away in 2007 and the permission to use this wonderful poem was given to me by his wife Joan and son Jim, to who I owe a debt of gratitude for such a lovely gesture.

THE LEGEND OF H.M.S. GANGES by John Douglas
There's a village they call Shotley to the East of Ipswich Town;
The port of Felixstowe across the way.
There's a concrete ship called Ganges near the Orwell flowing down,
And skirted by the shores of Harwich Bay.

We joined as Nozzers new, the sailor-boys in blue,
And punched our oppo's teeth out in the Gym,
We marched, we doubled fast, we climbed that bloody mast;
The Foreign Legion never was as grim!

Ten Divisions - Admirals all - parade-ground, Nelson Hall,
And Nozzer's Lane tucked out of sight away,
There was Collingwood & Blake, there was Benbow, Hawke & Drake;
And Grenville down the long, Long Covered Way.

The 'dabtoes' learned to sail a boat, correct a starboard list,
And take evasive action from the bombs,
They could 'bend' & 'splice' & hitch; they could knot a 'monkey's-fist,'
There was semaphore and flashing for the 'Comms.'

Down Laundry Hill on jankers, tin-hat shades the sweating-frown,
And bayonet bangin' 'ard against the thigh.
Rifles chafed our collar-bones, the hot sun scorching down,
From inverted bowl of blue, the summer sky.

"Do just as you are told, lad, make do with what you got!
Obey the orders, Boy! No 'ifs' or 'buts'!"
Ganges discipline was 'hot', and some went 'on the trot,'
But they dragged 'em back and lashed 'em with twelve 'cuts.'

We had Faith and we had Hope, we had Charity as well;
But these were not just virtues - as you know!
We stumbled and we fell - on those concrete steps to Hell.
Our souls were signed to Ganges - be it so.

What faith? What Hope? What Charity? Was there really no comparity?
As we staggered up those steps with muscle-pain,
We-e-ell, we knew we'd had enough - but assumed that we were tough -
So they made us double up and down again!

GANGES motto states at length, that "Wisdom, it is strength!"
Is there one of you who wouldn't go agen?
Tho' you flogged us an' you flayed us, by the livin' God what made us;
You took us on as boys - and made us men!

Copyright John Douglas 1978.

HMS Dunkirk (D09) - (20th Nov. 1959 – 18th Nov. 1960)

After a couple of long train journeys I found myself in Plymouth. I joined HMS Dunkirk at Devonport the day after leaving the comparative safety of Shotley

HMS Dunkirk - My first actual ship!

Village and HMS Ganges. I have to admit that pretty much straight away I didn't like it very much. We all come across this situation in our lives and I was just too young to accept it. I had left Ganges as one of the oldest and most senior ratings (which held a lot of sway at such an establishment) to find myself totally at the bottom of the poxy food chain again. I was the general dogsbody for absolutely bloody everyone and this can make your attitude to life change dramatically. I started to become a rebel. I hated my instant superiors, who in turn seemed to hate me. Any small thing that seemed to go wrong was naturally my bloody fault. I had to run the most ridiculous errands and was the signalling department's tea boy. One idiotic gesture certainly springs to mind. 'Knocker' White, the Leading Signalman was the second in charge of the visual signalling department. He told me to go down to the ship's engine room and get some green oil for the starboard light and some red oil for the port light. I, like an innocent child went happily on the errand. Of course the Chief Stoker was not amused and told me there was no such fucking thing and to piss off and bother someone else! 'Oil is fucking oil son, it doesn't come in pretty bloody colours!' On returning to the flag deck everyone was falling about laughing and pointing fingers at me and proclaiming how bloody thick I was. Bastards! The yeoman, who was in charge of the signalling branch and shall remain nameless, was always pissed and I seemed to be his whipping boy for everything and anything that went wrong.

HMS Dunkirk was destined to do a year in the Mediterranean and it wasn't too long before we said goodbye to good old Blighty. The only memorably good thing about my time on HMS Dunkirk, was when we eventually arrived at Gibraltar we had to go into dry dock for some serious repairs to the ship's steering column and screws. The ship also had to be fumigated because of a cockroach invasion. Fucking charming! So the senior signalling staff weren't the only bloody pests on board! We spent a few wonderful months in Gibraltar and I fell in love with the place. Well, in actual fact, I fell in love for the first time in Gibraltar.

Most nights we would go out drinking down Main Street, and in one bar, which I believe was called the Universal Bar there was a stage at one end, where lady Spanish dancers did their traditional dances throughout the evening. There was a young and extremely pretty girl named, Juanita and we made eyes at each other and smiled a lot at each other. Sadly, she was only fifteen and I the princely age of seventeen. This of course was no problem but everywhere she went she had to have a bloody chaperone. And so sadly nothing became of this pathetic affair but she was the first girl to really capture my heart.

It was also on this ship that I fell in lust! After Gibraltar we moved on to Naples, which was and probably still is the home of the United States Navy's Mediterranean fleet. With a couple of my mates we had gone ashore with our cameras to snap up the local scenery and indeed to have a few beverages. After a long day we found ourselves in a club for United States servicemen called the Bluebell Club. We had been drinking

Getting pissed with mates from HMS Dunkirk!

since lunchtime and were slightly the worse for wear. We were made very welcome and sat ourselves at a round table and started to drink the local beer. After about quarter of an hour we were accosted by three women, who promptly sat on our laps and asked if we would buy them a drink. Mine wasn't too bad looking but quite a few years older. After buying her a drink she asked if I would like to accompany her to her place for naughties! I enthusiastically agreed but she then told me how much it would cost me! I enthusiastically disagreed but she was extremely insistent. I just didn't have enough money and told her repeatedly. She then started to rub her hands gently over my John Thomas, which had now risen to its full height and was probably about to bloody salute! Again I told her about the pathetic monetary situation and showed her all the Lire that I had left. She then said she would be willing if I would throw in the camera as well! It was only a cheap Kodak jobbie and so I agreed, much to the mirth of my two mates, especially one called Clive, who fell about laughing as I left with the young lady. We walked down a few back streets and eventually into a dingy looking dwelling. I was led to a room that had very little furniture, with an unmade bed in its centre. She told me to undress and she did likewise. I was extremely shy and took forever to disrobe. She was undressed and lying on the bed in less than twenty bloody seconds. Her legs were wide open as she beckoned me to hurry up and get on top of her. It wasn't a pretty sight and this was to be my very first time at the real thing. I was seventeen years of age and reasonably pissed and for the life of me I couldn't obtain an erection and so with expert hands she helped me rise to the occasion! It was like trying to breathe life into a fucking sausage! Eventually, I climbed on top and after a bit of shuffling about it was all over. To my utter astonishment, she quickly rolled off the bed and filled up a bowl full of water. She straddled this bowl and started to douse her private parts. This worried me a little and I asked her what she was bloody doing. She replied that she was washing herself in case I had an infection. What a fucking cheek! I was a virgin up until then and she was a bloody prostitute but in some ways I suppose it was comforting to know that she probably hadn't got anything horrible. She informed me it was time to go and so I hurriedly and embarrassingly got dressed. This took about half the time it took to get undressed! As we started to leave there was a lot of puffing, panting and giggling from another room along the corridor which only had a piece of sacking for a door. I recognised one of these voices and quickly pulled back the sack curtain to find Clive having it away with my girl's mother! Mine was pretty average but his was bloody horrible and was all tits, teeth and toenails! So I threatened him to say absolutely nothing about my paying the balance with my camera and I would say nothing about his geriatric shenanigans! What a way to start your sex life. So that was goodbye to my virginity. It was a miracle that I wasn't put off for bloody life! I then made my way slowly back to the ship through the back streets of Naples. When you look back you see how stupid you were. First of all, having unprotected sex with a dubious lady and secondly walking back to the ship, on my own through the back streets of Naples! This story in a more fictional scenario formed a chapter in my book *Wild Oats*, in the *Wild Oats in Smoke* section.

The only other thing to happen on this voyage happened in the Bay of Biscay. It was extremely rough and our mess deck was at the stern of the ship. All the ratings took turns to collect the meals for the whole mess deck and on this day it was my turn. I made it to the galley okay and indeed back to the mess deck all in one piece but it was on the return voyage that I nearly lost my life. You were forbidden to wear flip-flops on the upper deck and on a really rough day when the deck was wet and slippery these would've been a nightmare. Of course, you can guess who decided that this was a very stupid rule and on my return journey to the galley with the empty trays the ship lurched horribly as we hit a huge wave. The trays flew into the air as my feet left me. In actual fact it was a good job I did let go of the trays, as I might not have been around to tell this tale. My body skidded across the wet deck and over the side of the ship. My hands shot out in desperation and luckily enough for me I caught the bottom wire of the guard railing. I hauled myself back on to the deck and picked up the empty trays, which were strewn about all over the place. My flip-flops had disappeared into the Bay of Biscay and so I made the trek back to the mess deck to put on some sensible footwear. It wasn't until later in my life that this really came home to me how close I had come to losing my life. There was nobody on that part of the ship and no one saw my near fatal slip. If the rough sea hadn't got me the ship's screws certainly would've, as I would've disappeared straight down and into those fast, churning propellers. Looking back I can see that somebody upstairs was looking down on me very favourably!

This was also the only ship in my naval career that I had to sleep in a bloody hammock! They are very comfortable but the lashing up of it every morning drove you to distress and then if it wasn't lashed up and stowed properly the leading hand of the mess whose surname was Hayter, made you do it all over again. Not a great way to wake up. Then, if that wasn't bad enough and if the ship was in port, the boys on the ship had to go for a run along the long pier and back again with the PTI. If you still had a hangover after this little lot then you must've swallowed the equivalent of the bloody Mediterranean the night before!

Mind you we did get our own back on Leading Seaman Hayter. He had been an absolute bastard to us generally and to one young lad especially. We used to put our hammocks up in the evening and then go for a wash and a pee before turning in. As Leading Seaman Hayter went for his wash and brush-up, this rating craftily unlashed one end of the hammock, the end where his head would be. He eventually returned to the mess deck and put away his washing gear. He swung himself up into his hammock and nothing happened. We all waited with baited breath. Sure enough and about fifteen seconds later the hammock collapsed and Leading Seaman Hayter was sent sprawling across the mess deck floor. We all wanted to laugh out loud but daren't. I pushed my face into my pillow and cried with silent laughter. Of course he wasn't amused to say the least and threatened us with all sorts of horrible punishments unless the guilty party came forward. No one came forward and we had to arise at some horrible hour for a fortnight and clean the mess deck floor and indeed anything else that could be remotely cleaned. The run along the pier also started a lot earlier and went on for much longer.

Another similar situation happened when we were in Gibraltar. One of the boys would get pissed most nights ashore and come back and dive into his hammock fully clothed. After about half an hour every night he would then get back out to have a pee. The lazy sod wouldn't go up the metal stairs to the ship's toilet but actually do it in his tin mug! This would stink to high heaven in the morning and this was a regular habit. So one of the boy electricians devised a small electrical device and wired it up to the offending tin mug. That night when the boy decided to have his regular pee in the tin mug he literally got the shock of his life. He screamed as the volts pierced his penis and immediately dropped the mug. Our electrician friend pulled hard with both hands and the wires came loose from the mug leaving no trace whatsoever of what had really happened. Needless to say, the *Phantom Pisser* never did it again.

Three months before I was due to leave HMS Dunkirk, I was awarded what was laughingly called, a Hurt Certificate. The actual date on the certificate for the accident was 25th August 1960. The reason for the awarding of this certificate was that on the said date above and whilst storing ship, yours truly dropped an 80lb sack of frozen beef on to my left foot, sustaining fractures of the first and second toes. I still have this certificate which is headed, Certificate for Wounds and Hurts. It was to be the only thing I was ever to be awarded on HMS Dunkirk. I only spent a year on HMS Dunkirk but it seemed like a bloody lifetime thanks to a few cretins. Of course there were some good times but in general I couldn't wait to leave. But sadly this was not to be my worst ship. That would be a little way off yet.

HMS Dunkirk was broken-up and scrapped at Faslane in November 1965. Anyway, this time my RN official record sheet stated: Character – VG, Efficiency – MOD. (TO3). Again, sadly MOD didn't stand for Ministry of Defence but for Moderate. Going downhill fast! TO3 was my new rating which stood for Tactical Operator 3rd Class. So a small jump from JTO1 to TO3 in a few days. Junior Tactical Operator 1st Class to Tactical Operator 3rd Class. Didn't sound quite as good, dropping down to 3rd class but this was a natural progression from the boy's navy to the men's navy.

HMS Rhyl (F129) - (2nd March 1961 – 25th Sept. 1961)

As you can see by the above dates HMS Rhyl was a ship that I was not on for very long. After HMS Dunkirk I had spent a transitory period at two shore bases, HMS Victory in Portsmouth and HMS Mercury in East Meon, near Petersfield. At the latter I passed my exam for TO2 which was one step up the ladder and which warranted a small pay rise.

And so I was then drafted on to HMS Rhyl, a Rothesay type, anti-submarine Frigate as a Tactical Operator 2nd Class but unluckily for me she was in mid-commission and her crew had been on board for quite a few months. As the comparative newcomer I just didn't fit in. Again, I seemed to be the scapegoat for all that went wrong in the signalling department. In the early days on this ship I tried to fit in but it seemed to no avail. The Yeoman in charge of the visual signalling department (who shall remain nameless for obvious reasons) was a real cretin and we definitely didn't hit it off from the very start. He was a weak man and was all fart and no faeces! As the new boy he thought he would take all his troubles out on me. The lads on the mess deck were all right and we had some fun when we went ashore. We did a stint as an Iceland

HMS Rhyl

Patrol vessel keeping an eye on our trawlers and making sure they didn't enter the forbidden fishing zone, which, at this time was a twelve-mile limit around the coast of Iceland. This was bloody rough and cold but quite fun. The fish and chips were wonderful as trawlers would draw up alongside and give us heaps of fresh fish. The chefs in the galley would fry a ton of chips along with this gorgeous fish and at least two or three times a week we feasted on the best fish and chips any of us had ever tasted. There were two Icelandic gunboats that used to fire warning shots over the bow of any offending trawler and generally threaten them with worse if they strayed any further into the forbidden zone. We would chase these two gunboats all over the bloody place. They were named after two Norse gods, Odin and Thor and were nippy little craft with just the one small gun up front. This patrol went on for six weeks and we all received a ship's certificate to say we had journeyed within the Arctic Circle. And then it was back to the UK. We visited places like Rhyl in North Wales, where we were given the freedom of the city for a week and if you went ashore in uniform with HMS Rhyl on your cap tally you couldn't go wrong. We visited Londonderry in Northern Ireland and of course Rothesay in Scotland just before and after our Icelandic stint.

I wasn't a bad little footballer but wasn't even considered for the ship's team, as this had already been picked months before and not long after the ship had been originally commissioned. It was a closed shop. Sadly for me, on our visit to Rhyl in North Wales the ship played the local team, Rhyl FC, which was a pretty good team and still is to this day. I wasn't even in the running to play and was quite chuffed when Rhyl FC beat HMS Rhyl by four goals to one.

Not for the first time it was this general shitty attitude which got to me and the rebel once again reared its ugly head. I would do as little as possible and just couldn't be bothered with life on the ship in general. It was a shame because it could've been a really good cruise but sadly thanks again to a few cretins it wasn't to be. The final straw came when we returned to Portsmouth and went into dry dock for a few weeks for some minor repairs to the ship's hull. The Yeoman had a small, red MG sports car that was his pride and joy and he used to park it alongside the dry dock when not in use. One morning, after a great night ashore with the lads, I was told to report to the bridge immediately with my cap in hand, which usually meant you were going to be in the shit for something or other. I arrived on the bridge of the ship to find a very disconsolate Yeoman, who I thought for a moment or two was going to have a pop at me. Good, I thought, the bastard's going to get what's coming to him! But no, he asked me about my movements the night before and what time did I get back to the ship and who with? Did I have any witnesses for the whole evening? I said why for goodness sake? I hadn't done anything wrong. He then took me to the side of the bridge and pointed down into the dry dock. At the bottom and piled up in a miserable heap was his beloved MG. It was in a terrible state and was most definitely a total write-off. It had obviously been picked up by a bunch of lads and physically thrown into the very deep dry dock. He blamed me from the very start but for once in my life I was

HMS Rhyl on Icelandic patrol (the Arctic Ocean bursting over the back of the ship and just look at the size of the waves!)

totally blameless. Luckily enough for me the police intervened and found muddy footprints all over the bonnet and the odd fingerprint. I had to produce my bloody shoes and of course they weren't the guilty pair, plus I had witnesses for the whole night. He still didn't believe me though I could tell and from that moment on my life on HMS Rhyl was even more hell. I began to wish I had been party to his car's demise but truthfully it had nothing to do with me.

Eventually life got absolutely unbearable and I was put under punishment for the slightest and most ridiculous types of misdemeanour. On the final occasion I was put on Captain's report for another absolutely pathetic reason. The Captain said he was sick and tired of seeing me at defaulters and gave me five days stoppage of leave and five days stoppage of pay. After saluting I turned and opened the door of the office, only to find the Yeoman outside with the biggest smile on his stupid face. This was too much for me and I threatened him then and there, calling him a greasy bastard and that I was going to punch his fucking lights out at the very next opportunity. Sadly for me, this was overheard by everyone at the Captain's table, and I was ordered to turn around and return to the table, where I received another five days stoppage of leave and another loss of five days pay. This was just too much and on returning to the MSO (Main Signal Office) I had to be physically restrained, as I was about to wipe the smug look off of the Yeoman's bloody face. Later that very same day the Navigation Officer called me to his office. He was the head of all navigation and communication ratings on board. He asked me if I was trying to work my ticket, which was the term for trying to get out of the RN. I told him that I wasn't and told him of my current plight and that it wasn't going to get any better. Within a week I had left the ship and was returned to HMS Mercury, the Royal Navy's signal school, where I would wait for another ship to come along. Surely things could only get better!

HMS Rhyl was purposely sunk off the West Coast of Ireland in 1985 after outstaying her welcome in the RN. Pity the bloody Yeoman wasn't on board! (Only joking). Anyway, this time my RN official record sheet stated: Character – VG* (Goodness knows what the bloody star was for. Perhaps they saw that I had some balls!), Efficiency – MOD. (TO2). No change there then!

HMS Aisne (D22) – (9th Jan. 1962 – 28th Jan. 1964)
After nearly four months at HMS Mercury brushing up on my communication skills, I was eventually given a new ship. This was a welcome relief as these months at Mercury were probably the worst in my whole naval career. After my experiences on HMS Rhyl I had turned into a rather rebellious character and had no intentions of bettering myself in any way, shape or form. I was put on Captain's report about five times in a fortnight for either not turning up to work on time or for a general scornful and insolent manner to anyone in authority. Finally, the Captain had had enough and instead of the usual stoppage of leave and pay, this time he awarded me five days in the cells. My charge was read out in front of the whole ship's company in the large dining room on the 18th November 1961 and was followed by a brief trip down to HMS Victory the shore base in Portsmouth and to the naval cells. I actually spent three days in these cells and got two days off of my sentence for good behaviour. This taught me a small lesson but my attitude to HMS Mercury and the RN in general hadn't changed.

HMS Aisne

Anyway, luckily for yours truly, (and probably a huge relief for them) it wasn't for much longer as my new ship awaited me in Chatham Dockyard. This was to be HMS Aisne, another Battle Class Destroyer, similar to HMS Dunkirk. Aisne was the name of a French river, situated in North-Eastern France and also the scene of three bitter battles in the First World War, in 1914, 1917 and 1918 between the German troops and the Allied forces. Well that's the history lesson out of the way and now on to my life on-board. This ship was the longest I actually served on in the RN, which was a few days over two years. Also it was to be the best so far by a long chalk, which wasn't that hard after the antics of HMS Dunkirk and HMS Rhyl. It was a little like Butlin's and Pontin's compared to Belsen and Auschwitz!

This time I joined the ship along with all the other ratings and made friends quickly. It was on this ship that I met and became great friends with TO2 Grinstead. If you have ever read, *Wild Oats* or *Wild Oats in Cornwall*, this was the man known to friends and enemies alike as, the dreaded Grimble! He was a great guy and found just about everything funny! He had no intentions of bettering himself by going up the rankings in the RN but made sure he was having a great time standing bloody still! With my current attitude to the RN he instantly became a hero! If you want a really good laugh and wish to find out more about what Grimble could get up to, can I suggest you purchase a copy of *Wild Oats* as I guarantee it will make you laugh and if it doesn't I'll give you your money back. (Well that's the advert over). It's worth buying just to read about Grimble's ghost, which incidentally is explained a little bit later in this chapter. I haven't repeated all those stories here, as this book is not a novel and is not really about Grimble, but what a guy.

Also another great friend appeared on this ship and his name was RO2 Green and better known as Doc' Green. RO2 stood for Radio Operator 2nd Class and he worked in the Wireless Office. Grimble came from Guildford and Doc' hailed from Oxford. Also, on Aisne we had a decent Yeoman this time and his name was Yeoman Greenfield. Next in charge was LTO Brooker and the signalling department was made up of, TO2 Beaven (Bev), TO2 Dobson (Dobbo), TO2 Grinstead (Grimble) and yours truly TO2 Phipps (Flip). As you could see everyone had a nickname and was only ever called by their rank and full names by the hierarchy and usually if you were receiving a bollocking! Then it was last names only.

After spending a while in the UK and completing what was called the Work-Up in Portland, we were to spend a year in the Mediterranean. The Work-Up lasted for around six weeks and our ship and a few others were put under war conditions for the whole period. If this was what real war was like then I sincerely hoped I never found myself in one. It was extremely hard work and very tiring. We were attacked by aircraft, submarines, other warships and even bloody frogmen whilst in harbour who tried to attach fake limpet mines to the hull of the ship.

Doc' Green and me mucking about in Malta!

Here is a small extract taken from the Royal Navy's website about the infamous Work-Up at Portland:

After 1945, Portland continued in its role as a base for the Home Fleet and the Training Squadron. HMS Osprey became a testing ground for the Royal Navy's new helicopters and soon became a busy Naval Air Station. Lord Mountbatten's 'Way Ahead' White Paper of 1958 established the post of Flag Officer Sea Training (FOST) whose organisation, and the name Portland, became bywords for naval training from the early 1960s until 1999. 'FOST' is an expression, which has been known to make the hardiest of naval souls quake in their steaming boots. The training packages undertaken at Portland by so many ships were renowned for their rigorous high standards. Every ship which went to Portland came under the operational command of FOST and emerged from the experience in better shape, with a ship's company worked up to the very peak of professional and operational efficiency.

We weren't allowed too much leave to relieve the pressure and everyone was glad when it was over and the ship and its crew received the magic words that it had passed this very severe test. I can see the common sense in this exercise as it made the ship and the whole crew really seaworthy, learning to work as a strong and efficient team and indeed ready for almost anything.

It was whilst doing this dreaded Work-Up that we were given a weekend's leave. It was too far to go home and so we spent the time in neighbouring Weymouth getting a little inebriated. I had gone ashore on the Sunday evening with my friend Doc' Green and after a very long pub crawl along the seaside front of Weymouth we found ourselves in a huge bar that was absolutely packed with locals and holidaymakers alike. Loud music erupted from a gigantic jukebox and it was all you could do to get a drink. Eventually, with pints in hand, we looked around for any spare female talent. All of a sudden I received a tap on the shoulder which was followed by the words, 'Phippsy my boy, it is you, isn't it?' I turned to see a school chum from Hemel Hempstead, Colin Ward who had been in my class at Adeyfield Secondary Modern. Colin had bright ginger hair and was a great guy and very much one of the lads. He was on a camping holiday with a few of his friends and they were touring the South of England for a couple of weeks engaging in the two most popular sports of the time, pulling and getting pissed. This was to be a dodgy meeting though, as we all teamed up and got pissed out of our tiny minds. After the pubs eventually closed we purchased a few bottles and continued with the merrymaking in their tents. This chance meeting instilled upon me all that I was missing in Civvy Street and how much I missed my friends and family back home. And so Doc' and I agreed to go on the trot and join up with this gang of guys on their holiday. Next morning they were going to make their way to Torquay, which of course was the place of my birth and seemed like a sign. We all awoke with huge hangovers and as we crawled out of the tents we saw that we were on a huge hill overlooking Portland Harbour in the distance, and Weymouth below. Even more disturbing was the fact that three destroyers were now making their way out of Portland Harbour, on their way out to sea. Our ship HMS Aisne was one of them! Doc' and I looked at each other and decided that we had better carry on with the plans made the night before and gave a hearty wave goodbye to the ships in the distance. The only trouble with this plan is the four lads only had the one car and that was a mini. All their camping gear was stowed on a roof rack and it was all the car could do to get started. So what would Doc' and I do? We decided we would hitchhike to Torquay and meet up with them there. They gave us the address of the campsite they would be staying at and we waved our fond farewells. Of course Doc' and I had no clothes, only what we stood up in and indeed no washing gear and not a lot of money. All of a sudden the idea started to fall a little flat and what seemed like a great idea under the influence of alcohol now didn't seem quite so clever. We trudged very slowly along the road in the direction the mini had taken a few minutes earlier. Every time we heard a car coming up behind us we thumbed for a lift. We hadn't been on the road twenty minutes when a car actually pulled up. But to our absolute horror it was a bloody police car! One of the policemen got out of the car and asked us where we were headed? We said we were holidaymakers and were hitchhiking to Devon but I think our short haircuts (which were definitely not the fashion in the mid-sixties) gave us away. It turned out that the ship had informed the local police of our absence and to keep a lookout for us. The policeman actually informed us of our bloody names which was a little embarrassing to say the least and so we were driven back to Weymouth police station and spent the day there in the company of the local constabulary. The ship was due back in that evening, having completed a day's exercises in the local area. Eventually, we were driven back to the ship as she docked in Portland harbour and had to report to the Officer of the Day. We were put on Captain's report and next day found ourselves before the Captain on defaulters. We obviously didn't inform him of our intentions to go on an extended unpaid holiday but just said that we missed the ship after booking in to a local bed and breakfast place and didn't actually hear our alarm call and had sadly overslept. We put on our looks of absolute innocence and that butter wouldn't melt in our mouths. All a load of bullshit of course but none of this fooled the Captain, as he gave us both seven days stoppage of pay and seven days stoppage of leave!

And so it was back to the dreaded Work-Up for another couple of weeks but eventually it was all over and in a few weeks time we would be off to the sunnier climes of the Mediterranean. Before sailing for the Mediterranean though, the ship docked in Portsmouth harbour for a few weeks where we would visit just about every bar in the town at some stage and believe me there were a few, to say the least.

On a Friday night we would go to the neighbouring town of Southsea and visit the Savoy dance hall. Friday night was the night for the big groups and singers and the Savoy would be absolutely packed. We watched and danced to, The Animals, Tom Jones, Gene Pitney, Brian Poole and the Tremeloes and many others. It was whilst watching The Animals that I took a good battering in the bar. The Animals had just finished their superb rendition of their great hit, *The House of the Rising Sun* and as it finished everyone quickly made for the bar. A support group came on to the stage but nearly everyone was in the bar hoping to get a drink or two before The Animals reappeared. I was with my good friend Doc' Green and it was my round. The crowd stood about five bloody deep at the bar and everyone shouted their orders to the bar staff. I got a little closer and started to shout my order out whilst waving a five pound note in the air. Big mistake! Before I even knew what had hit me I was spun round and punched squarely on the jaw. I hit the ground with a thud and the next thing I knew I was viciously kicked in the neck. I totally blacked out. I eventually came round on one of the bar's benches and asked if I was okay. I stood up and gingerly started to try and move my neck. This was nigh impossible and so I made my way to the toilet. I was bleeding from the mouth and there was a large red lump on my neck where the kick had found its mark. As I came out of the toilet my good friend Doc' appeared and asked if I was okay. I asked him what had bloody happened and where the fuck was he? He told me the gory details. As I was busily waving the five-pound note around this guy just turned me around and smacked me in the chin. Doc' told me I went down like the Titanic with my hand still in the air holding the said fiver. My attacker just casually took the note from my hand, said thanks and kicked me in the bloody neck. I quickly enquired of my so-called friend, where the hell were you? Doc's reply was that there was a whole gang of them and it would've been useless to intervene. Great buddy! Later on, one of the bar staff told me this was a regular happening in the Savoy and the police were on the lookout for these guys. Another one of the staff said that this was true but that also I had danced with my attacker's girlfriend a little earlier in the evening. Absolutely brilliant, why hadn't anyone informed me? When The Animals did eventually arrive back on stage, their first number was, *We Gotta Get Out Of This Place*. Ha, fucking ha! Couldn't have put it better myself. Doc' even had the audacity to smile. Now I was a cripple with no bloody cash and I couldn't move my damned neck properly for weeks and this taught me a very painful lesson. If you do have any money, stop bloody waving it about! The last comical thing in this scenario is that the girl in question had been dumped by her boyfriend and on seeing that I was leaving asked if she could come with me. I remember she wore glasses but she was very pretty and petite with all the right bits in all the right places. I said of course and said goodbye to Doc'. He could have no bloody complaints after his brave attack of cowardice in the bar. The girl and I walked slowly back to Portsmouth hand in hand, stopping every now and then for a kiss and a cuddle. I now felt extremely randy even with my current injuries and I was glad to say so was she. We walked up a small and quiet side road in the town and made wild, passionate love on somebody's front lawn. We both promised to see each other on the very next evening but I bottled out and felt like shit with my painful injuries and didn't venture ashore again for a few nights. But what a night! I had seen one of the best groups of the sixties, had a few drinks, got beaten up and had a bloody shag to boot. Now that's what you call a night out!

A couple of weeks later and after returning to the ship in Portsmouth harbour from a weekend's leave at home in Hemel Hempstead I met a very disconsolate Grimble on the mess deck of the ship. I used to catch the very last train from Waterloo on the Sunday evening that arrived at Portsmouth station in the early hours of Monday morning. I then walked to the dockyard and on to the ship. On arrival in our mess deck, there sat Grimble looking very strangely upset with a cup of tea in his hand. He had caught the train before mine and had been back onboard about an hour. Normally he would be in his bed asleep and trying to catch up on a few hours shuteye before the new morning and a new week. The mess deck itself was very eerie, as all of those ratings that hadn't gone on weekend leave were asleep in their bunks and the only light came from a dim, red nightlight. I whispered hi and how did he enjoy his weekend leave? Instead of the usual happy Grimble and his various tales of frolic and fun, he just answered in a miserable voice that it was okay. I could see something was on his mind and asked him whatever was the matter? And so began a tale of impish fun and spookiness that made the hairs on the back of my neck stand on end. He said the weekend had started out great with him and one of his many friends pulling a fast one on the train journey from Portsmouth to London. Grimble's friend was brassic and hadn't got two pennies to rub together. He wanted so bad to go on weekend leave to see his loved one but just couldn't afford it. Grimble said leave it to him. On the ship there were two other *Jack the Lads* who were always boasting of their little train scam. One would buy a ticket to London and the other just a platform ticket. Once on the platform at Portsmouth both would actually board the train. When the ticket collector was spotted a carriage or two away, they would both dive into the small toilet together. When the ticket collector knocked on the toilet door and shouted, 'Tickets please', the door would gingerly open and a hand would produce the one ticket. After thanking the person in the toilet the ticket collector would go on his way. At the other end in London, one of these chap's girlfriends would purchase two platform tickets and be on the platform awaiting the arrival of the train. Off the train the two would jump and she would give one of them one of the platform tickets and off they went merrily on their way with only one paying for the journey. Grimble had got a little pissed off with these two continually boasting about their amazing ticket prowess and decided to concoct one of his own. Grimble and his friend boarded the same train as our two ticket cheats but Grimble was the only one with a valid ticket. His friend only had a platform ticket but again both would board the train. Grimble lived in Guildford and would be getting off the train at this stop so the scam he had in mind had to be worked well before then. All four sat in the same carriage but not together and Grimble watched the two ticket cheats with an eagle eye. What he did next was ingenious. He got up to go to the toilet and on returning had let half the carriage know that the ticket collector was in the next carriage. Our two ticket cheats started to put their scam into operation and made for the toilet. Once they had been inside for a little while, Grimble rose from his seat and made for the same toilet. He knocked loudly on the door and in a gruff voice shouted, 'Tickets please'. The door opened and sure enough there was the hand with the ticket in it. Grimble took the ticket and asked for the person to shut the door and he would return the ticket when the person inside had finished their toilet business. The door gingerly shut and Grimble made off with the ticket and gave it to his friend. When the ticket collector did eventually arrive, Grimble and his friend both had tickets and the two in the loo had none. It turned out that the two in the toilet had to pay the full fare and they were very lucky not to get prosecuted, as they accused the ticket collector of taking one of their bloody tickets whilst in the toilet. Of course the ticket collector denied this crap, which led to him asking why they had both been in the toilet together in the first place. They came up with some bullshit story but they weren't believed and both of them had to pay the full single fare or take the consequences and be taken to court. I couldn't stop laughing. I had to stop myself, as a voice from a distant bunk told me to shut the fuck up. What a brilliant scam but Grimble wasn't laughing. He said that that was the happy part of the weekend but there was more to come. I asked him to carry on and he told a very ghostly story, which I thought he had made up but I knew Grimble too well and he most definitely was not joking or telling a lie. He continued. When on leave Grimble drove a Norton 650cc motorbike. It was his pride and joy and it turned out that on the Saturday night of the weekend he had attended a party a few miles away in a village near his home town of Guildford. He said he hadn't drunk too much as he was on the bike. It was the wee small hours of the morning when he did eventually decide to start the trek home and as he had had a couple of drinks decided to go home by the scenic route through the back lanes. About halfway home and through these quiet lanes and in the distance, a girl stepped out from behind a tree and waved him down. Being the gentleman he was, he stopped and asked her what the matter was. She explained that she was riding pillion on her boyfriend's motorbike when they had had a huge argument. The boyfriend, in a temper told her to get off the bloody bike and fucking walk home. So she asked Grimble if he would give her a lift home. This he agreed to and she mounted the pillion on Grimble's machine, put her arms around his waist and he took her to her parent's house on the outskirts of Guildford. She thanked him as she dismounted from his bike. Grimble asked her for her name and would she fancy going for a meal or a drink one evening. She said her name was Helen and that she would love to. They said a brief goodbye and she walked down the path and into her house. Grimble then drove home. Next afternoon he plucked up the courage to go and visit her at her parent's house and see if she fancied that drink. On arriving at the house, he parked his bike and strode down the path and knocked on the door. A man opened it and asked Grimble what he wanted. Grimble said he would like to see Helen. The man gave a menacing look in Grimble's direction and asked him to repeat what he had just said. Grimble repeated that he would like to see Helen. The man said that Helen didn't live at the house anymore to which Grimble replied that he had brought her home the previous night. The man broke down on the doorstep. Grimble put his arm around his shoulders and they went into the man's living room. After giving Grimble a drink he told Grimble that Helen had died nearly three months ago in a motorcycle accident. It turned out that she was on her way home with her boyfriend from a night out when they had had an argument. The bike had swerved badly and crashed. She was thrown over the handlebars and into the very tree that she had appeared from when Grimble picked her up. She was stone dead on impact. Grimble had literally seen her ghost.

The hairs still stand up on the back of my neck when I tell this story. First of all, I thought Grimble was giving me one of his tall stories but no, he most definitely wasn't, as I detected tears in his eyes. I said something like, bloody hell, how awful. Grimble wiped his eyes and asked me not to repeat the story to anyone on the ship, lest they thought he had lost his marbles. Up until then I had never believed in ghosts and am still not sure but I know for a fact that Grimble does. We never, ever discussed this again, which, in a strange way, is proof that Grimble was telling the truth. For if Grimble had a joke or a good story to tell, every one and his bloody dog would have heard it from him a million and one times! (There is a paraphrased version of this story in my novel, *Wild Oats*).

On another weekend's leave, a friend of mine Able Seaman Baldy Baldwin and I decided to have a laugh in London. We visited Carnaby Street during the day and bought some outrageous clothes and in the evening visited the bars of Soho. It was here that I nearly got done over again. We were drinking at the bar when in walked this very smartly dressed bloke with the most stunningly gorgeous girl on his arm. They sat near the door and he made his way over to the bar to order their drinks. I couldn't take my eyes off of this beautiful girl and our friend noticed this. He took his drinks over to his girlfriend and then made his way over to me. I was sat on a barstool and he spun me round and asked me, What the fuck I was looking at? I pathetically replied, What do you mean? He told me if I looked at his girl once more he would drop me where I stood. It was obvious to me at this point that he knew what he was doing, so I quickly apologised and turned back toward the bar. He stomped off and sat back down with his girlfriend. I could see them in a mirror behind the bar and he hardly ever took his eyes off of me. Baldy was no use either, as he certainly was no fighter and so we both sat facing the bar, sipping our drinks and talking in whispers. After about twenty minutes the couple stood up, put their coats on and left. I instantly became the real hard man and said to Baldy that it was a good job he didn't start anything. The barman heard my silly boast and totally agreed. His next remark nearly made me shit myself. He said that I was a very lucky boy, as this guy was known to nigh on kill people for less. He said he was a relation to the infamous Kray family and hadn't long been out of prison for GBH for nearly killing a guy. Fucking hell! I don't think I looked at another bird for a bloody week!

The tattoo parlours were also very busy in Portsmouth and many of us had the odd tattoo somewhere on our bodies. One rating in our ship's company had the word BOLLOCKS tattooed on the edge of his right hand just below his little finger. So now, whenever he executed the naval salute to an officer this wonderful word greeted whomever he was saluting at the time. From a distance he could get away with it and indeed did for a month or so but eventually whilst getting paid and saluting the Pay Officer he got caught. He was punished with a huge stoppage of leave and pay and told to get the infamous tattoo removed. He couldn't actually get it taken off but had the offending word covered up with a row of tattooed daisy-like flowers! There were many very funny tattoos and some were a work of art. One chap had a row of small footprints across his belly button and stomach with the words, NAVEL PATROL etched below the footprints. Although the spelling of naval/navel was slightly different, it still got its message across and was a very funny tattoo. Another had CUT ALONG THE DOTTED LINE around his neck with a row of dots encompassing his throat. One chap even had his eyelids tattooed with a small three-letter word on each eyelid, so that when they eventually closed them on his death the words, THE END would greet the undertaker. Across one rating's whole back was the crucifixion scene of Jesus and on another rating's back was an English fox-hunting scene with the foxes tail just visible out of the sailor's arse. There were just too many to mention but some were extremely funny.

But our time in England was quickly running out. We had some home leave and said goodbye to our loved ones and prepared for a year away from them and the UK.

My year in the Mediterranean on this ship had to be one of the most enjoyable in my naval career. It was the early 1960's and the world seemed to be a very different place with the music, the clothes, the haircuts and a hugely diverse attitude to life in general. The ship visited many ports in many countries in the Mediterranean but my favourite was the good old RN stronghold of Malta. Being a destroyer, HMS Aisne used to moor up on to buoys in the centre of Sliema Creek, a harbour that was used for the slightly smaller RN vessels, destroyers, frigates and the like, with the really big ships docking in Valletta Grand Harbour. We used to board the little Maltese boats called dyso's by the sailors but actually spelt dghajsa. These very colourful little water taxis, plied their trade in Sliema Creek and Valletta Grand Harbour and would ferry passengers, usually sailors from their ships to land and of course vice versa. We would land on shore and go straight in to the closest bar and after a few beverages would make our way to Valletta either by taxi or karozzin, which was a horse drawn cab and a little cheaper than the taxi but also of course took a little longer. Jolly Jack Tar's name for these was karry. We seemed to have a bloody slang name for just about anything! Once in Valletta we would make for the infamous, Strait Street, which was aptly named The Gut. This was a cobbled street that went slowly downhill for about half a mile. Downhill probably being the right word for this infamous street, as just about every establishment was either a bar, cheap restaurant or knocking shop! But it was cheap and nasty and of course a magnet for sailors. We used to start at the top and see how far down we could get before falling over, totally pissed out of our brains. The music of the late fifties and early sixties used to blare out from the hundreds of bars from their huge Wurlitzer jukeboxes. There would be Elvis telling us that it was *Now or Never*, Roy Orbison informed us it was *Only the Lonely*, Paul Anka raved on about *Diana* and Chris Montez sang *Let's Dance*. It was most definitely a fun place to be with all the prostitutes trying to get their man in just about nearly every bar.

On many an occasion you would see lines of sailors doing their impression of the seven dwarfs. We would roll up our trousers and get on our knees in a long line. We would hold on to the shoulder of the person in front with our left hand and with our right hand pretended to have an imaginary shovel over our right shoulder. The line, which was sometimes massive looked a little like *The Conga* for vertically challenged people and went in and out of bars and restaurants, weaving its way down The Gut. People could join on the end at any time and so the line steadily got longer. A song was also sung as we marched on our sore knees and was to the famous tune from the Walt Disney hit film, *Snow White and the Seven Dwarfs*. Hi, Ho, Hi, Ho, it's off to work we go, With a shovel and pick and a walking stick, Hi, Ho, Hi, Ho, Hi, Ho, Hi, Ho, etc... This was followed by a pathetic attempt at whistling, as in the film version, with Jolly Jack Tar falling over in convulsions and crying with laughter. The words were not quite the same as the film version but who cared. It was indeed a sight for sore eyes for any onlookers and for those who were participating sore bloody knees!

But I personally used to enjoy the bars along the front at Sliema Creek more. One or two of these had large dance floors, with again the jukebox blaring out the music of the day. Also, you didn't have to pay for travel to and from Valletta and this of course gave you more money to piss up against the wall!

It was here that my sex life would multiply immensely. I had met a girl called Shirley in one of these bars-cum-dancehalls. She was about seventeen or eighteen years of age and I would've been about twenty-one. She had the body of an angel and wasn't too bad looking either. Her mother was Maltese and her father was either a Chief Petty Officer or Petty Officer stationed somewhere in Malta. I immediately fell in lust! On and off for the next few months, (on and off being the right words and depending on the ship's itinerary) I had more sexual encounters with Shirley than the rest of the crew's sex lives put together. We were always at it. The only trouble was that when my ship was at sea, someone else was filling my boots. Shirley was a nymphomaniac but what a lay! We used to hire a room for the night, which was easily done in Malta at that time and probably, in most cases, for the sole purpose of what we were using it for as well. The only trouble with knowing Shirley like this was that other sailors also knew her the same way. And so the obvious eventually happened and I found myself in a punch-up in a bar's toilet with a sailor off of HMS Trafalgar. Nothing much really happened. A couple of punches were thrown in anger and it all got broken up by people wanting a piss in peace and without the sideshow of two idiotic sailors trying to punch each other's lights out. I think I was losing the fight but I won the battle as Shirley went back with me to a small flat we had hired. I had a cut on my head where I had been punched and she bathed and kissed it better. I wish now I'd have got kicked in the bollocks! Anyway, eventually this came to a halt as I was getting fed up with too much of a good thing. Pathetic isn't it and there have been many times in my life when I have thoroughly regretted this poor and very sad decision. But all was not lost as another slightly older lady came to my rescue.

Yours truly!

I was with my great friend Doc' Green and we were dancing in another of these bar-cum-dancehalls to the loud music of the day. A lady on another table kept looking my way and smiling. It is one of those situations where you think something is bloody wrong with yourself. So I made for the toilet to check that everything was in order. In the said toilet one of my shipmates, an Able Seaman Benfield was pissed out of his tiny mind and started to throw-up all over the place including on me. I cursed this bloody idiot, who briefly and pathetically apologised as I started to wash the sick off of my trousers and shoes. Anyway, this done I went back to the dancehall a little damper and smellier than when I had left. I will always remember the next bit as my luck changed dramatically. Little Eva came on the jukebox with her 1962 hit *The Loco-Motion*. Loads of us got up to do our poor impressions of the dance, which accompanied this song. It was a sight for sore eyes to see all these sailors and women trying to look like bloody train engines. Anyway, my spewing friend had now come out of the toilet and was heading straight for me. He was as pissed as a fart and was swearing that he was going to knock my fucking head off. He was restrained for a while by a couple of his mates and at the same time the bar staff had informed the RN patrol by telephone of impending trouble. Sure enough, our friend stood up and broke a bottle on his table and shouted, that he was about to make my face a little uglier than it already was. Funnily enough though, it didn't bother me too much, as he was wobbling all over the place, as he shouted these obscenities in my direction. Hardly anyone took any notice of this scenario as the dancing carried on. Just as I was about to move defiantly toward my drunken opponent, there was a hell of a commotion coming from the entrance to the bar, with whistles blowing and much screaming and shouting. It was the arrival of The RN patrol.

Just as I thought that I would be in trouble, I was turned quickly around and instead of having a bottle thrust in my face, there was a very beautiful lady there instead. She put her arms around me and lightly kissed me on the lips and told me to keep dancing. This had the desired effect as the RN patrol whisked away Able Seaman Benfield and left everybody else in peace. I thanked this lady, which of course was the same lady that was making eyes at me a little earlier in the evening. She asked if Doc' and I would like to join her and her mate at their table, to which we quickly obliged. She said her name was Moira and that she came from Weston-super-Mare. She was the wife of a submariner, who at that moment in time was at sea. She lived in a flat in Sliema in the RN married quarters which I was told later was a hotbed of sex and lust. The rest of the story is relatively obvious and I will not go into any sordid details but needless to say the next few weeks were absolutely wonderful. I just couldn't wait to go ashore and swapped shifts and duties like they were going out of fashion. Cost me a bloody fortune but by golly she was worth it.

She would've been about five or six years older than yours truly and she certainly knew her way around the boudoir and the male physique. Like Shirley before her she certainly had nymphomaniac tendencies. Up till this period of time in my life in Malta, I thought that a nymph was some sort of bloody female elf that pranced around forests! How wrong could you be? They were scantily clad females and pranced around Malta! The only trouble with all of these wonderful encounters was that all of the ship's company somehow knew of my sexual shenanigans and on many occasions would rib me about these mercilessly. I received many a clip around the ear from my peers for replying to their many taunts and calling them jealous bastards!

The ship's company got the last laugh though as my poor old, overworked genital organ started to sting! It hurt to go for a pee and I feared the worst. I made my way to the ship's sickbay and reported this to the ship's medical orderly. After a few tests it was diagnosed as just being overworked and that I had suffered a serious strain somewhere in the urethra. I was going to inform the medical staff that I had never been to 'Urethra' but quickly thought better of it as my genitalia were placed in their hands at the time! I had to take it easy on the sexual front, well in actual fact I had to bloody stop! I also had to take some sort of penicillin pills but this wasn't the main problem. The ship's medical orderly was also the manager of the ship's football team and I was in the bloody team. Of course word got about very quickly and everybody took the piss (an unfortunate turn of phrase!) Some of the team would cross over to the other side of the dressing room shouting and pointing towards yours truly, 'Unclean!' This was usually followed by a little naval ditty chanted at the unfortunate victim, 'Dhobi, Dhobi, Dhobi, never go ashore, Never have to muster at the Sickbay door'. To dhobi in the RN was to wash ones clothing and was an Indian word that literally meant, washing. This was very embarrassing to say the least and lasted for quite a few weeks. But after this period of time was eventually over, this subject didn't raise its ugly head again until the ship crossed the Equator.

In these earlier years of my life it seemed that I could pull the ladies no problem, but now all I can pull is a fucking muscle or a Christmas bloody cracker! But I was very choosy in those halcyon days - they had to have a pulse!

Another funny episode was whilst the ship was at sea on a very hot and sunny day. Once in a while the captain would totally stop the ship's engines and order, 'Hands to bathe and away sea boat's crew.' This meant you could dive or jump off the ship on either the port or starboard side, depending on which side had been chosen. You could swim or muck around in the sea for about half an hour and this was a welcome relaxation from the day's work and the very hot Mediterranean sun. A large rope, scrambling net was placed over the side of the ship that had been chosen so that the swimmers were able to get back on-board the ship. There are sharks in the Mediterranean, so the small lifeboat was always lowered before the swimmers entered the water and patrolled in a large semi-circle, within which the swimmers had to stay. On-board the lifeboat was a seaman with a .303 rifle who looked out for any such animal appearing anywhere near the swimmers. On this day though, a wicked prank was to be played by a rating on-board, Roy Scarborough. Roy was a fantastic swimmer who had a brilliant sense of humour, and unbeknown to just about everyone on-board, had made a large shark's fin, which he would secure with a strap to his chest. He wore goggles and had a small tube coming from his mouth, which was totally undetectable from a distance. This was similar to a snorkelling tube but much smaller. He had innocently boarded the lifeboat as one of the crew but already stowed in the boat was the fake fin, the goggles, a pair of flippers and his crude breathing apparatus. The captain and all those on the bridge knew about his little ruse and so all was well with the hierarchy. I was on watch on the bridge with the captain and the officer of the watch and so had a wonderful view of the farce that was about to unfold below.

There were loads of people in the water splashing about, swimming and generally having a great time on this very hot day. On the lifeboat Roy prepared by stripping off his normal working clothes and donning his shark disguise. He dropped silently into the water from the lifeboat on the blind side of all the swimmers. The fin was strapped to his chest and he was now ready with the goggles, flippers and breathing tube in place. He swam on his back and just under the water, so the only thing a swimmer could see was the dreaded fin coming towards them. I have never seen so much panic in my entire life. Someone from the lifeboat shouted, 'Shark!' Roy slowly swam towards the swimmers, who on seeing the fin coming towards them just about shit themselves. Hairy-arsed sailors were absolutely wetting themselves and shouting, 'For fuck's sake shoot the bleeding thing!' The gunman on the lifeboat just informed them that he couldn't as he might hit one of the swimmers. Olympic records were probably shattered as about fifty sailors swam for the safety of the scrambling net on the side of the ship. There were people dangling from all parts of the net. Bums were hanging in the water as everyone shouted to the people above them to, 'Fucking hurry up!'

I was crying with laughter on the bridge and the captain and the officer of the watch also found the scene below absolutely hilarious. The sea was cleared in about thirty seconds flat and this whole episode will stay with me for the rest of my days. It was one of the only times that I was pleased to be on duty!

With our twelve month trip to the Mediterranean nearly over and everyone excited at getting back to dear old Blighty, HMS Aisne was instructed by the powers that be at MOD Navy in Whitehall, that our tour to the Mediterranean would be extended for another six weeks. In actual fact we would be travelling down the Suez Canal and into the Red Sea and making our way to Aden in the Yemen. After this we would be visiting Mombasa and Zanzibar in Africa and then making our way back to Aden and eventually home. Aden was a terrorist hotspot in those days and there had been some trouble with these terrorists, who had thrown a grenade on to a school bus of British children, killing quite a few of the children and a couple of teachers. HMS Aisne was to show the muscle of Great Britain and do anything in its power to help stop these horrors.

This decision to extend our tour was met with much derision by the crew but sadly there was absolutely nothing we could do about it, except moan. The only good thing about this was that the ship would now cross the Equator.

On the day that we were actually due to pass the actual Equator, a large canvas swimming pool was set up on the bow of the ship. A chair was made up as a throne as we all waited for the signal from the Captain that we were passing over the centre of the earth. When the signal eventually came the ship came to a stop and all hell let loose. All the ship's company, officers included, mustered on the bow of the ship by the makeshift pool. Now enthroned in the pool was his Oceanic Majesty King Neptune! This was a large hairy-arsed able seaman that was dressed up as King Neptune with beard, robes and crown. In his hand he held a DIY three-pronged trident. In the pool with him were about three or four of his so-called helpers, known affectionately as the Bears. These were all dressed in a variety of weird apparel, trying to look like something Neptune might call on in an emergency! Again, all of these were of the hairy-arsed able seaman or stoker variety as well!

King Neptune had a list of all of those who had never crossed the Equator in their naval careers, with a special mention to certain ratings that deserved a more dubious accolade. Your name was called out and you made your way to the pool, led by the Bears, who then lathered you up with foam and who then proceeded to shave you with a gigantic, fake wooden cut-throat razor. You were then, what was aptly called, thrown to the Bears and ducked unceremoniously in the pool a number of times. Then, after being pronounced a true and worthy seagoing rating by Neptune himself, you were allowed to leave and get a shower and get properly dressed. As a novice you were now initiated into the Brotherhood of the Sea. Then it was the turn of the special people! You can guess who was bloody first? A long list was read out by King Neptune, which contained all my sexual conquests in Malta with Shirley and Moira, followed by a false sickbay report. Everyone jeered at every new line, shouting 'Duck him, duck him!' On these special occasions it was the duty of the said accused to try and escape but although I made a pathetic try at avoiding the obvious, I was soon caught by Neptune's Bears and dragged screaming to the pool. 'How do you plead?' Neptune directed his question to me. I was now stood in the pool surrounded by his hairy-arsed Bears!

'Not guilty, sir'

'Utter bollocks! You are guilty of gross misconduct in that you brought the good name of this ship and the RN into dubious shame. You are charged with being severely over-sexed. Shave and duck him ten times!' I was then lathered with the foam and roughly shaved with the huge wooden razor, which I am glad to say wasn't sharp. Then I was ducked ten times and each time I came up for air, the ship's company let out a huge cheer. After this was eventually over, Neptune informed me to leave and never darken his pool again and to keep my pecker well and truly hidden in my trousers! It was all great fun though and a couple of days after we were all presented with a certificate stating that we had crossed the Equator on Her Majesty's Destroyer, HMS Aisne.

Football was my one passion, well after women of course! HMS Aisne had a decent team for a destroyer and if you were good enough you were picked to play for the 7th Destroyer Squadron, of which we belonged to and both had decent teams. I played either left midfield or left wing. I was lucky to be relatively decent with both feet, so usually got lumbered on the left side with most people preferring either the right side or indeed the centre. We played some fantastic teams. The only trouble was that England had a great name in soccer and every team we played in every country thought they were playing bloody England. We usually got hammered but having said that put up a decent show on the whole. Our worst defeat was at the hands of the Italian club, Bordighera who played in one of the lower leagues in Italy. We got well and truly thrashed 7-0 but it was still a good match (well, especially if you were Italian!) We were all presented with a medal by the Italian FC and afterwards had a brilliant free meal and booze up. We all sat around one huge, long table with our Italian friends and the red wine just kept flowing.

When we arrived in Mombasa on the last leg of our Mediterranean/African journey we had a match against the local team. The pitch was a little sparse and on the edge of the jungle but what I couldn't believe was that the African team played in bare feet. We were all kitted out smartly in our Adidas boots and they played in Adidas bloody feet. Anyway, just over halfway through the match there was a huge commotion from the African team and everyone ran away from the jungle area. I was playing on the left wing and was quite a way from the furore. Now, there were all twenty-two players at the far end of the pitch and nobody gave a damn about the ball! All of a sudden, a spokesman from the African team shouted, 'Snake!' That was enough for me. I was up the far end of the pitch before you could say boo! A load of African spectators, all waving huge palm tree leaves came on to the area of the pitch that the offending reptile was supposed to be inhabiting and beat the ground as they shouted. Eventually, the snake disappeared back into the jungle and all was well. Later we were told that it was probably a Black Mamba, an extremely large and deadly variety and indeed the bloody fastest snake on the planet! The game then carried on but none of the English team could concentrate properly, as we couldn't stop looking at the ground for more venomous creatures. When the snake first appeared the score was 1-1. At the end of the match they had beaten us 4-1. Perhaps this was a clever ploy but I didn't stick around to find out! I wonder if it would work at Molineux?

Another match was against the Israeli Army in Haifa in Israel. This time the crowd was huge and we asked our Israeli opponents why so many spectators? Again it was the English football heritage that seemed to follow us around and it turned out that the leader of the Israeli base had insisted that the whole camp turned out to watch the match. Again I was playing on the left wing, which was definitely a mistake. There are many women in the Israeli Army and they all seemed to be stunningly beautiful and all on my bloody side of the pitch. Could I concentrate, could I bollocks! I'm sure this was another cunning ploy as yet again we bloody lost!

HMS Aisne's team against Samsoun of Turkey
(Yours truly in the centre of the front line)

Other excellent teams we played were Limassol from Cyprus, Samsoun from Turkey, Limnos (sometimes spelt Lemnos) from Greece, and a Russian Naval Team. Sadly, we were beaten in all of these matches but usually only by the odd goal, except against the Russians who hammered us 7-1 and of course Bordighera. Seven seemed to be our unlucky number! Where we did do well though was against other RN ships and HM Forces shore bases, where we could hold our own and in the main were victorious.

Generally though the trip was a successful one and eventually and six weeks later than expected, we arrived home at Portsmouth. There were many adventures over these two years with my friends, too many to mention to be honest and so far HMS Aisne was easily the best ship I had served on. After about three weeks leave I was told to report to HMS Warrior in Northwood in Middlesex, which was absolutely wonderful as this was reasonably close to my home town of Hemel Hempstead and I could catch the 347 bus right to the base.

Sadly, HMS Aisne was broken up and scrapped at Inverkeithing in June 1970. Another part of my life had vanished forever. Scrapped seemed an appropriate word! This time my RN official record sheet stated: Character – VG (No bloody star this time!), Efficiency – SAT. RO2(T). Whilst on this ship the RN in its great wisdom decided to change the title from TO2 Tactical Operator 2nd Class to RO2(T) Radio Operator 2nd Class (Tactical). Still meant exactly the same bloody thing though! This time though there was a little footnote on my record sheet. It stated: *Bridge and MSO duties. Has improved greatly and will eventually reach LRO(T) standard.* LRO(T) was Leading Radio Operator (Tactical) and was usually the person who was second-in-command of the signalling branch on a destroyer or frigate. MSO stood for Main Signal Office and the bridge of the ship is where we actually worked, standing with the Captain and the officer of the watch. Blimey, on the way up!

HMS WARRIOR – (29th Jan. 1964 – 24th March 1965)

This posting couldn't have been any better. I was within a bus ride from my parent's house and with the shift pattern we worked this meant I could spend about half the week at my home at 100 Lime Walk in the Bennetts End part of Hemel Hempstead. We worked a pattern of two days on and two days off. The first day comprised of working all morning and then an evening shift. The second day was taken up by working an afternoon shift and then all night from 10pm until 8am next morning. Then it was two glorious days off. I used to catch the first bus home from the bus stop right outside the camp's main gate. On arriving at my mum and dad's house I used to go straight to bed to catch up on my sleep and slowly awaken in the late afternoon. After a wonderful meal from my lovely mum and a wash and brush up it was then off to the pub. What a wonderful life!

Crest of HMS Warrior

HMS Warrior was a small naval contingent that made its home at an RAF base at Northwood. There were some very high-flying senior HM Forces personnel at the base and indeed quite a few from the USA. RAF Northwood was a NATO base and was the HQ for CINC HF (Commander in Chief Home Fleet). It was also the HQ for CINC EASTLANT (Commander in Chief Eastern Atlantic) and the UK HQ for SACLANT (Supreme Allied Commander Atlantic). We were all sworn in to the Official Secret's Act and were actually given passports in case we had to dash off anywhere within the NATO network. There were many other senior bods at the camp but I cannot remember all of their initials and titles. This last passage in the book is not against the Official Secret's Act as all these titles and many more were on a large board situated at the main gate.

We worked our shifts in the MSO (Main Signal Office) at the camp and this was stationed underground. You had to travel down quite a few flights of stairs to get to the various offices and pass a couple of Royal Marine security guards as you entered what was lovingly called, 'The Hole'. It was said to be nuclear bomb proof but I'm glad we never needed to find out.

The work here was pretty easy and was all to do with typing and teleprinters. The discipline was also very relaxed and was such a wonderful change from my life in the RN so far. The food was excellent and the NAAFI Club, where we all congregated when off watch, was great fun. There were many WRAF (Women's Royal Air Force) ratings on the camp and a few WRNS as well, so life was absolutely idyllic.

It was still the mid-1960's and the music and general attitude to life in the UK was extremely exciting. On my trips to my mum and dad's house I used to eat and live like a king. I frequented my local pub, 'The Boot' and spent loads of time with my civilian mates, Smut, Buzz, Bert and Brian Trundell (who I played football with at school and who has been a good friend ever since). On the odd occasion we would be joined by another old school chum Terry Tapping, who had also played for our school team in the early days before changing schools. Terry was a brilliant footballer and was on Arsenal's books and I believe actually played for them on one or two occasions. For many years he was the captain of Barnet FC and gets a mention in the autobiography of Jimmy Greaves. A mutual friend informed me that Terry was pissed off about the autobiography, as they had spelt his name wrong, leaving the 'g' off of the end. I believe Terry eventually finished his footballing career at Romford FC. These were great nights though, drinking, playing darts, listening to the jukebox and just generally having a great time.

I remember one time in particular when we played a wicked hoax on Smut. He was smoking a *Jamaican Woodbine* and happily boasting about the fact. We were all playing darts when he decided to go for a crap. Whilst he was comfortably seated in the little lock-up shithouse, one of our gang opened the main door to the toilet and shouted that the police had just entered the pub. Of course you could smell Smut's joint for bloody miles. All was quiet for a while and the next thing we heard was Smut screaming, 'Shit!' We all wondered what the bloody hell had happened as the police thing was only a gag. Anyway, after about a minute in walks Smut to the bar rubbing his arse. We told him of our little ruse and at first he was not amused to say the least. Then he burst out laughing and told us his side of the story. He really had gone in for a crap and he was accustomed to putting a load of paper in the toilet bowl beforehand so as to stop any splash back. On hearing that the police were in the building, he had quickly thrown his joint through his parted legs and into the toilet bowl. He then sat quietly, hoping and praying that the police wouldn't come into the toilet and detect the sweet, pungent aroma that filled the small room. The next thing is the joint actually sets light to the ton of bloody toilet paper he has placed at the bottom of the bowl and the flames burnt him on his backside. Well, we just fell about and cried with laughter. He laughed with us but was very careful next time he sat down. He told us the flames had actually blistered his arse!

My dad played darts for 'The Boot' and the daughter of the landlord and landlady, Paula Watts fancied me. This may sound a bit big-headed but is a story in itself. My hero was Bob Dylan and I used to wear a scruffy old Levi jacket and jeans to match. These were the most fashionable items of the day. I also used to wear this trendy navy blue, peaked cap very similar to my musical hero in those days. This seemed to be my personal trademark and I didn't feel one bit uncomfortable in it as in the RN we had to wear bloody strange hats all the time! Anyway, Paula used to make eyes at me on a very regular basis. She was very pretty with beautiful long hair and the body to match but sadly she was only sixteen. I was all of twenty-one but this seemed to be a chasm of a difference and so all I ever did was smile and say hallo. Much later in life I met her at a caravan park near Milton Keynes. I was with my wife Tracey and her parents. They had a nice weekend caravan on this site and we were there for a couple of day's holiday. In the evening we visited the camp's bar for a beverage or two, when guess who taps me on the shoulder,

Paula. We had a laugh about the old days and she told me right then and there and in front of Tracey that she fancied the pants off of me in those earlier days. Bloody typical, missed out again. She was still very attractive but was now married and lived in Australia and was just over for a brief family visit.

Being at Northwood was just like having a real civilian job and I had lived the life of Old Riley! I spent many wonderful times with my naval and civilian mates enjoying the fun of the sixties but after about fourteen months of this utter bliss another change reared its ugly head! Without a doubt, I had spent the best year of my naval career so far at HMS Warrior. I had made some fantastic friends at the base, such as Ian Scraggs who hailed from Borehamwood, Willie Dunningham from Colchester, Artie Artiss from Harpenden and the Petty Officer in charge of our actual team, Yeoman Dennis from the Chatham area in Kent. Personally, I would've been extremely happy to actually spend the rest of my time in the navy at Northwood but the RN had other ideas. Sadly, I was informed that it was to be another destroyer for me and this one was to be the Daring Class destroyer, HMS Decoy.

My RN official record sheet from HMS Warrior stated: Character – VG, Efficiency – SAT. RO2(T). No change again then. My character was obviously okay but my efficiency left a lot to be desired. Sounded a little like my sex life! It was here on 24th December 1964 whilst serving at HMS Warrior that I received my first Good Conduct Badge, which meant I could wear a stripe on the left sleeve of my uniform. No big deal as everyone eventually received these once you had served enough time. Just meant more bloody sewing!

HMS DECOY (D106) – (25th March 1965 – 16th July 1965)
HMS Decoy was stationed in Portsmouth harbour. She was tied up to the dockside and in a terrible state. There were dockyard personnel working from top to bottom on her and I had never seen a ship in such a dilapidated condition. The paintwork was horrible and she looked ready for the scrapyard let alone a commission in the Far East.

Obviously we couldn't live on-board and so we were stationed at the huge shore base in Portsmouth, HMS Victory. On weekdays and after breakfast each morning we marched down to the dockyard and on to HMS Decoy. There was just nothing to do except chip away at old paint work, preparing for the day when the dockyard had finished whatever they were doing to her and we could then paint her and make her seaworthy again. We marched back to Victory again for lunch and then back to Decoy again for the afternoon shift. Weekends were our own and we could either spend them in Portsmouth or go home.

It got a bit expensive going home every weekend by train and so many times we used to hitchhike. We used to catch a bus to Portsdown Hill, which is just outside

Portsmouth and on to the A3 towards London and the north and then start hitching a ride. Some of the crew used to go home in uniform and this was usually a good way to guarantee a lift. Others of us couldn't wait to get out of uniform and made the trip in civvies. The trick here though was to tie your naval hat to the side of your case or holdall and this had about the same affect as actually being in uniform. Most people would give Jolly Jack Tar a lift, especially ex-service personnel.

Again, this was a very cushy life and the ship's crew were a great bunch of lads.We played a lot of five-aside-football in the huge gymnasium at HMS Victory after our daily grind of doing absolutely sod all and after about an hour of this, showered and changed into our civilian clothes and had a night on the town. Portsmouth is a great and very vibrant town and there were many places and drinking holes to visit. We were spoilt for choice. This wonderful existence lasted for nearly four months but was to all change rather dramatically. The ship it seemed was beyond repair, certainly for the near future and so we were told that we would be joining HMS Delight, another Daring Class destroyer for the rest of the commission. The only snag with this was that HMS Delight was being refitted in Rosyth in bonny Scotland and so a few of the ship's company travelled by train to join up with her in Rosyth. I was amongst these and enjoyed the long journey immensely and spent most of the time in the refreshment carriage of the train downing the odd beer or ten! The rest of the crew stayed behind at HMS Victory and awaited the arrival of HMS Delight, which was to be a week or two later. On arrival in Scotland, HMS Delight was certainly in a better state than her sister ship HMS Decoy in Portsmouth but the only thing against her was that the engines did not work properly. We were told this was a job that had to be done in Portsmouth Dockyard and so HMS Delight made her way slowly and painfully down the east coast of England being towed unceremoniously by a tug! Could you imagine if war was imminent with an unknown foreign nation and they saw this pathetic sight of a warship being towed by a bloody tug! If I remember rightly, the trip took around five days door to door but eventually and indeed safely we arrived in Portsmouth harbour and joined up with the rest of the crew. And so it was goodbye to good old HMS Decoy. I would miss these times of doing just about nothing, as now it was back to being on a real warship!

HMS Decoy was eventually sold to the Peruvian Navy in 1970 and she was known as, BAP Ferre (DM-74). She was decommissioned in 2007. Probably now razorblades! There were to be no RN official records for HMS Decoy for any of us, as these just naturally transferred to HMS Delight, as it was still the same commission. Of course I probably would've been wonderful in both character and efficiency ratings, as how could you be average at doing absolutely fuck all!

HMS DELIGHT (D119) – (17th July 1965 – 28th March 1966)
And so we packed our kitbags and left HMS Victory for the last time and made our home on our new ship, HMS Delight. The ship was still not seaworthy but the living

HMS Delight

quarters, galley and offices etc. were up and running. The ship still had something quite seriously wrong in the boiler room but this was constantly being worked on by the dockyard work force.

We cleaned the ship up and painted her. She sparkled and for a change so did I. This ship's crew was the best I had ever been a part of and indeed had the best football team. Probably thanks to all the training we had on the five-a-side pitch at HMS Victory. We never lost a single game whilst in Portsmouth and were the first small ship's team to beat the mighty HMS Excellent, the large gunnery school on their home ground by two goals to one. We were ecstatic. The man in charge of the visual signalling branch was an absolute diamond. He was extremely tall and fit and a very good rugby player and had played at the highest level in the RN. His name was Yeoman Alfie Gore and I believe he came from Bristol. He encouraged sport and therefore we hit it off straight away and he would do anything in his power to see me play football for the ship's team.

Instead of me running around like a blue-arsed fly trying to swap shifts every time a game was on, he would do it for me. He was a real gentleman and one that was extremely good at his job as well. He was by far the best Yeoman I had had on any of my seagoing ships. It was a lesson I would put into operation much later in my life in the karate dojo as a sensei. Be encouraging but be fair. No one likes a bully or a big mouth. You have to earn respect, not demand it! And Yeoman Gore had certainly earned my respect. I loved being a part of this ship's company and for a change did my job to the very best of my ability. We had some great characters on-board and two of my best mates were telegraphists in the wireless office. One was from Harold Hill, Romford and went by the name of Smudger Smith and the other a bright ginger headed lad from Liverpool, Ginge Garner. Ginge was a huge Bob Dylan fan and used to go round quoting lines from the musical genius. Most of these would have no bearing on any current situation but he was so funny. He would just walk up to you and in a Bob Dylan accent quote something like, *The sun's not yellow, it's chicken*, or, *When you've got nothing you've got nothing to lose*, and then just walk off whistling or singing. Another of his favourites was from one of Dylan's more comical songs. *I sat my monkey on a log and ordered him to do the dog! He shook his tail and wagged his head, went and did the cat instead. He's a weird monkey!* Ginge had a whole bloody host of these sayings and being a Dylan fan myself I found him extremely funny.

Eventually the ship's boiler problems were sorted out and we did many trials in the Solent. Everything seemed to be okay with the ship and so next on the agenda was the dreaded Work-Up at Portland. For some reason (perhaps it was the great crew on-board) this seemed to go really well and seemed to fly by. The ship passed this six-week test with flying colours and was now ready for its Far East commission. Totally the opposite to any similar experiences on the two other destroyers I had served on, HMS Dunkirk and HMS Aisne, where the Work-Up had been a real pain in the arse!

It was now close to Christmas 1965 and indeed the worst Christmas of my entire life. The ship had been chosen to actually work at Christmas as the emergency destroyer in the English Channel. This was just to keep an eye on shipping in this busy part of the maritime world. We would sail as far as the Medway in Kent, turn around and back to Portsmouth and then turn back again. You just kept this monotony up until your allotted time was over, which I believe was about a week. We would go on our Christmas leave around the 28th of December and spend New Year with our families instead. Well that was the plan but not exactly how things turned out for me.

My beloved brother Martin (literally weeks before his death!)

I had just come off watch at nearly midnight on the 22nd December and was preparing to go to bed. As I was about to dive into my bunk my divisional officer and one of the duty telegraphists said they needed to see me urgently in the Wireless Office. I quickly donned some clothing and followed them along the passageway to the office. Once inside the officer told me to sit down. He told me he had some bad news for me. A million and one things shot through my brain. A coded message had been received from MOD Navy in London that my dear brother Martin had either committed or had attempted suicide. The worst thing though is that the coded word for either committed or attempted had come through garbled. They showed me the message and told me they had asked for an urgent reply to what the garbled word could be. It took about five minutes but it seemed more like five hours. The word was, COMMITTED. I was numb. I couldn't cry. I wanted to but just couldn't, as my whole body froze and I was in a state of suspended animation. I just kept shaking my head from side to side. The officer quickly left the Wireless Office and went to see the Captain. After about ten minutes he returned and said that the Captain had decided to turn the ship round and head back to Portsmouth harbour. The destroyer picked up speed and literally flew through the English Channel. The sea was rough but by golly could these Daring Class destroyers shift. At very early daylight we arrived outside the harbour but it was much too rough for the ship to enter through the narrow harbour entrance. So a tug was signalled to come out to the ship and pick me up. After about half an hour the tug arrived and tied itself up very gingerly alongside. I had to make a daring jump on to the deck of the tug as the rough sea threw both ship and tug up and down like corks. I more or less fell on to the wet deck of the tug and my suitcase was thrown to one of the tug's crew. The trip into the harbour only took about twenty minutes and before I knew it I was on Portsmouth and Southsea train station waiting for the train to Waterloo. The two main train journeys to Hemel Hempstead and the tube ride across London were just a blur. I was in another world. I just wouldn't accept the horrible news I had received only a few hours earlier. It wasn't until I rang the doorbell of my parent's home in Bennetts End that anything really hit home. My mum answered the door and her eyes and face were swollen with tears. I just broke down. I didn't know what to do or where to turn. I hugged my mum and dad and indeed my nan and grandad, who were at the house consoling my stricken mum and dad. Luckily enough they only lived about half a mile away. I don't think I stopped crying for many hours and even as I type this passage in the book, tears are streaming down my face. I believe my brother was in the hospital morgue and then an undertaker's parlour, I'm not totally sure. My mum and dad asked if I wished to see his body one last time but I just couldn't bring myself to do it. Firstly, because I had never seen a real dead body before and secondly, because it just seemed so final. Many years later I wished I actually had, just to say one last goodbye. But I know we will meet again one day, of this I'm sure.

It was only a few days before this terrible tragedy that we had spent the weekend together. We had had a few drinks in the local pub and had finished up in a nightclub in Watford. Martin was a Mod and was always smartly groomed and dressed. He loved the music of The Who, The Kinks and of all those wonderful groups of the day. His hero was Keith Moon, The Who's drummer. He spent many a night in the clubs of Wardour Street in the Soho part of London, especially the Marquee, dancing and just having a great time following his heroes and sadly, as we found out later popping pills. We used to take the piss out of each other's love of music, as I veered towards Bob Dylan and the Folk/Rock scene and he certainly didn't. But I must admit I did really enjoy the music that Martin loved and still do to this very day especially, The Who, The Kinks, The Animals, The Small Faces and The Hollies. I know he was looking forward to Christmas, although I wouldn't be there until just after and we laughed and joked and on waving goodbye on the Sunday evening both said how much we looked forward to seeing each other again and what a great time we would have. I could never have guessed in a million years that that would be the last time I would see him here on earth. I have never spent such an awful Christmas in all my life. I sat with mum and dad and we slowly opened the presents we had bought for him and indeed the one's he had bought for us. I had purchased a copy of his favourite groups first LP record, *My Generation* by The Who and a pair of desert boots. He had bought me a pair of football shin pads, as he knew mine had seen better days.

My dad explained what had actually happened on that fateful day. Martin had once or twice threatened to take his own life in the few months previous but these had only been threats. He worked as a trainee pharmacist at a chemist's shop in Borehamwood. On the day in question he had overslept. This was no big deal but he had been given the shop's keys by the owner and asked to open up. I was told that he never made it on this awful day but instead rang my mum at the hospital and told her of his plight and what he was going to do. Mum worked as a receptionist at the local hospital and she detected something in his voice that just didn't seem right. She couldn't get away from her hospital duties so immediately rang my dad. Dad worked as a bus conductor and worked locally at the Two Waters Bus Garage. On receiving this message from my mum he dashed home but sadly was too late. Martin was in his pyjamas and lying on the living room floor. The electric bar fire was on and on the hearth lay his watch, gold ring and wallet all in a neat pile. He had passed away peacefully. We didn't have a private telephone in those days but literally just opposite the house was a public telephone. Dad rang for an ambulance. In minutes it arrived and announced that Martin was dead. The ambulance took his body to the hospital where of course my mum feared the worst. As they took his body out of the ambulance and unbeknown to them, mum was watching their every move with baited breath. It was pronounced that he had taken an overdose of some very strong barbiturates that he had procured from the chemist where he worked.

The case went to the Coroner's Court where the coroner announced that Martin was a schizophrenic and with his mind in a state of turmoil had taken his own life. Before the actual hearing the coroner had to come round to our house and search Martin's bedroom. In a locked cupboard they found a huge, sealed bag of purple hearts (the in-drug in the clubs and dancehalls of the day) and a syringe. The syringe had never been used. The coroner was a lovely man and seeing that mum and dad could take no more, flushed the pills down the toilet and put the syringe in his briefcase and said, 'We'll just forget about these shall we?' This was a lovely gesture as a report of Martin's death appeared in the following week's local paper but nothing was said of the coroner's find.

The Who's fantastic film, *Quadrophenia* says it all. I have to be in the right mood to watch this excellent film, which is a wonderful review of those times and I cringe when the father screams at the lad, Jimmy (Phil Daniels), that he is a bloody schizophrenic. Everything is in the film, the pill popping, the music, the violence, the one night stands, the good times and indeed the sad times. Young people who were searching for the meaning of life. I believe Martin truthfully was searching but sadly never found it. We'll never know!

Since that awful, awful day I have always worn the gold ring that he was so proud of and that was one of the very first things he had purchased with his first month's wages. Even to this very day, I cannot call to account any one day of my life so vividly. It seemed so unfair that the youngest member of our family would be the first to die. He died eight days before his 18th Birthday! Martin was cremated at the West Herts. Crematorium in Garston, Watford and his name placed in the book of remembrance.

I was granted a few days extra leave on compassionate grounds but once this was over reported back to the ship, which was now docked in Portsmouth harbour. After a few days my Divisional Officer called me to his office. He explained that a letter had been received from my mum and dad's doctor, a Dr. Walton in Hemel Hempstead regarding the current state of affairs. The letter explained that due to my mum and dad's mental health and as I was now their only offspring and was about to be posted to the Far East for a year he wondered if the RN could do something about this dismal situation. My Divisional Officer told me he would be willing to either get me posted back to HMS Warrior at Northwood, or indeed see about getting me a compassionate discharge from the RN. He gave me a few days to think things over and have a word with mum and dad and then let him know my decision. After chatting with mum and dad it was decided that going back to Northwood would probably be the better of the two options. I wasn't really skilled in anything other than semaphore and the Morse code and there wasn't a lot of call for these two skills in Civvy Street. I could type but it was agreed that it would probably be best for all concerned to get posted back to HMS Warrior. And so this is what actually happened. I would miss my friends on HMS Delight, as this was by far the best crew that I'd ever served with and indeed the best football team. So after a couple of more weeks on HMS Delight it was time to say goodbye to all of my friends and head back to Northwood. The strangest of things happened on the very same day. My best friend on HMS Delight was Smudger Smith from the wireless office and he had put in a request to buy himself out of the RN. This eventually came through and on the very same day that I left the ship, he also left the RN. So we travelled up to London together on the train and said goodbye in London as he made his way to his home in Harold Hill, Romford and I made my trip to Northwood and then on to Hemel Hempstead.

HMS Delight was eventually broken up and scrapped at Inverkeithing in May 1971. This time my RN official record sheet from HMS Decoy/Delight stated: Character – VG, Efficiency – SAT. RO2(T). Once again still the same. Extremely consistent but no nice footnote this time!

HMS WARRIOR – (29th March 1966 – 5th March 1967)
And so it was to be another posting to Northwood and the life of a part time civilian, or as close as damn it. Things hadn't changed much since my departure a year previous but nearly all of the personnel were different. All my close friends from my last visit had now gone to other postings. My actual job was the same as before, down 'The Hole' in the NATO Main Signal Office working the shift pattern of two days on and two days off.

Again, we had a decent football team and won most of our matches. We became runners-up in a prestigious West Herts. senior cup competition, just losing out in the final 2-1 to Clements of Watford at Woodside Stadium in North Watford. My mum and dad were there to watch a very close match and one in which yours truly scored an offside goal that would've taken the match to extra time. Of course my biased view of the goal was that there was absolutely nothing wrong with it but the referee and linesman disagreed. We did really well considering the opposition had two Luton Town FC players playing. They weren't regular first team players for Luton but they were both just a bit good to say the least.

I still enjoyed my time with my mates in Hemel Hempstead and whilst at Northwood started dating one of the

Best man at Nick Byatt's wedding (Just look at that suit!)

WRAF's. She worked down 'The Hole' in the PABX Telephone Exchange and was on many of the shifts that I worked on. Being in the Women's Royal Air Force her shift pattern was a little different than mine but often our paths collided. Her name was Janet Elizabeth Flynn and she came from Pembury, near Tunbridge Wells in Kent. Over the months ahead I saw a lot of her and eventually fell in love and Jan would eventually become my first wife.

My time at Northwood this time was very similar to my last experience. I had new friends and one of these asked me to be his best man. His name was Nick Byatt and his wife-to-be was Kay. They married at a church in Northchurch near Berkhamsted, which is the next town to Hemel Hempstead and this was my very first time at being the best man. I was very honoured. I can't even remember the speech but you can bet your sweet life it was crap! But my life would never be the same again without Martin. I started to drink too much and lose my temper a lot. I just couldn't comprehend what had happened and it made me very angry. Why me? This became my password for life.

I remember the captain of our football team was injured and couldn't play for one of our league matches and right out of the blue, they made me captain. Anyway, to cut a long story short I got sent off for the first time in my football career and I was the bloody captain! There had been a strong and rather late tackle between one of the opposition's fullbacks and myself. I don't think anyone was really to blame, it was just a hard tackle. After we had picked ourselves up, and the referees whistle had blown, I squared up to my opponent and told him I was going to punch his fucking lights out. He replied, you and whose army? Just as I was about to throw the first punch, the referee split us up and put our names in his little black book (This was before the yellow and red cards of today). He told us off in no uncertain terms but I was not finished yet. The next time the fullback and I came together I upended him about a million miles in the air with the latest tackle you have ever seen in your life. Again, the whistle blew and I was sent off. As I walked off towards the changing rooms, I told this guy that I would be waiting for him in the changing rooms when the match was over. Again, the referee called me over and gave me a right bollocking and said he was going to report me to my Divisional Officer back at Northwood. This seemed to have the right affect on me and I miserably made my way to the changing rooms and the showers. I believe the match was a draw and afterwards my team mates made damned sure I didn't go anywhere near the opposing team's dressing room and so I thought that that was that. Wrong! The very next day my Divisional Officer, a certain Lt. Franks called me into his office. (Lt. is the abbreviation for Lieutenant for those who are not sure). I didn't like this little man and he didn't like me. He had made his way through the lower ranks of the RN and made it to officer rank. He came from Liverpool and was pretty much disliked by the whole communication branch at Northwood. He dressed me down proper about being the captain of the football team and setting an example and banned me from playing football for a month and told me if anything like this happened again then I would really be in trouble. I semi-sneered and told him that I couldn't care less if I never played for the team again and that it wasn't my idea to make me captain. He blew his top and told me that he would be watching out for me the next time I so much as thought about putting a foot wrong. Sadly though, he would have the last bloody laugh, as you will see in a few paragraphs time.

I did start to play again for the team after my ban was served and was very glad I did. One of our games was against Tring Town FC under their floodlights at Pendley Manor, Tring. We were all looking forward to this big time but expected to get absolutely thrashed, as this was a proper team in a proper league. It was to be a pre-season friendly for Tring Town but as you probably know, there is no such thing as a bloody friendly. There was too much honour at stake. I played on the left wing and had a blinder of a game, as indeed did our goalkeeper. At halftime it was 1-1 but it was in the second half that I scored one of the best goals of my life. I beat a couple of players and raced in from the wing and just let fly. The ball absolutely flew into the far, top corner of the goal. This was to be the winning goal and our team could not believe that we had beaten such a prestigious team. We were absolutely elated. After getting changed and in the bar afterwards the barman said that one of the officials of the club wanted to speak to our goalkeeper and me. After a brief word or two about our footballing backgrounds, the club actually signed us up there and then. I was on cloud nine but sadly not for too long!

A lot of my mates in Hemel Hempstead and indeed one or two at Northwood seemed to be getting married. Jan and I had been going out with each other for a few months and had decided also that it was time to tie the knot. And so the day eventually arrived. My best man was another signalman from HMS Warrior and a good friend who was on the same watch as me, Alan Henwood. The wedding was held on 21st January 1967 in Jan's home village of Pembury at St. Peter Upper Church. Her family were all there, as indeed were mine. Jan's dad had died a few years earlier and so she was to be given away by her eldest brother Eric. The service went really well, as did the reception in a local hall afterwards. We honeymooned for a week in St Ives in Cornwall and stayed at a small guesthouse in Carbis Bay. Then it was back to Northwood for me and out of the WRAF for Jan. You were not allowed to be married in the WRAF's unless you were an officer in those days, so Jan's Air Force days were over. For the foreseeable future she lived

Wedding No.1 - Left to right: Dad, Mum, Alan Henwood (Best man), Me, Jan, Maureen (Jan's sister and bridesmaid), Jan's mum and her brother Eric who gave her away

with my parents in Hemel Hempstead. My wonderful nan had just made my wedding day, as she promised she would. You could tell she was very ill and sadly in the middle of February she passed away with a heart attack. She was 79 years old and I loved her so very much and will never forget her and the wonderful times we had in my early years at Wealdstone. My grandad was absolutely devastated, as they had been married for well over fifty years. I still miss her to this very day and she was an absolutely wonderful lady. She was a shoulder to cry on throughout all of my younger years and I was so glad she made my wedding day. Other than this horrible incident, life wasn't too bad and I enjoyed my married existence to the full. But sadly, every silver lining has a fucking cloud!

One morning at Northwood, also around the middle of February 1967 and just after my nan's death, I was called in to the office of the dreaded Lt. Franks. I thought I must've done something wrong but couldn't think what. He asked me to sit down. He then told me the unthinkable. I was to be drafted from HMS Warrior at the beginning of March to HMS Jufair, a shore base in Bahrain. I asked if I could take my new wife Jan with me and he said no, as it was a single person's posting. I couldn't believe my ears and told him what he could do with the draft. I detected a sly smile on his face as he said there was nothing he could do about it. I told him why I had been drafted to Northwood in the first place but he said he obviously knew all of this and as I was now married, my mum and dad were no longer my next of kin and so things would change. I had spent the customary year at

Nan (just made my wedding day, as she promised)

Northwood and would now be drafted to Bahrain for a year. I just couldn't conceive being without Jan for a year and told him of my plight. I also told him of my nan's death and the state of my mum's health, due to first Martin dying and now the death of her mum. Again that horrible sly little grin as he stated that his hands were tied. I honestly felt like decking him but knew this would land me up in even more trouble and I didn't want to spend time in some HM Force's prison somewhere, so this idea was quickly put on hold. I panicked and told him that I'd rather go on the run than go to bloody Bahrain. This was a silly thing to actually threaten, as he then forbid me any leave from Northwood from that moment on and told me not to leave the camp under any circumstances. This meant I couldn't go home to see mum and dad or of course Jan, who now had to make the journey to Northwood to see me on my days off. I was on some sort of probation and had to sign in at the RN Regulation Office about four times a day. The day before I was due to fly to Bahrain, Jan, mum and dad had travelled to the camp to say their last goodbyes. It was a very sad affair with many tears but I promised them faithfully that I would do everything in my power to get out of the RN as quickly as was humanly possible. The next day absolutely flew by and was mainly taken up with packing. That evening two Royal Marines escorted me in an RN car all the way to RAF Lyneham in Swindon. Once there, they had to actually watch me board the RAF VC10 for Bahrain just in case I decided to do a last minute runner. I gave them a wave as I walked up the steps of the plane. To my surprise they even waved back. And so my second time at Northwood had come to an abrupt end. I now made a very serious pact with myself to buy myself out of the RN at the earliest opportunity, as had my friend Smudger Smith on HMS Delight.

This time my RN official record sheet from HMS Warrior stated: Character – VG, Efficiency – SAT. RO2(T).Yet again more of the same but with no mention of my shenanigans with Lt. Franks!

HMS JUFAIR - (6th March 1967 – 14th February 1968)
I can still remember to this very day the moment I stepped out of the plane at RAF Muharraq, the RAF base and airport in Bahrain. I had never in my life felt heat like it. It was like hitting a solid wall. I thought to myself, fucking wonderful, I'm only here

for a bloody year! I had now built up a real hate for the RN and this damned heat wasn't going to help matters one bloody iota!

After settling into my living quarters and into my job in the Main Signal Office, my sole purpose in life was to get out of the RN. I arranged for a meeting between my new Divisional Officer, a certain Lt. Mitten and myself. Talk about chalk and cheese, as Lt. Mitten was the total opposite to Lt. Franks at Northwood. This chap was human and listened intently to my sad story about the current events that had happened in my family life over the last year or so. He too thought that a discharge from the RN was the answer but wasn't absolutely sure I would obtain it on compassionate grounds alone. I told him that I would be willing to buy myself out and he said he would put this to the Captain. This he did and the Captain agreed there was a genuine case to answer here. They would use the compassionate angle and this would give me a bit of leverage in buying my way out of the RN. Just because you had the cash (which I didn't have at the time) didn't mean they would let you out when you felt like it. It had to go before a board at MOD Navy in London and they would decide. The RN had put a lot of cash into training its personnel and so wouldn't let them leave when they felt like it. Blimey, there would be nobody left in if this were the case! The other painful thing was this procedure could take up to a year to actually happen and so wasn't the perfect answer.

But Lt. Mitten had another ace up his sleeve. He asked if I knew any of the ratings at HMS Jufair that were on a married drafting. These couples were at Bahrain for two years and had very nice married quarters, whereas the single fellows were there for just twelve months and lived on the camp. Luckily for me, I had a great friend staying at the married quarters and one whom I had spent my first year at HMS Warrior in Northwood with. This was Willie Dunningham from Colchester who had also married one of the WRAF's at Northwood and whose name was Bernie (short for Bernadette I guess). This was a huge stroke of luck and Willie and Bernie said they would love to have Jan and me staying with them. We would pay them a small rent so everything was tickety-boo. Lt. Mitten said he would set it all up and get Jan a visa and a cheap flight, care of the RN funds! What a wonderful man and someone I immediately looked up to and would work hard for. Just shows you what a bit of interest and enthusiasm can do for one's fellow man. Jan could only get a visa for three months in Bahrain but Lt. Mitten stated that the authorities very rarely checked-up on this and he was sure she could stay for the duration. So after about six weeks on my own at HMS Jufair, Jan came out to join me and we moved in with Willie and Bernie. This was much better and life started to take an upward turn again.

Willie was a brilliant guitarist and I do mean brilliant. He would play loads of stuff by Chet Atkins, a country guitarist from the USA and indeed one of the very best guitarists in the world. I had tinkered around on other people's instruments but was totally useless. I think I could play the theme from the original *Batman* series on television but so could a fucking chimpanzee! I asked Willie if he would teach me.

I think he found this a small honour and proceeded to teach me three chords, so as to be able to play quite a bit of rock and roll and folk music. After mastering the chords of, C, F and G he then showed me another chord pattern of, A, E and D. The hardest thing though was getting from one chord to another and this seemed to take forever. But slowly and surely something started to sound like a tune. Two of my musical heroes, Buddy Holly and Bob Dylan played many of their hits in these two chord patterns and so I was well and truly hooked. The occupants of the married quarters for miles around were now totally sick of *Peggy Sue* and *Blowing in the Wind*!

On our days off we would make for the sheikh's beach. This was a man-made beach on the other side of the island. You could only get there by taxi or private car but it was certainly worth the trip. Bahrain is not naturally sandy and the sheikh, whose full name was Sheikh Isa Bin-Salman Al Khalifah had invested heavily in shiploads of sand being transported to this part of the island to make up this wonderful beach. It had a small pier and the sheikh's beach house residence sat in all its glory behind the beach itself. The sea was beautifully clear and warm and we used to spend the whole day there just sunbathing and swimming. The sheikh's favourite music was that of the country and western star, Jim Reeves and his velvet voice wafted daily from large speakers situated on the beach house. *Welcome to my World*. It was idyllic.

Sheikh of Bahrain (Sheikh Isa Bin-Salman Al Khalifah)

The sheikh's servants, at certain intervals, would bring out free coffee and biscuits for the people on the beach. This sounds a wonderful and very expensive gesture but the truth of the matter was that Bahrainis were not allowed anywhere near this very private and select beach. It was reserved for HM Forces personnel who had their wives with them and for the many European and USA oil companies residents and their wives. You were not allowed on the beach unless accompanied by your wife or girlfriend, or perhaps someone else's!

If you were really unbelievably lucky you would get an invite from the sheikh to attend a party that same evening at his private beach house. The sheikh's personal manservant, a chap called Mohammed, used to come to your table and give you a personal invite from the sheikh. Around half a dozen couples would be invited and how could you refuse? In our time at Bahrain this happened to Jan and me on two separate occasions. We would dash back home and make ourselves presentable, returning at eight o'clock prompt that same evening. It was a wonderful experience to mix with royalty and see how the other half live. The beach house was so very plush, as you would expect and done out in a beautiful red velvet. A few of the sheikh's male relations would also be present and the alcohol flowed. Of course the sheikh and his family did not drink as this is against their religion but there was plenty for us westerners. British and American pop music would be playing and the sheikh and his family would dance with the wives and girlfriends of the male guests. He was a very short man and his nose would come up to approximately the height of the western women's breasts. A sight for sore eyes indeed! These were absolutely brilliant nights and would finish around midnight. On leaving, each couple received a gift from the sheikh personally as they left. On our first visit to the beach house, Jan and I got presented with a plain envelope. We thanked the sheikh but still didn't know its contents. When we got into the taxi we hurriedly opened the envelope to find the equivalent of three hundred pounds sterling in the local Bahraini currency, the dinar. We were over the moon, as this could be used for eventually buying my way out of the RN. What a stroke of luck!

On our second visit a few months later and on leaving, I was presented with a solid gold Omega watch and Jan a beautiful multi-faced and multi-strapped Rotary watch. This fine gesture gave me my first love of wristwatches, which I still have to this very day. These were the only two times we personally visited the sheikh and his family but something that will stay in my memory forever.

We visited the beach on many occasions but other than the above two times, a couple of other instances stand out in my mind. Mohammed the manservant, sometimes would walk around with a beautiful falcon secured to his arm. It was always hooded but it was a magnificent bird. On the day in question and at the sheikh's private table on the beach, a beautiful white dove was secured firmly to one of the legs of the table. Nobody could understand the reason for this but would soon find out. At the sheikh's command, Mohammed appeared at the sheikh's table with the hooded falcon on his arm. He bent down and untied the dove from the table leg and let it fly away. I thought this was a really nice and humane gesture. Wrong! He then took the hood off of the falcon and let it go. Well, I'm sure you can guess the rest. It looked quickly around and then on sighting the dove above flew straight into the air and with its sharp talons, killed it stone dead. This was bad enough but then the falcon landed by the sheikh's table with the poor dove in its talons and started to pluck and eat it. After about ten minutes there was nothing left except for a load of white feathers which were now scattering across the sand in the light breeze.

Hours before the dreaded sunburn (that is the tiller between my legs - honest!)

Another time we were walking along the small pier when someone spotted a huge ray in the shallow water just below the pier. A few commands were given between the sheikh and his entourage and then one of them appeared with a bloody twelve-bore shotgun. The sheikh ran down the pier with the gun in hand and blasted the poor ray out of the water. These things personally made me cringe and I found them extremely cruel at the time and indeed still do today. Different culture perhaps, who knows?

On one occasion and before Jan had actually arrived in Bahrain I suffered one of the worst cases of sunburn known to man! A few of the lads had hired a small wooden boat, called an Arab dhow for the day. It had a small engine and you didn't need a degree in seamanship or boat handling to be able to work it. We stocked up with beer and sandwiches and made for a huge wreck just off of the coast of Bahrain. This was a tanker of some sort that had run aground many years previous. Nobody was actually allowed on the wreck as it was rusting and very dangerous but you could swim around it if you so wished. All I wore all day was just a pair of swimming trunks and it was the hottest bloody day imaginable. We had a lot of great fun playing silly games in the water and eating and drinking merrily on the boat. I remember vividly just diving into the water from the boat when one of my mates shouted, 'Sea snakes!' I nearly shit myself and couldn't get back into the boat fast enough. I thought he was pulling my leg until he pointed to two of these creatures swimming in unison past our boat. I don't know whether they were highly venomous or not and I certainly didn't stop to bloody ask. That was it for me, no more bloody swimming. Of course this was the worst thing that could happen as the sun scorched my puny body. It wasn't until I got back to the camp that I started to feel ill. My shoulders and parts of my face were badly blistered and it even hurt to have a shower. I couldn't put a shirt on and had to sleep without the customary top sheet and nearly bloody froze to death in the air-conditioned mess deck. I used bottle after bottle of calamine lotion, which was the only thing that felt good on my burnt skin. I also had to make sure that I turned up for my shifts in the MSO on time, as sunburn was considered a self-inflicted injury and was very much frowned on by the hierarchy of the RN, especially if it stopped you from performing your job properly. On those early duties and for quite a few days, my bloody shirt killed me and sometimes got stuck to my skin! Silly boy!

Another snake story was when all the locals were making a hell of a fuss outside our block of flats. We went outside to see what the commotion was all about. Eventually we found an Arab that could speak a little English and he told us that a snake had crawled up a pipe and into the air conditioning unit of one of the flats. Thank goodness it wasn't ours. Anyway, there was a lot of banging around on the pipe outside and from inside the flat as well and eventually the snake made a run for it and I believe escaped. To this very day I couldn't tell you whether it was venomous or not but I know I couldn't sleep for a bloody week, especially as our bed was right up against our flat's air conditioning unit. We immediately moved the bed away from the wall and I used to spray a ton of fly spray into the unit before going to bed at night and cover the unit with a big blanket, tucking it in at the sides. Anyway, I'm glad to say our slithery friend never made another guest appearance!

On the whole though life carried on as normal and was very relaxed at HMS Jufair. I think a lot of this was to do with the heat, as it was the hottest place on the planet that I'd visited to date. Jan and I went to watch camel racing on one day and this was different to say the least, and I for one didn't realise how fast these large creatures could run. We made small bets and the whole day was real fun.

HMS Jufair 1967 swimming cup winners

A sort of Bahraini Ascot for animals that had the hump!

We visited Manama, the capital of Bahrain on quite a few occasions, mainly to buy presents and things for when we went back home to England. It used to make us laugh at the difference in cultures. Here, men would walk hand in hand with each other, whilst women would walk a few paces behind. On the local television channels even kissing was not allowed. It was very funny to see a Hollywood couple going in for a kiss, the film was then quickly cut and the next thing was they were on the way out again! We were forbidden to make any sexual gestures to the opposite sex in public and were not allowed to kiss or even hold hands with our loved ones.

I even won a small cup for swimming, as our mixed team of communication ratings and Royal Marines won the HMS Jufair Annual Swimming Cup. I think this was mainly due to the Royal Marine contingent as they swam like bloody dolphins. Yours truly swam more like a pregnant earwig and took on more bloody water than a sponge! But at least we won.

I also played football for HMS Jufair but the heat was so crippling and there was certainly no grass. Sliding tackles would take the skin off of half of your leg. We would play the game and then jump straight into the swimming pool, which was very close to the football pitch and then go for a few cold beers in the Ace of Clubs. The Ace of Clubs was the only place at HMS Jufair where you could purchase alcoholic beverages. Bahrain is a dry country and drinking is strictly against their religion, so there were no bars or clubs to visit outside of the camp. So the Ace of Clubs and other HM Forces bases such as RAF Muharraq were the only watering holes for us Brits.

It was in the Ace of Clubs that we first came into contact with Clint Eastwood. Not literally of course, but on film. Once a week we would have film night and chairs were placed out in cinema fashion in the club and we bought our beers and anything we fancied munching ready for the show. On this particular day the film was a western. It was called *A Fistful of Dollars*. The film had been out in England for the best part of two years but it took that long for the RN to catch up. We watched in utter amazement and the one thing that stood out was that the good guy was also a baddie. The music by Ennio Morricone was absolutely out of this world and we sat and watched the film three times through with only small toilet breaks in between the showings. That was it. Many of the ship's company went in to Manama to try to buy toy guns and holsters. Some clever bastards even made their own holsters but everywhere you looked on the camp for at least three months there were gunfights. People went around whistling the catchy tune and quickly drawing imaginary six-shooters. There were lists drawn up to see who had the fastest gun and some ratings even greased their holsters with something horrible from the ship's galley. Amazing what a good film and the blistering heat could do!

When I look back I suppose on the whole we enjoyed ourselves but it was just so boring and the year seemed to take an eternity to go. It was a bit like a prison sentence where you literally counted the days until your release.

Near the end of our days in Bahrain, Jan fell pregnant. She took all the tests and sure enough they were positive. She was also way over her visa limit but nobody had said anything and so neither did we. She could not travel home with me as she would have to go home on a private airline, courtesy of BOAC and I would be going home courtesy of the RAF. Also due to the pregnancy it was agreed by the doctoring staff that the earlier the better. And so Jan left to go back to England about six weeks before I was due to depart. I remember waving her off at Bahrain Airport and just knew that the next six weeks would seem like six years.

But good news was very close at hand. Jan had only been back in England for around two weeks when I was called to the office of my Divisional Officer. He sat me down and told me the good news. Well, in actual fact he showed me the good news and there on a draft from MOD Navy in London was my name amongst those who had been successful in purchasing their freedom.

I was absolutely elated but he told me that I would have to finish the four weeks I had left at HMS Jufair and then I would be sent to HMS Victory in Portsmouth for my release. Yippeee! I immediately telephoned the good news to Jan and my parents and couldn't wait for the following four weeks to vanish. The international telephone call cost a £1 a minute but it was well worth it!

Eventually, the four weeks passed and I said goodbye to my friends on the base. I was driven to RAF Muharraq and boarded another VC10 and headed for home. On arrival at RAF Lyneham, we made our way across the tarmac and into a large building. We all stood around waiting to go through the customs. Before this actually happened though, a huge Royal Marine got on to a platform and informed us that if anyone had any pornography, drugs of any kind that were not personally prescribed, or weapons of any kind, now would be a good time to get rid of them. He continued and told the gathering, that if you were caught with any of the aforementioned, any leave you had coming to you would be spent in an HM Forces prison somewhere nasty. For a few moments there was absolute still in the crowd. The calm before the storm! Then all of a sudden, first one, then a couple and then an absolute deluge made their way to the toilets. My curiosity got the better of me and I went to see what this was all about. Either everyone had a sudden urge to go to the loo to get rid of some bodily waste matter, or perhaps and even more likely, thanks to the Royal Marine's drastic and threatening message needed to get rid of some, not such bodily matter. The scene that greeted me was one of absolute hilarity. There were pornographic magazines and photographs everywhere and also pocket-knives of all shapes and sizes, especially flick-knives. Also you could see the odd dubious container full of some sort of pills. I thought to myself, what happens to all this dodgy gear when we leave? Either it gets thrown away or our Royal Marine friend is going to make a bloody packet on the black market! Anyway, eventually everyone was ready and we made our way through the custom's posts. I hadn't got a lot to declare as Jan had taken most of the stuff we had purchased with her earlier. The RAF chap in front of me, though, got absolutely clobbered. I had never seen anyone with so much camera equipment. He had about four new Nikon and Pentax cameras around his neck and enough lenses to set up shop. They charged him an absolute fortune and he hadn't enough money on him to pay. Luckily enough his wife was on the other side of the barrier to meet him and they had to call her over to pay the difference. Now I started to panic. Had I got enough money and how much would they clobber me for the gold watch. I only had two items to declare and these were my two watches. I had the gold Omega from the sheikh and one I had purchased before this wonderful present from the ruler. It was a Seiko and a sort of a diver's watch. I got charged a few pounds for the Seiko as I wore the gold one on my wrist and told the customs officer it was for personal use, which of course was true and even more importantly, he believed.

And so my Middle East experience had come to an end and now it was home to Hemel Hempstead for about three weeks leave. This time my final record in the RN stated: Character – VG, Efficiency – SAT. RO2(T). This time though there was a small paragraph added. An excellent operator, employed in MSO (Main Signal Office) using Teleprinter procedure. Bloody typical! Only any good when I'm about to leave the RN!

HMS VICTORY - (15th February 1968 – 25th April 1968)
After my three wonderful weeks of paid leave had expired then it was back to HMS Victory for my release from the RN. But there was still one more cock up to come! On arrival at the Main Gate of the shore base HMS Victory I was told that I had to report to Nelson's bloody flagship, HMS Victory, which of course is dry-docked in Portsmouth harbour. So off I traipsed, kitbag over my shoulder and suitcase in hand. I walked up the gangplank of this wonderful vessel and was directed to an

Wrong bloody ship!

office. Here I was told that there had been a mistake and I should definitely be at the shore base HMS Victory. So off again I trudged back to the shore base. This time they searched and studied my documents a little closer and after a brief apology stated that I was now in the right place. I was well and truly knackered by this time. Nelson's famous saying came to mind, 'Kiss me, Hardy'. Malcolm's famous saying was even better, 'Kiss my arse, navy!'

I spent the final two months of my ten-year naval career at HMS Victory, returning my gas mask and certain parts of my kit. All the paperwork was now in place and I had paid the £100 for my discharge out of my last month's wages. This may not seem a lot now but was a tidy sum in 1968. And so the day eventually arrived. I was dressed in my civilian clothes and now just had a suitcase to contend with. I would kill anyone who suggested I should go anywhere near Nelson's bloody flagship! I made my last salute at the main gate and then made for Portsmouth train station. And so it was goodbye to the RN and ten years of my life.

I was enrolled in the RFR (Royal Fleet Reserve) from the 26th April 1968 until the 18th December 1969. This was compulsory on leaving the RN and I received a small cheque every month for being a part of this group. It didn't actually entail any training as such but you just had to stand by in case of a war.

Civvy Street

Part One (1968-1973)

It is one thing coming out of the RN but then of course you have to find a bloody job! The only thing I stood a chance in, was something that involved communications and preferably teleprinting or telex, as semaphore and the Morse code had gone out with the bloody ark! There was nothing on offer in Hemel Hempstead and so I was pointed to an agency in London that dealt with these types of jobs. The agency was called The Three T's Agency and its offices were in Fleet Street. The three T's stood for, Telephone, Telex and Teleprinter operators. So off I trudged hoping for some temp work and even more hopefully full time employment.

For the last few months Jan had got herself a job as a telephonist at a local firm in Hemel Hempstead and I had enough pay from the RN to last a while but it wouldn't last for too long. We lived with my mum and dad and had our names down for a council house. After a couple of small temporary posts, I eventually got lucky and found some full time employment. It was shift work in the City of London and in a road named St Mary Axe. The name of the company was Bunge and Co. Ltd who were and probably still are an extremely successful Merchant Bank. I worked in the Communication Department of the company, using the many teleprinters and telex machines that adorned the office walls. There were basically three shifts, the morning shift from 8am until 2pm, the afternoon shift from 2pm until 10pm and the dreaded nightshift from 10pm until 8am. Sundays were off if I remember rightly and a skeleton staff worked for a few hours on a Saturday morning. You also had one other day off in the week. The worst thing though was the crippling train fares from Hemel Hempstead to Bank Underground Station, which was the station closest to work. I met some good friends at Bunge and Co. and two of these, Ian Rutherford from Chelmsford and John Montague from Stratford in East London, were both on the same shift as me. We did have some laughs as all three of us had the same sick sense of humour.

The biggest trouble on coming out of the HM Forces for many blokes is that you still want to be one of the lads and this is not the best recipe for a successful marriage. Our immediate boss was the Communication Department supervisor. His name was Bill Brockie and he was a Scotsman. Bill was very good at his job and had also been in the Royal Navy many years before me. But Bill was gay and this was before this became fashionable. This didn't bother me in the least but it was blindingly obvious that he started to fancy me a little. He used to ask me out for drinks and I would only go if Ian and John accompanied me. Bill was very good with his money and wouldn't let any of us buy a round. But every once in a while his hand would find its way on to my knee and start to make its way up my thigh. I used to push him away and told him in a very deep and scrotum swinging voice that I wasn't like that and that I was a very happily married man. I think he eventually got the message but it did take a while. Eventually the manager of the

81

department, Charlie Paul retired and Bill became the office manager. A new supervisor was appointed and his name was Bill Cowell. Another bloody Bill but at least this one kept his hands to himself!

On the 30th September at 9.40am of that very first year at Bunge and Co. (1968), my daughter Tracey was born. She was a bonny, bouncing 7lbs 5oz. Tracey my daughter, many years later would change the spelling of her Christian name to Tracie. It may have been that later in life, as I actually married a Tracey that she wanted her name spelt slightly differently. Jan gave birth at St Paul's Hospital, which in those days was the maternity hospital for the Hemel Hempstead region. The hospital itself is no longer there as they pulled it down and built a small housing estate on the site. Blimey, I was now a dad. Jan had had a few stitches after the birth but on the whole both mum and baby were fit and well. Here is an extract from Jan's diary from that day: *Baby started about 4am. Went to St. Pauls about 5am. Tracey Jane born at 9.40am. 7lbs 5ozs and gorgeous. Had stitches in ward at 2pm. Fed Tracey at 6pm. She was fast asleep when the best daddy and hubby in the world came to see his beautiful daughter and worn out but very, very happy wife. Was woken up at 5am after a bad night's sleep. Fed Tracey, got up a few times. Fed again at 9am. Done a few exercises at 11.30am.*

Tracey, my lovely baby daughter

Because of our family increase and the overcrowding at mum and dad's we were eventually given a brand new three-bedroom council house. We had lived with mum and dad for all of 1968 and early in 1969 moved into number 15, Hanger Close in the Lockers Park part of Hemel Hempstead. The house should've been number 13 but because of superstitious reasons the council had missed out the number 13 and jumped from 11 straight to 15. Sadly, and as luck had it, number 13 might've been the right number if you believe in such rubbish!

I was over the moon and now was a proud father, but sadly not a very good one. Over the next couple of years my drinking habit was becoming too regular and extremely dangerous. I started to miss days at work getting Jan to phone in to tell them of my false sicknesses, which in all truthfulness were gigantic hangovers. Even after the morning or afternoon shifts, Ian, John and me would go to the local pub and down a few pints listening to the music of the day from the jukebox. On the odd occasion I wouldn't even go home and dossed down somewhere, usually a friend's house or a train station until the first train home the following morning. This, of course meant I would miss work the next day and Jan would again phone me in sick.

Even my football started to suffer. I played for a Sunday team, Boxmoor and after a good night on the town the previous night, would often turn up with a huge hangover and of course this was not acceptable. When I wasn't drinking in London then it was at my local, 'The Anchor' or the pub I played football out of, 'The Three Blackbirds' both in the Boxmoor region of Hemel Hempstead. After closing time I would sometimes then go off to a nightclub in Watford called 'The New Penny' and drink and dance until the wee small hours of the morning.

I was now starting to mistreat Jan and my family life in general was becoming a disaster area. Obviously she complained about my very erratic and poor behaviour but sadly this had little effect. It was just that I couldn't cope and wasn't ready for this kind of life yet. Coming out of the RN had been such a shock and I just couldn't take on board my responsibilities. Many men find that coming out of HM Forces is such a huge shock to the system and many, like me just couldn't handle it. Lynda La Plante's book and television series, *Civvies* highlighted this dilemma perfectly. After a while of putting up with all my horrible abuse, Jan left me. She went to work and live in a Jewish home for old people, looking after the residents and obviously she had Tracey with her. I pleaded with her to come back on many an occasion, promising that I would change my way of life and eventually and after a couple of months she believed me. The trouble with this type of panic promise is that they are sometimes very hard to keep. And of course it wasn't long before I fell by the wayside again. This time though, I actually landed up in court. It was New Year's Eve and the imminent arrival of 1972. I had to work on the morning shift with Ian and John but of course as soon as this shift was over we started to celebrate at the local pub which was very close to Bunge and Co. By early evening all of us were pretty much pissed and then a couple of others from the next shift joined us. Bill Brockie the manager was one of these and as was his way bought most of the drinks. I was as pissed as a fart. Like ET I hadn't phoned home either and eventually just made the last train home from Euston to Hemel Hempstead. Sadly though, I fell asleep and totally missed my station. The next thing I heard was, 'End of the Line. Bletchley Station, all change.' The guard who was clearing the train asked me where I was going and I told him Hemel Hempstead. He informed me that there were no trains at this time of night and the first one back to Hemel Hempstead was about 5.30am next morning. Well, the same morning actually, as it was now about 1.30am in the bloody morning. I didn't know what to do and stupidly decided to walk. I'm not sure of the exact distance between Bletchley and Hemel Hempstead but it must be getting on for twenty-five miles and it was a bitterly cold night. As I walked out of the station I spotted a bike shed and a couple of bicycles that weren't padlocked. In my stupid drunken state I nicked one of these and started the long trek home. I hadn't got a bloody

Jan and me at the Bunge and Co. Christmas party (look at that crazy moustache!)

clue in what direction to go, so just started to pedal down the road in which the bike was pointing and hoping to find a signpost soon. I fell off the bloody bike twice to my knowledge. The first time was on trying to mount the damn thing. Bloody Lance Armstrong I wasn't! Anyway, these shenanigans had been well and truly witnessed by certain railway staff on the nightshift in one of the many signal boxes at the station. They had informed the police and after about a mile, I fell off again at the sound of a police siren. I tried to hide the bike in the bushes but this was to no avail. I think the two police officers found the whole charade quite funny but even so I was taken back to a local police station and charged. Shit! Could you imagine my criminal record sheet reading, drunk in charge of a bloody bike! Of course it was a little more serious than this and I was charged with the theft of the said bike. In England we had had the Kray twins, the Richardsons, Jack the Ripper and now the infamous, Phipps the Bike Pilferer! As I write this autobiography I am glad to say that this was my very first and only time to appear in court to date. Perhaps I had learned my lesson. I appeared at the magistrate's court in Fenny Stratford a few days later and as it was my very first offence just received a small fine and told to keep the peace. Fucking, Happy New Year! In actual fact when I informed Bill Brockie our manager of the whole pathetic incident he offered to actually pay the fine for me, as he felt a lot of the blame was his in getting me pissed in the first place. Not quite true but still a nice gesture.

But again Jan had had enough. I had abused her in just about every way possible and obviously still hadn't learnt my lesson. She spent the odd few days with my parents and many times she would visit her family in Pembury in Kent, sometimes for a good week or two. First of all I didn't mind this, as now I could get pissed as much as I liked without any nagging. But soon this stupid attitude wore off and I realised I had some serious growing up to do. I wasn't an alcoholic and indeed wasn't actually addicted to alcohol. I was just addicted to having a good time and alcohol was a huge part of this. In all truthfulness I just hadn't grown up. But this time I really did try and for a while life got so much better on all fronts. I became a husband and father again. I was really fed up with my job though and still had too much time off or turned up late for my shifts, usually blaming it on good old British Rail. I had worked at Bunge and Co. for five years and after a few too many bollockings from the hierarchy decided it might be time to leave. Well, in actual fact they thought it best if I left. They said they didn't want to actually sack me and thought it best if I looked for other employment. They didn't know what a huge favour they were doing me, as my next job was an excellent one. I was sick and tired of working at Bunge and Co. anyway and as they say, a change is as good as a rest. And so it was back to The Three T's Agency to look for another job.

Part Two (1973-1978)

After a couple of decent temporary jobs the agency found me another full time position. The name of the firm was Wilson, Smithett and Cope, which was part of the Lewis Peat Group and their offices were in Mincing Lane in the City. They were actually Commodity Brokers and I was put on a week's trial. I worked in the Metal

Department and we mainly dealt in silver, copper, tin and lead. I really loved working for them and my immediate boss was a real diamond. His name was Hans Oosterhuis and was the father of the world famous golfer Peter Oosterhuis. I passed the week's trial period with flying colours, so I was told and so it was down to full time employment again. This time there was no shift work and we didn't work at weekends. Heavenly!

I made some good friends quickly at this new job and the atmosphere was brilliant especially after the last five years. Here it was interesting, as you felt a part of a successful team. If a large coup happened in any of the separate metal departments and a large transaction was successful, then everybody cheered. It was great fun and a real challenge. Other than Hans Oosterhuis our boss, there was Terry Kane, who became a good friend and George Reptowski an absolute brilliant trader and later there would be others. I had only been there for a few months when the whole company changed offices and indeed titles as we were swallowed up by a much bigger fish. We moved to brand new premises near Tower Bridge and the company became part of the large Guinness Mahon Group. We would now be known as the Guinness Peat Group. These new offices were totally different and we, the metal department had now joined up with the sugar, cocoa, coffee and rubber departments of the company. The huge office was an open space affair and our communication section was the hub in the centre. This made it easy for the traders in all of the departments to get their messages and bids across to us. I worked with the other communications operator from the other commodities we dealt in, who in Mincing Lane was in a totally different office. His name was Dave Hunt and he came from Kent. I really enjoyed this new job and when Dave Hunt was asked if he would like to become part of the cocoa trading team, there became a vacancy in the communication department. Mr Oosterhuis asked if I knew of anyone who might like to take up the vacancy and I said that I just might. I immediately got in touch with my good friend from Bunge and Co. Ian Rutherford and told him about the current vacancy and what a brilliant firm it was to work for. I told him that there was no shift work and that the pay was much better. How could he refuse? He had to work a month's notice though and for this month I was absolutely snowed under but had help from anyone who had the slightest knowledge of trading and typing. After Ian had been there for a few months the work load just seemed to treble and it was obvious that we were going to need another operator to be able to cope with all this new business. They advertised for a new operator and sure enough within a couple of weeks he arrived. His name was Fergus Sheridan and was affectionately known as Gus. He was an Irishman living in London and was a great guy. The really nice thing about all this though, was that I was now the most senior operator, a position I had never been in before. The following Christmas, when we would all go in one at a time to Mr. Oosterhuis's office to receive our annual bonus, he told me he was making me the Communication Department Supervisor. You could've knocked me over with a feather, as no one had ever shown this trust in me before. Of course I accepted both the large bonus and the new position with absolute glee.

Practising Nunchaku in my dinner hour!

It was at about this time that I started training in Shotokan karate. (I have written about this in the chapter headed Karate, so I won't repeat everything again here). I absolutely loved it and it gave me a new interest in life. It wasn't too long before Dave Hunt also started training in Kent in a different style from mine, Kyokushinkai. Due to the huge risk of heart attacks in our very demanding job, the company had given everyone who worked in all of its departments, free membership to a very up market squash club and gymnasium. The club itself was actually in the parapets of London Bridge and was owned and run by an English squash and hockey international, Mike Corby. Many of the firm used to play squash after work or during their lunch hours but Dave and I used to purposefully have a late lunch from 2pm till 3pm and use a squash court for karate practice. There was also a small gymnasium where we could use all the weight training equipment and the bikes and rowing machines. We used to spend about half an hour just sparring with each other plus of course kata training. I had never been so fit.

In my time at this company I actually achieved my first dan black belt grade. I was over the moon and it really felt as though my life was going somewhere at last.

In 1975 I became a Christian (also written about in the chapter headed, Follow Me) and after spending quite a long time at Sunnyhill Fellowship eventually joined a more traditional church, Belmont Road Baptist Church. The minister was a fully qualified concert pianist and his name was David Trafford. He was an absolutely brilliant man and a wonderful musician who used to give concerts in some very prestigious venues. He was the man who baptised my mum and dad at this very church and it was here that Jan and I became leaders of the youth group of the church. Also, it was at this church that eventually I would start my own karate club on a Saturday afternoon. The year was 1977 and this year would be a two-edged sword in my life.

On the good side I had convinced David and the church deacons that karate was not some sort of satanic, Japanese ritualistic, mumbo-jumbo and they gave me permission to use the small church hall on a Saturday afternoon for a couple of hours. Many members of our youth group actually wanted to start training in karate so this was perfect. After the club had been running successfully for a few months it was actually added to the church service times on the big board outside the church, facing the road. It was professionally painted into the day-to-day events of the church and I reckon at that time we would be the only church in the whole country to have its own karate club written into its weekly events. Jan and I became so embroiled with the youth group and indeed the karate club that we decided to move house and therefore be a lot closer to the church. We moved into another three-bedroom council house at 58 Sempill Road, which was only a short walk from the church. Life here was excellent to begin with and the karate club thrived. But again every silver lining has a bloody cloud! The karate club had around fifteen students, who of course were all beginners. I was ably helped by a friend of mine John Lawrence who at that time was a purple and white belt in the local SKI club that we both trained at. The church group was also going well and we used to meet every Sunday morning, an hour before the main service began.

The sad side of 1977 was that my wonderful dad passed away. It was only weeks after he had been baptised at the church. During

My dear dad, with mum and dad's cocker spaniel, Tess

the early part of the night in question he had suffered a heart attack at his home in Bennetts End and had died in St Albans City Hospital after suffering another massive heart attack as they tried to fit him with a pacemaker. Mum, Jan, Tracey and I waited most of the night in the hospital waiting room and soon were sadly given the news that we dreaded. We filed in to see dad's body on the operating table and you could visibly see the scar where they had inserted the pacemaker. He died at 5.15am on the 8th July 1977 three days before his 59th birthday. After an autopsy a few days later, the doctor explained to my mum that his lungs were black through a lifetime of smoking and his heart just couldn't cope any longer. He was one of the greatest men, if not the greatest that I have ever known and I miss him like crazy. Although not my actual blood father, this man was the man I was proud to call my dad and who was a real father to me. I know one day we will be together again but until that day I miss him so very much. Three legends passed away in 1977. Charlie Chaplin, Elvis Presley and the legend that was my dad.

Also, and not long after this sad event, my marriage took a turn for the worse. Obviously all was not well in my relationship with Jan and although things were certainly a lot better and I was not drinking at all at the time, something was missing from the marriage. We struggled on for a while but it became obvious that I couldn't cope with married life anymore. Eventually, Jan had had enough and left to live with her mum in Pembury in Kent. It was a mutual agreement but of course we had to give up the church youth leadership job but the karate club carried on for a little while. I now lived on my own and paid the rent and had to feed myself and do all the jobs the running of a house required. My mum as usual came to the rescue and fed me a few times a week.

After dad's death she just couldn't live at the house any longer, the home in which my brother Martin and my dad had both tragically died. And so she became the warden of an old people's complex in Mayflower Avenue and had a lovely two bedroom flat to live in that came with the job. She had got the job quite easily, as working at the local hospital and then for a doctor's surgery, had made her more than qualified. And so I would find myself on her doorstep on many an occasion wanting to be fed. Of course being her only son now, she would never turn me away and her cooking was wonderful. On the odd occasion I would also sleep in the spare bedroom and wake up to a wonderful cooked breakfast. We had some laughs at Mayflower Avenue and they are times I miss very much.

My karate club had slowly outstayed its welcome at the church in Belmont Road due mainly to my current marriage status and also we were becoming amazingly larger. So we moved to bigger premises which were about a quarter of a mile up the road. The dojo was Bennetts End Community Centre. It was also obvious that we needed to train more than once a week and so a second night was set up at the Carey Baptist Church hall in the town centre of Hemel Hempstead. The club just took off and we had started to make a name for ourselves. So much so, that I was approached by St Albans College if I would teach there as well. I couldn't believe my luck. I had a small interview with the college hierarchy and within a few weeks was up and running in the college gym. The club was advertised throughout the college and on the first lesson I had nearly fifty students of all shapes and sizes. Again, the college was so impressed they asked me if I would consider teaching during the day for Hertfordshire County Council. The college was made up of the normal college and the Building College next door. Students were given option schemes throughout the week where they could choose a myriad of things to try and the college wanted karate to be one of these subjects. I stated that sadly I couldn't as I had a full time job in London and could only work in the evenings. The PE teacher said that this was a real shame and had I ever thought about teaching karate and self-defence for a living. In all truthfulness it hadn't entered my head at the time but it certainly did from then on. I approached my boss at work Mr. Oosterhuis and told him of my current dilemma. He again was absolutely brilliant and suggested that I go for it. He said he would hate to lose me as I was a vibrant part of a very successful team but opportunities like this didn't come along in one's life very often. He said he understood my situation fully as he had had a similar experience with his famous golfing son, Peter Oosterhuis. And so I approached the college, telling them that there was a good chance of being able to do these option schemes in the future. Once more Mr Oosterhuis intervened and said that he would give me a day off a week to teach at the college. What a guy! The college agreed to this and once every week I used to spend the whole day at the college teaching karate and self-defence on these option schemes. With my very successful clubs in Hemel Hempstead and St Albans College and indeed with a small wage now from Hertfordshire County Council, it looked as though there was a good chance that I could make a go of it. And so after a couple of months of this routine, I handed in my notice to the company in London. Yet again, Hans came to the rescue and said that although I had to give a month's notice, I didn't actually have to work it but I would be paid in full for this month. Blimey, I'd never had so much money. And so this was the beginning of things to come.

Jan had been gone for about three months and I had slowly started drinking again. Not heavily, but pretty regularly. I went to my local 'The Boot', only to find that all my old mates had changed pubs and were now drinking just down the road in 'The Albion'. My late dad had played darts for both of these pubs and so I knew my way around this new venue quite well. Sure enough, there were all my old friends and they made a big fuss of my arrival. This drew attention to one young lady, who was with her boyfriend at the bar. Her name was Carol Butler and there was obviously some attraction on both sides. Our eyes met across a crowded room! Well, across a crowded bar to be truthful. By this time I had passed my karate black belt exam at Featherstone School in Southall, Middlesex and a black belt in those days was indeed still quite a rarity. Of course all my chums were full of this and expected to have the next Bruce Lee in their very midst. This was obviously a talking point and maybe an attraction, as Carol started to ask me where I trained and did I teach etc. It was obvious that there was some chemistry between the two of us and I fancied her very much. She had a great sense of humour and had a sexy and slim body. Mind you, anyone who found me attractive had to have a sense of humour!

I used to go to the pub hoping like crazy that she would be there and was chuffed to bits when she was. It wasn't long before we started to see each other properly. The first few occasions were very secretive, as she still kept her boyfriend but after a while she packed him in for yours truly. She had also started training at the karate club and was doing reasonably well, so we were seeing a lot of each other. Life with Carol was sexy, exciting and absolutely wonderful and we had a ball in those early months. After a while we decided we would live together and moved into a grotty flat in Leighton Buzzard. Carol worked for Trewins the large department store in Watford, which was approximately twenty miles away, so she had a fair old drive every working day but it was worth it. This idyllic little lifestyle lasted for quite a few months but then we found out that sex wasn't everything in a relationship and started to argue and drift apart. We had been seeing each other for the best part of a year and Carol had reached green belt in karate. But eventually the inevitable happened and we parted company. Carol went back to live with her mum and dad in the Gadebridge part of Hemel Hempstead and regrettably packed in her karate training. Luckily for me, my wonderful mum took me in, as whilst all this was going on Jan had moved back into Sempill Road with Tracey and was citing me for divorce. Although I hadn't left Jan for anyone else, the solicitors thought it would be a much easier transition if Jan would cite me for adultery with Carol. Carol agreed to this and so the proceedings went ahead. It went reasonably smoothly and I had to pay a small maintenance fee to Jan each month for Tracey and after the usual decree nisi nonsense and different solicitors farting about, the divorce was eventually made final on the 19th December 1979. What a coincidence, as this was exactly the date of my thirty-seventh birthday. And so I was single again and it was goodbye to over twelve years of marriage.

Sadly, as all this was going on, another piece of distressing news came to pass. The minister of Belmont Road Baptist Church, David Trafford had committed suicide. I was told that his wife had left him for some other bloke and David had given up his post at the church and moved to London somewhere. He obviously couldn't stand the grief and took his own life. He was not only an excellent minister and concert pianist but also a wonderful man who was very sadly missed.

The karate clubs were going really well but still I didn't have quite enough money to equal my weekly wages from my London job. So I decided that I would try my hand at some sort of women's yoga-type, keep fit classes. There was not a lot of call for a daily karate club but there were loads of women who would like some sort of keep fit during the day, after they had sent their little charges to school. I just used karate exercises mixed in with a few yoga exercises that I had learnt, plus a bit of meditation at the end. To my utter amazement it worked.

At that time, I had a very attractive young lady training at the karate dojo at Bennetts End Community Centre and she said she would get her mum and some of her mum's mates interested. This she did and these sessions just took off. I was getting around twenty ladies each lesson. I remember at the end of one karate class actually thanking the pretty, young karate lady for her help and just made a joke that I would take her out for a drink sometime. She grinned and said she would hold me to that. I nearly fell through the dojo floor. Of course this was the perfect opening and immediately the very next lesson I asked her out for that drink. To my utter amazement and extreme happiness she agreed. She was a good deal younger than me but neither of us seemed to let this bother us. Her name became a legend in English karate and was none other than Tracey Smith later to become the English International fighter and British and English kumite champion, Tracey Phipps. To this very day, I have never seen a lady kick as well and as fast as Tracey. She was phenomenal with her rapid and very accurate roundhouse kicks and off of both legs.

These last five years of my life were very important for both happy and sad reasons. On the sad side I had lost my wonderful dad and David Trafford the Baptist minister had also sadly passed away. I had been divorced. I had figured out there was much more to life than we all think and had become a Christian. I had made it to the dizzy height of Communications Supervisor in the best civilian job I had ever had. I had started training in the art of Shotokan karate and had passed all my grades up to and including my black belt first dan. I had started my own very successful karate clubs and was now doing what I really loved doing for a living. I had lived with another woman for a few months and then finally met the girl of my dreams. These were definitely some of the most productive and interesting years of my whole life. But there was much more to come.

Karate (1973 - Present Day)

Some of my life's story will slightly overlap at this juncture, as I now want to go back to the beginning of my actual karate life in 1973 in much more detail. Some of this has been touched on in the last chapter but I will try not to repeat myself word for word and hope you will not be bored.

It was on the 1st February 1974 that I first entered an actual dojo. The place was Broadfield School in Adeyfield, a part of Hemel Hempstead and the instructor was, John Van Weenen sensei, who was then a 2nd Dan black belt. The seed was first sown back in my naval days where I had witnessed a certain Scotsman, Jock Scott kicking and punching ten bells out of his kitbag on the mess deck. I had quietly made my way down the ladder and on to the mess deck of the destroyer I was then serving on to make a cup of coffee. There was Jock kicking and punching his kitbag, which was hanging from a hammock hook on the ceiling. Dust was flying everywhere and he let out a piercing scream with the odd kick or punch. He didn't know I was there, such was his concentration. I was totally mesmerized. Eventually, I plucked up the courage and asked him what it was he was actually doing and this made him jump as he thought he was on his own. On this momentous occasion he only made two statements. The first of these was to inform me that he was training in the Japanese art of karate and the second was to fuck off! I immediately took on board the second statement, especially after witnessing the pounding of the kitbag.

I was still playing football twice a week for local teams but late in 1973, I, like many other would-be martial artists, had been to see *Enter the Dragon* at the old Empire Cinema in Watford. I think I saw it three times. I was absolutely hooked by this new way of life and started to pathetically train myself at home copying a cheap book I had purchased at a second-hand shop by a man who went by the name of Bruce Tegner. I still believe to this day, if the Shaolin Monks had seen me trying to perform they would've taken up knitting! But in my defence, I was still enjoying football and didn't know where to go to start karate or kung fu lessons. Then, my prayers were answered. There in the local paper was an advert for Shotokan karate. I tried to get some of the members of the football teams I was playing for interested but to no avail. And so, on the 1st February 1974, I nervously made my way to the school. I actually walked the couple of miles from my house, as I still hadn't mastered the art of driving a car at this time. Up till then I hadn't needed to drive. I left school in December 1957, a few days after my fifteenth birthday and on the 10th June 1958 I joined the Royal Navy. I had tried my hand at a couple of unsuccessful jobs in this interim period, with the first of these as an apprentice printer at John Dickinsons in Apsley, where I was very unhappy, then as a shop assistant in Milletts, where I was very happy but had no prospects. I spent the next ten years in the RN and then the following ten years commuting by train to London to work in various offices, so for just over twenty years after leaving school there had been no actual need of a car. So travel for me in 1973/4 was either by London Transport, British Rail or Shank's Pony! I chose the latter. It didn't cost anything.

I arrived at the school and followed my ears. I could hear many strained and weird shouts coming from the direction of the school hall and so I tentatively made my way to the closed doors. These doors were of solid wood with a small square window in each. I nervously peered in through one of these windows to see the karate class in action. It was absolutely heaving with bodies and it was extremely obvious to me by now, that many more people than just yours truly, were going to be the next Bruce Lee. I watched the instructor in absolute awe as he gave out his commands in Japanese. I followed his every move as he walked around the class, correcting students as he went. Then, he disappeared. He very quickly appeared again as he opened the door I was looking through. I jumped a million miles in the air and didn't know whether to bow, run or shit myself. I came close to the latter but this nice man broke the eerie silence and politely asked if I would like to come in and watch the class in action. How could I refuse? And so I was sat down on a school chair and for the next hour or so was absolutely mesmerized at what I was witnessing. I was hooked and at the end of the lesson had put my name down to join the club – I would be along on the very next lesson. And so, the journey had begun.

I then searched the For Sale columns in the local papers for the appropriate attire. I was in luck. There was a judo suit for sale for £3. What a bargain! I immediately got in touch with the seller and purchased the suit, which came with a yellow belt. I felt the very business. Sadly, I hadn't gone in to the subject quite deeply enough and couldn't understand why all these people, on my first few lessons, were all dressed in these beautifully thin, white cotton suits whilst I was in an off-white, poxy, quilted eiderdown. The jacket was much too big and the trousers were very short and I looked like a reject from the film, *Teahouse of the August Moon*. I didn't dare wear the yellow belt and couldn't find a shop anywhere that sold martial arts equipment. Nevertheless, I had been extremely clever, so I thought, and used a long, white elastic bandage as an obi (belt). I looked like a sack of potatoes and felt much worse. I was sweating profusely and was losing weight at an incredible rate. The only thing that gave me any comfort was that the guy next to me, on two of those earlier occasions was dressed in a pair of his dad's striped pyjamas! The jacket was worn on the outside of his pants and his mum had sewn up the front of the trousers so nothing horrible would pop out. He also had some sort of white, cotton tape surrounding his zebra-like attire, keeping him together and doubling up as an obi. What was the collective term for such a sad sight? Probably a pair of prats!

The other thing which makes me chuckle now is that those early lessons were only seventy pence each and that the dojo was always packed. We trained diligently twice weekly at the school and in those early days there were hardly any coloured belts in the class. We had an excellent first kyu, who was also a dan grade in judo,

Richard Saint. Richard often took the exercise routines and was a powerfully built and strong karateka. Another exceptionally good student was Mick Dobby, who in those very early days was a fourth kyu. These guys seemed to be on another planet to us mere mortals. There was a smattering of lower coloured belts in the class but in the main it was nearly all beginners and with around fifty people in each class, that was a hell of a lot of beginners! It was actually Mick Dobby that taught me my first painful lesson. We were practising kihon ippon kumite (basic one-step sparring) and this was the first time I had actually partnered someone who knew what they were really doing. As he went back into gedan barai (lower area block) to attack, he screamed, 'JODAN!' His face was so stern and this along with the severity of the word made me smile. In came the attack and smashed me straight in the forehead. I literally saw stars. My blocking arm hadn't even started to move. My head ached and I thought I was going to collapse. I shook my throbbing head and made it very slowly back to my starting position (yoi). I gave him an extremely stern look, which said, 'What the fuck was that for?' He could see my concern and just quietly said, 'Never smile in kumite!'

Lesson one learnt - Karate is fun but certainly not funny!

I remember my first grading day in Picketts Lock in North London. It was 1974 and the grading panel consisted of, Kanazawa sensei, the late Eddie Whitcher sensei and my own instructor John Van Weenen sensei. In the morning we trained with the great Kanazawa sensei and two things immediately spring to mind. Sensei was demonstrating the art of kime (focus of power) to the students and had asked us all to gather round in a circle. His English wasn't brilliant in those early days and he was struggling a little trying to get over what he wanted us to learn. He then said, 'I show'. He pulled his gi jacket over his shoulders and released his arms and let the jacket hang loosely from his belt. I looked at his slim body but didn't think it was anything really special. Then he sent out a punch and tensed his upper body. I had never seen so many muscles. They popped up every bloody where and I was so impressed. There were two lady students stood directly in front of me and one whispered to the other that it was worth the grading and lesson fee just to see him perform this amazing feat. I had to agree. Alongside me were two famous Arsenal football players, Bob Wilson and Frank McLintock and their children, all in their new, white suits. Both looked at each other, totally amazed at what they had just witnessed. 'That is kime!' Sensei informed the class. 'That is fucking phenomenal!' I informed myself. Later in the same class I first saw the humility of the great man. He was to demonstrate the kata, Heian Nidan to the class and went into yoi (position of readiness). He stated the kata's name with great karate spirit. 'Heian Nidan!' We all stood and waited with baited breath. Sensei then burst into the first two moves of Heian Shodan and immediately stopped dead. He came back to yoi and apologised to the whole class. 'So sorry, wrong kata,' he smiled. After watching the kime demonstration and muscles popping out of everywhere, he was certainly the only one who did actually smile. He named the kata again and gave a fantastic display of karate finesse and awesome power. He bowed at the end of the kata and we all bowed back. He just got on with his teaching as though nothing had happened and this I thought at the time was a wonderful display of true humility. It reminded me of a saying I once heard. *The sensei is not always right - but they are always the sensei!*

It was at one of these very first grading examinations that one of the funniest things I have ever witnessed in a dojo took place. I was sat waiting to be called up when a couple of groups before me were called to the floor. The grading was at Picketts Lock in London and was held in a large room, as opposed to the main hall of the centre. Kanazawa sensei was the main grading officer and this group, now on the floor performed their kihon (basics) up and down the dojo. Eventually, it came to the kata part of the test and one chap was most definitely standing much too close by the wall to his left to perform the kata properly. Kanazawa sensei looked and informed the group in general to make sure that they had enough room to perform the kata, Heian shodan. Our friend didn't budge an inch. So Kanazawa sensei then asked the group to turn to face the wall, the one which our friend was nearly hugging. The class turned but still our friend didn't budge. He had turned with everyone else but still hadn't moved away from the wall. Kanazawa sensei informed the class to begin the kata. Our friend, along with the class named the kata and at sensei's command, 'Hajime!' proceeded with the first five movements. But on move number six, the gedan barai (downward block) he now faced the wall and a closed door. This door was the door into the men's toilets and as our dear friend proceeded with the three age uke blocks (upper rising blocks) he found himself confronting this door after the first block. I couldn't believe what he did next. On seeing that he had no room to manoeuvre, he actually opened the door and stepped inside. The door quickly shut behind him on its severe spring-loaded hinges as our colleague disappeared from sight.

We all heard a muffled kiai from inside the toilet and a few seconds later the door reopened and out came our friend with the three oi-zuki (lunge punches) of the kata. Well, I found it hard not to laugh, as did all the people watching but nothing on the face of Kanazawa sensei. The whole grading eventually came to a close and it was time for the results. We all waited with baited breath, not just for our own results but the result of our toilet-trained colleague. Eventually, his name was called out and he made his way to the desk. He bowed deeply to Kanazawa sensei. Sensei smiled and bowed back and stated that he had passed his grading and that he was very impressed with his initiative but next time would he please make sure he had enough room to perform the kata properly. It was the first kata and indeed the last kata I've ever witnessed that actually had a toilet break in it! When the grading was finally over and we were now safely back in the changing rooms, we all just howled with laughter at the antics and the quick thinking of our karate comrade.

I was thoroughly enjoying my karate, so much so that at the yellow belt level I gave up playing football. I was thirty years of age and wasn't enjoying the challenge of local football anywhere near the challenge that karate now placed before me. I looked back at my young life and realised that at thirty years of age I had done really nothing with it whatsoever. So the challenge was set before me – try to make a go of it in the world of Shotokan karate. For a yellow belt this indeed was a challenge but one I just knew I was going to enjoy – well most of the time!

It was whilst I was taking my green belt exam in the Bunyan Centre in Bedford that I seriously decided that I would like to become a karate instructor one day. I was sat with a karate colleague of mine at the time, Tony Larke, an architect from our home town of Hemel Hempstead and we looked on in awe as students took their dan gradings. This was the first time I had actually witnessed anyone taking the prestigious black belt, as on most other occasions the dojo had been cleared of all personnel, other than those taking the exam and of course the examiners. It was whilst four lads were taking their second dan exam that I turned to Tony and whispered, that one day that would optimistically be me. My dream continued, as I told him that I would hopefully become a sensei and run my own club one day and again Tony nodded his approval and

As a green belt at a local demo. (Note the stance and the hair!)

stated that he wanted the same. At this time in my karate career this was only a dream of course but one that stayed firmly rooted somewhere at the back of my brain. Sadly, Tony was forced to retire from karate training at the purple belt level due to an extremely painful haemorrhoid condition, better known in the Royal Navy as 'bum plums'!

It was a shame because he could've been really good. I have met him in Hemel Hempstead a couple of times and he rues the day he had to stop training and we laughed, as we remembered the day we made those promises to each other. He has always followed my successes in the local press and congratulated me on these each time we met. It was the first thing in my life that I had actually stuck at and this gave me a wonderful feeling of self belief and something I have tried to instill into my young students, that sometimes dreams can come true but you do have to work at them.

During the purple belt stage of my karate journey I had my first break from training. It only lasted a few weeks and was the time when I was searching my soul for a more spiritual contentment and enlightenment and on eventually becoming a Christian.

The break only lasted for about four to five weeks and on returning to the dojo, Van

Weenen sensei had asked me where I had been? I didn't have the courage of my convictions in those early days and I lied about my non-attendance and told him it was through some sort of injury. The class itself only had two purple belts at that time, myself and one other chap who was supposedly a decent footballer and I believe was playing for Berkhamsted Town at the time. I know his first name was Russell. Anyway, he hadn't been training very hard either due to his football training commitments. Approximately halfway through the lesson Van Weenen sensei asked the class to sit down. He then asked the purple belts to stay on the floor and perform their rendition of their next grading kata, Heian Godan. Before we actually started, he told the black and brown belts to watch for any mistakes that we would make, as he would question them after our performance. Anyway, on his command off we went. I can't speak for Russell but mine felt reasonably okay. Wrong! He then asked the senior grades one by one to pick holes in our performances. This they did with great verve and I felt absolutely deflated by the end of their comments. At the end of the lesson Van Weenen sensei came over to me and informed me that the kata wasn't too bad but would've been a damned sight better had I not had any time off.

Lesson two, well and truly learnt - Don't have time off and if you do, have the balls to tell the truth why you were not in attendance at the dojo.

The second line of the dojo kun (morals of the dojo) came springing to mind. Hitotsu! Makoto No Michi O Mamoru Koto! (One! To defend the paths of truth!)

As Kato sensei once stated, on one of his courses at my dojo many years ago. 'Training is like going to the toilet. Needs to be regular!'

My next standout performance was just after passing my third kyu brown belt and a physically more painful one. In our club we were not allowed to start jiyu kumite (free sparring or free fighting) until we had passed this grade. As junior grades we watched in awe as the seniors progressed in this part of the art and although only watching, still picked up the odd move here and there in our minds. It was probably around the third lesson after my brown belt grading that I had my first taste of this kumite freedom. Van Weenen sensei had told the senior grades to partner up and I found myself with an extremely competent and stocky first kyu, Pete Batty. We stalked around each other like a couple of prowling lions. I noticed that his front leg was very close to mine and so I thought I would be daring and try a front leg sweep. My instep tapped him in the ankle region and to my utter surprise it worked! His body semi-collapsed as he tried to regain his balance, but sadly I didn't follow it up with a decent counter attack. I thought to myself, 'Hey, this is easy. Perhaps I could be world champion one day at this rate'. He nodded and said, 'Oss', as off we went again, pursuing each other around the dojo floor. The gyaku-zuki he then threw hit me square in the solar plexus and I thought for a moment had appeared out the other side. I collapsed in a big heap, gasping for breath. Van Weenen sensei had seen me crawling around on all fours trying to suck air into my lungs. He lifted me up, told me I looked green and proceeded to bring me back to life. On returning to my normal colour he told me to continue. I thought he was seriously joking and he could see the despair on my face. 'Best thing to do when you fall off a horse is to get back on!' I was going to say, 'Yes, but what if you've just been hit by a fucking horse!' But I thought better of it. I pranced around for another thirty seconds, keeping well out of the way of my partner and certainly keeping my bloody legs to myself!

Lesson three, very painfully learnt – Be ready for anything and tense your bloody stomach when your opponent attacks.

Another major lesson I learnt was a different type of experience totally. It materialised on the day of my second kyu brown belt grading, which was to be held at Dacorum Sports Centre in my local town of Hemel Hempstead. This was the very first grading I had taken on home soil and was looking forward to it immensely, if not a little tentatively. Mum and dad said they would come and watch but I asked them not to, as I was nervous enough as it was. Gradings up till then had been taken at either, Picketts Lock in North-east London, John Bunyan Centre in Bedford, Nottingham University and on one occasion at the USAF base at Chicksands in Bedfordshire. These had all been with Kanazawa sensei or Asano sensei, with lower graded English sensei seated on the panel. These included the late, Eddie Whitcher and indeed my own instructor, John Van Weenen.

On this occasion the grading instructor was Asano Sensei and sat on the table with him was my very own sensei, John Van Weenen. The grading progressed with the lower belts first and worked its way up to the seniors. I eventually took my place on the dojo floor and followed the commands for the kihon (basics). It then came to my favourite part of karate in those days, the kata. After performing two of the Heian kata as shitei kata (designated kata) we were to perform Bassai-Dai kata. After the command to begin, we proceeded to execute the kata to the very best of our ability. This done, we then went through the kumite drills and were eventually told to sit down as the grading was now finished. There was a fairly long delay as Asano sensei signed and stamped the licenses of the successful participants. After what seemed like a lifetime, our names were called out one by one by Van Weenen sensei and we made our way to the grading table. The moment had arrived. 'Malcolm Phipps!' I bowed and shouted, 'Oss, sensei!' And made my way briskly up to the desk and bowed deeply to Asano sensei. He looked me in the eyes and said, 'Second kyu!' He gave me a bow and I returned the gesture. I was about to turn and make my way back to my place in the class, when he spoke again, 'Very good Bassai-Dai!' I bowed even more deeply this time as I thanked him for this wonderful accolade. I felt absolutely elated and walked around the Sports Centre feeling like a million dollars. Just then my mum and dad appeared and congratulated me. They had hidden themselves away on the balcony of the Sports Centre on the pretence of playing table tennis. Secretly though, I was pleased that they had made the effort. At least they now knew what was involved in karate training and from that moment on I found it easy to talk to them about my love for my chosen martial art.

I was now training three times a week and the third session was with a second dan black belt from the St Albans area, Stewart Vousden. His club trained at the London Colney Community Centre and I thoroughly enjoyed these sessions, as they were slightly different. One thing that was most definitely different is that Stewart didn't care too much for the politics of karate and with this in mind, let anybody train at his dojo. This included our SKI group and a couple of very good black belts from a local KUGB club, Gary Hunt and his brother. We had heard all sorts of horrific stories about the KUGB but of course these were total cobblers. These lads were not only excellent in their karate but also in their attitude. We all used to have a drink at the bar after these sessions and got to know each other quite well.

It was on the first of these sessions, after my successful grading that the next big lesson was learnt. The class was coming to an end and Stewart congratulated all those who had passed their grades and were now wearing their new belts with pride. He stated that he was especially proud of one of our students, who had been congratulated personally by Asano sensei for his great Bassai-Dai. My heart skipped a beat. 'Well done, Malcolm an excellent kata'. The whole class agreed and everyone clapped. I blushed and felt very pleased with myself. 'I think Malcolm should now show us his excellent rendition of Bassai-Dai, do you agree?' In unison there was a huge, 'Oss!' I nearly let out a huge, 'Shit!' But I thought better of it. 'Off you go then, Malcolm,' Stewart pointed toward the centre of the dojo. I made my way out on to the dojo floor and proceeded to give the worst rendition of Bassai-Dai ever known to man. On finishing, Stewart politely said, 'Thank you', and nicely informed the class, that it was much better on the grading day.

Lesson four – Karate has no place for a big head!

Following on from this story and indeed the very same year I attended the SKI UK National Championships as a spectator. The venue was Nottingham University. Asano sensei was the host and he was dressed smartly in a three-piece suit as indeed was Kato sensei. Kanazawa sensei and a few other senior Japanese instructors were in karate suits and refereed and judged the day's proceedings. I was sat in the bleachers with my good friend John Lawrence who had driven me up the M1 in his sports car to the tournament. Asano sensei was walking around with Kato sensei doing his *mein host* bit and as they passed the seating that we occupied, he waved in my direction. I was halfway up these uncomfortable wooden seats and truthfully thought he was waving at somebody behind me. I looked around but couldn't see anyone waving back. I looked back at Asano sensei and he was pointing directly at me. I stupidly pointed at myself saying, 'Who, me?' He nodded and waved again. I smiled and waved back. He then smiled and gave a little nod and said, 'Oss!' I immediately returned the gesture and was extremely chuffed. In fact it made my day. Yours truly, a lowly brown belt being recognised by a world class sensei. Amazing what a half-decent kata could do! At that time it didn't get any better than that. My mate John was so impressed and said something like, 'Jammy bastard!' To quote Helen Nielsen: *'Humility is like underwear. Essential, but indecent if it shows!'*

Also, whilst at the second kyu grade of my karate life, another stupid thing happened. I had trained with Van Weenen sensei at the Dacorum Sports Centre (as it was then known) in Hemel Hempstead and on that very same evening the England football team were playing Holland at Wembley and the second half was to be on the television. After the lesson, I changed quickly and ran as fast as I could home so as not to miss the second half of the match. I ran along Heath

Can't see any bloody nail holes!

Lane by the school fields of Hemel Hempstead School. In those days these school fields were well fenced off from the road by a wooden fence and in certain places this fence had seen better days. I don't know whether it was vandals that had pulled the odd panel loose or maybe the wind, or indeed for that matter fate. But as I raced along this road with my mind firmly fixed on the football match, I inadvertently stood on one of these loose panels. A nail went straight through the sole of my Adidas trainer and into my right foot. I flapped around like a pregnant bloody penguin with this board stuck to my foot. Eventually and indeed painfully, I pulled the offending board from my foot and limped miserably home. Jan looked at my foot and thought I should go immediately to the outpatient's at the local hospital. This of course meant missing the football, so I declined this offer and sat with my foot in a bowl of warm, disinfected water and watched the match. After the football was over I made for bed with a hot drink and a couple of aspirins.

Next morning, as I put my foot to the floor I screamed and jumped back on to the bed. The pain was excruciating and I could hardly put this foot to the floor. And so the outpatient's was a must. We got a taxi to the West Herts. Hospital in Hillfield Road and after a lengthy wait in the waiting room I was eventually shown in to see the doctor. He was a very old chap and I believe Polish. I explained the previous night's events in some detail to him, leaving out the football bit, to which he just grunted. I removed my shoe and sock on his command and he stared at the offending foot and called me all the stupid idiots under the sun. I thought, bloody charming! I've come here in immense discomfort and all he can do is insult me. He then asked the attendant nurse if she would get him a scalpel. I nearly bloody wet myself and thought that amputation was taking it a bit too far! He then made two deep diagonal cuts across the wound and proceeded to squeeze out any muck. He informed me that I was very lucky, as the foot could've become gangrenous and then I would have been in real trouble. He told me what Jan had suggested the night before that I should've gone to the hospital straight away after the accident. I was going to ask him if he enjoyed the match but thought better of it, especially as he was still holding the bloody scalpel! Anyway, after the bollocking and painful squeezing he passed me over to the nurse to get the wound cleaned up and bandaged. This was followed by the customary tetanus injection. I don't know what was hurting the most, my pride or my bloody foot!

The saddest and most annoying thing in all of this was that I couldn't train for the best part of a month, as it took this long for the damned foot to heal. Not so much a legend in the dojo, more of a fucking leg end! Eventually, and on returning to the dojo, Van Weenen sensei asked me where the hell I had been. I hadn't had the balls to go to the dojo and explain my stupidity but even more foolishly hadn't watched any of these missed lessons. I was told by sensei that I should've been there to watch and to explain my injury. He told me to stay behind after the class was over. This I did and eventually when the dojo was empty Van Weenen sensei said that we would do some light sparring. I got absolutely battered and couldn't get away from the dojo wall. He had me pinned there and hit me with an array of various punches and kicks but not once did he hurt me. His control was superb and the only thing that actually hurt was my pride. Once this lesson was over he bowed and told me not to miss classes in the future and that if I was injured at any time, to let him know and at least come and watch the lessons.

Another time I can look back on now and laugh, is when I had had a very average lesson, again as a brown belt. Nothing would go right. At the end of the lesson and in front of the whole class, Van Weenen sensei directed his final comment to me personally. 'Mr. Phipps, you only made one mistake tonight.'
'Thank you sensei,' I courteously replied as I bowed.
'Turning up!'
My head dropped as the class thought that this was extremely hilarious. We finished the class with the traditional bowing routine and sensei asked me to come over to him. He could see that I was extremely deflated and asked me what was the matter? I wanted to tell him that I didn't find his comment very fucking funny but instead I apologised and told him that it just hadn't been my night. He asked me, was I in anyway disturbed at his final comments? I said, no not really but that I was a little hurt as I was trying my best but nothing seemed to go right. It was just one of those nights we all have every now and then. He then said something that has stayed with me since that day. He said that he thought that I had something worth pursuing in the art and that he only spoke to students like this when they actually mattered. He continued and said it was when your name was never, ever mentioned that you might be falling short of the mark and this silence from the

instructor was usually aimed at those students who just weren't trying or being sloppy. These were the ones that a sensei just hadn't got too much time for. These were the students that trained as though they didn't really want to be in the dojo in the first place and were only practicing karate as a hobby and not as a martial art.

He told me to go on my way and that he would see me at the very next lesson. I bowed and with the conventional, 'Oss sensei.' left to go home. I felt a little bit better but was not totally convinced but knew I would give my very all at that next class. I remember another time when the whole class was not working as hard as it should and Van Weenen sensei stated that we all gave him the assurance that there was definitely life after death!

Flying through the air with the greatest of ease - bollocking to follow!

I also remember receiving a bollocking from another sensei for literally flying around the Harpenden dojo. I had arrived early and changed quickly into my gi, as the Sports Centre main hall was empty. So I did a very quick warm up and started to practice my favourite kick, tobi-yoko-geri (jumping side kick). I took run ups and flew through the air with the greatest of ease. I then tried it from a standing start, as I had seen Kanazawa sensei performing this incredible feat a couple of years previous but this was nigh impossible to do. So it was back to the runway and flying for me! A couple of students had now entered the dojo and were extremely impressed at my Concorde type antics. Then the dojo started to fill up and I carried on showing off. All of a sudden the sensei, who had quietly entered the dojo unbeknown to me, called me over. 'What do you think you are doing?' he asked.
'Tobi-yoko-geri, sensei', I confidently replied.
'Why?'
I was stumped for an answer. I shrugged my shoulders and spluttered, 'Just practising, sensei.'
'Well, when you can perform your basic kicks properly then you can start practising this kick. Oss?'
I bowed deeply and said, 'Oss, sensei.' He bowed back and I went on my miserable way, my tail between my legs. Whoops! My flying days had come to an abrupt halt. Well, for the immediate future anyway. I look back now and could see

what the instructor meant. But it was a kick I could do pretty well but now I need a fucking crane and a prayer to be able to get that high!

It was also around this time that I first saw Kanazawa sensei lose his cool. We had trained with sensei in Hemel Hempstead Sports Centre and after the training was over and after sensei had signed his autograph about a million times, that I found myself in the changing room almost alone with the great man. I had taken my copy of Nakayama sensei's brilliant book, *Dynamic Karate*, to the dojo and hoped that I could get Kanazawa sensei to sign it for me on the page where he has his gi top off and is showing the musculature of the upper body (page 103, hardback edition) titled, Muscles used in tsuki (punching). I opened the book and asked him if he would sign it for me. Being the gentleman that he is he agreed and took up the pen and the book. He then spoke to me stating that he thought the photograph could have been done better. I looked on in awe and asked how? This photograph has muscles on it I didn't know even bloody existed! He said the photograph itself was okay but he thought the names of the muscles, which appear underneath this photograph and are numbered, should have had lines pointing to the muscle in question. He then scratched a line in my book from the words underneath to the picture above with the closed biro. I saw what he meant and hastily agreed. He then signed my book underneath the piece we had been talking about with his wonderful flamboyant Mount Fuji signature. Not only is his autograph very special to me in this book but also the scratch mark!

Still bloody flying - this time at Carol Butler!

Also sat very quietly in the changing room was a little Japanese gentleman dressed in civilian clothes with a peaked cap on. Kanazawa sensei then introduced him to me personally and it was sensei's brother who was visiting England. I bowed and he stood and bowed back but he couldn't speak any English whatsoever, so that was where the introduction stopped. Just at that very moment a black belt arrived in the changing room and started to undress. He took off his obi (belt) and literally threw it at one of the coat hooks. Sadly for him it miserably missed and fell in a heap on the floor. Kanazawa sensei went berserk. He screamed at the black belt to pick up his belt and place it neatly on the hook, stating that a black belt in Shotokan karate had been painstakingly earned and should be highly respected and never be thrown around like that. The black belt bowed deeply, picked up his obi and placed it neatly on the hook and apologised to sensei. It was at that very moment that I could see how this great man had been JKA kumite champion. His eyes blazed as his temper rose but went straight back down in a few seconds to the humble gentleman most people witness all the time. It was a chance encounter that I would never forget, not only for the autograph and the small chat but for the lesson I had witnessed about one's kuro obi (black belt).

It was whilst at the brown belt level that I witnessed another pathetic event and one that has stayed with me ever since. We had been training at the Harpenden Sports Centre dojo and as the lesson came to an end the sensei informed us of the imminent weekend course with the legendary Kanazawa sensei. We then bowed out of the lesson and went and changed into our civilian clothes. There is a pub that is very close to this dojo called, 'The Silver Cup' and many of the lower graded students and also the black belts used to visit this pub after the training session was over, for a pint of whatever and a general chat. It was a case of never the twain shall meet, as the black belts all gathered on one table in a circle with the lower grades at another table, also in a large circle. A colleague of mine and a good friend, Fred Hoskins, who was also a brown belt, asked me if I could remember the times of the up and coming Kanazawa sensei seminar. I gave him an answer but said I couldn't be absolutely sure, so Fred made his way to the black belt's table and politely asked the senior instructor for the times of the course. The next most senior black belt then rigidly stood up and screamed at Fred to stand to attention and bow to the sensei, say, 'Oss' and give him the proper respect. Fred politely stated that he thought that as this was a pub and we were all dressed in civvies he didn't have to stand to attention and bow. Fred had already called him sensei anyway and thought that that was enough. The young black belt again screamed at Fred not to argue with a black belt and told him to listen harder next time in the dojo. Fred eventually came back to our table absolutely seething. He was a really nice guy and a very good brown belt, in his early thirties who dearly loved his karate but this had sent him over the top. Our table had witnessed this horrible event as indeed had all the regulars in the pub. Fred stated that that was it for him and that he would never train again in the art of karate. I tried hard to talk him round but he would have none of it. He kept to his word and to this day never trained

My first sensei, John Van Weenen and me many years later

again to my knowledge. How bloody sad is that! This wanker of a black belt eventually stopped training himself and I have to say that karate is a lot better off without the likes of him!

On the whole though, everything was going well in my karate life. It was at the first kyu level that I was asked by the youngsters at my church if I would think about opening up a small club in the church hall. This I mentioned earlier in the book. I asked Van Weenen sensei if this would be at all possible at my grade and he agreed and thought that I could make a half decent instructor. All he asked was that I would invite him to my dojo once every couple of months to see that all was going well, to which I of course agreed. There weren't many black belts around in those days, especially in our area and so the club started on a Saturday afternoon in the church hall. The club absolutely blossomed and all of the youngsters looked so smart in their new karate suits and I was extremely proud of them. We started with around twelve students.

Then came the unthinkable. Van Weenen sensei ceased to be the local instructor at the SKI club in Hemel Hempstead. I just couldn't figure out what had happened but there were enough rumours flying about to fill a Sunday newspaper. Some of these rumours included Kanazawa sensei but I do not wish to fill this book with hearsay and I believe John tells the story best in his autobiography, *In Funakoshi's Footsteps*, page 258.

It turned out that John had gone on his honeymoon and when he returned home nearly all of his students, for some reason or other, had defected to his second in

Me, Dan and Blanti

command. I know this created a lot of bad feeling between them and I remember being in the Hemel Hempstead Sports Centre dojo, in seiza (Japanese sitting position) when all of a sudden the dojo doors opened and there stood John in blue jeans and jacket. He threw into the dojo a load of silver coins and just said to the other instructor, 'There you are Judas, thirty pieces of silver!' Very dramatic indeed and of course the rumours now became even worse.

With this new instructor taking over I wasn't sure what would happen to my small club. The answer to this question was soon to arrive as he gathered the senior grades around one lesson. He informed us that all the little satellite clubs would now have to close down, and all students would have to train with him at the Hemel Hempstead Sports Centre dojo. This was okay to a point but the club at the Sports Centre didn't finish until quite late and this was not really acceptable to my very young students. So I was placed in a dilemma, and one that was not of my own making for a change. I could understand the 'new broom sweeps clean syndrome', but this was going to be of no use to me.

In those days, like many karate students I used to get *Combat* magazine on a regular monthly basis. It was one of the monthly highlights and I used to dash down to W.H. Smiths and usually purchase it on the day it came out. In the current issue that I was reading at the time there was a huge article about the MAC (Martial Arts Commission) and so I decided to give them a ring and tell them of my situation. I was put in touch with a wonderful man, a Mr. Dan Bradley and he listened intently to my problem. He suggested that the best thing I could do was to probably join another Shotokan group. He said that he personally trained in Shotokan karate and that he belonged to a group, the Amateur Shotokan Karate Association (ASKA) that basically, in the south of England, ran out of the Southall and Hounslow areas and which was reasonably close to me. The Chief Instructor for the south of England was a fifth dan instructor by the name of Balwant Sahans sensei and if I liked, he (Dan) would ask Blanti (as Balwant Sahans sensei was affectionately known) to visit my club on a Saturday afternoon in the very near future. This I happily agreed to and told my students the good news. They were obviously chuffed to bits. The day approached and I had the dojo looking spic and span. The students, that now numbered fifteen, looked excellent in their bright, white karate suits. I remember waiting by the gate of the church for the car to arrive. It turned up a quarter of an hour early and I was shaking at the knees. The car door opened and Dan courteously introduced me to Blanti. Of course I had to introduce myself to both of them, as I had only spoken to Dan via the phone. I had wondered what nationality or indeed what race or religion the name Balwant Sahans came from and on that first meeting was pleasantly surprised to see that Blanti was a Sikh. He was a big jovial fellow and he shook my hand and I took them both into the vestry of the church where we changed into our karate suits. The students all bowed courteously as Blanti, Dan and myself entered the dojo doors. The lesson was absolutely brilliant and one in which Blanti had obviously struck up a respect and a friendship with and from the students. After this lesson was over we retired to the vestry to get changed back into our street clothes. Blanti shook my hand and told me he was very impressed with the youngsters and that we would be very welcome to join the ASKA if we so wished. He stated that Dan was the actual secretary of the Association and he would inform me of the correct licensing procedures and the like. I instantly agreed to join and again we shook hands and Blanti and Dan welcomed my group to the ASKA and made their way home. I went into the dojo, which was full of expectant young students and told them the good news. They all let out a cheer. They could now be properly licensed and graded in the art of Shotokan karate. Luckily enough, as the club hadn't been going that long we hadn't had to take out SKI licences, so no monies were lost or wasted. And so my SKI days were over. I was sad in some ways and in others very happy. My sensei was sadly no longer around and I would miss the training with Kanazawa sensei. But things had to change, for if they didn't karate would've lost fifteen very enthusiastic young students and I was not willing to let this happen.

I sent a letter to Van Weenen sensei at his home address and he sent me a really nice reply. He stated that I was a sensible man of the world and one that knew what had happened and wished me the very best for my future. I hardly ever see him now but we have been friends ever since. I did miss training with him, as he was my very first sensei and the man that planted my feet firmly on the road of karate for those important first four years.

And so the next part of my karate journey had started. The one huge difference between my old club and the new Association was that ASKA actually competed on the big stage. I hadn't competed at all whilst in SKI, as our club was not really encouraged to do so. So slowly but surely we learnt the art of competition kumite and kata. I always wondered why we were never encouraged to compete, as in *Combat* and *Karate and Oriental Arts* magazines, I was constantly reading about the many competition successes of great Shotokan personnel, names such as, Terry O'Neill, Billy Higgins, Andy Sherry, Bob Poynton, Bob Rhodes and of course the legendary Ticky Donovan of Ishinryu.

As I was still only a first kyu, I was asked by Blanti and Dan to go for my black belt in the April of 1978. Before this though, there would be another dan grading at the Trent Lock dojo in Nottingham. They said they would like me to just go along to this and do a sort of mock grading to see how I got on with their syllabus. I was extremely pleased to be asked and thought better of declining the offer, as I didn't want to start my life in my new Association on the wrong foot, and so this is what I did. The instructor at the Trent Lock dojo was Jack Warner sensei who was also a fifth dan and was the Chief Instructor for the northern branch of the Association. He was an absolutely lovely man and made me feel very welcome. I went to this grading a bag of nerves even though I knew I couldn't actually pass anything, as for me it was really just a dress rehearsal. A couple of my students accompanied me on the journey to watch how a dan grading went in our new Association. I didn't do too badly considering a different syllabus and a different Association but I'm not sure I would've passed even if it had been the real thing. I came away knowing I had a lot of work to do especially in the free-fighting part of the exam. The time passed quickly and soon it was to be the real thing. As I said earlier in the book, I didn't drive in those days and so made the journey to Featherstone School in Southall by bus. I caught the 347 from Hemel Hempstead to Uxbridge and then another bus from Uxbridge to Southall, and walked the short distance to the school. I was so nervous for two reasons. First of all, this was the real thing and secondly this time I was on my own. I remember that in the morning we trained with Blanti and then we had a couple of hours for lunch. Then it was the grading. My name was called out and I stood in a line of very nervous first kyu students and off we went, kihon, kata and kumite – the three K's of Shotokan karate and in that order. It is hard to know how well you actually did yourself but at the end of the pretty tough exam I was told I had passed. I was presented with my black belt by Jack Warner sensei and Blanti sensei gave me my stamped up licence. Dan Bradley congratulated me and I was over the moon. I then had to make the long trek back to Hemel Hempstead by the return bus route. I can still remember sitting on the top deck of both buses, perched in the back seat on purpose, so as to be on my own, and every now and then I would open my holdall, take out the black belt and just look at it in awe. Then I would take out my stamped up licence and gaze at the signature in the box marked 1st Dan. The date was the 8th of April 1978 and I was now a shodan black belt in the art of Shotokan karate. I was absolutely elated. All the hard work and ups and downs of the last four years had been most definitely worth it. I still have that original belt but like many new shodans I went straight out and purchased a brand new, silk Tokaido one, which is the one I wear every so often and is now pure white. Full circle then, from white to black and back again. Sounds a little bit like life really, which is extremely deep and highly philosophical. Sage on the bloody hill again!

My club had had its first grading at the church hall and all the youngsters had passed their first belt. But we were very quickly outgrowing this venue and so we moved up the road to Bennetts End Community Centre and changed our training day from Saturdays to a Wednesday evening. This is where the club would take off. But like all good clubs we needed a second night and couldn't get one at the Community Centre. So a second night was set up on a Monday evening at the Carey Baptist Church hall in the town centre.

The club absolutely thrived at these two venues and the classes were packed. Of course we advertised but I believe one of the things which took us to the dizzy heights of being the most successful club for miles around was competition karate. There was nothing wrong with our Shotokan karate but it would be on the competition circuit that we would make our name. Blanti would come to my dojo once in a while and we would go and train at his dojo in Featherstone School in Southall, Middlesex. And slowly but surely we became quite adept at competition kumite. Our kata training was already quite decent and so there was no real need to do too much extra in this side of competitive karate, other than get used to team kata. At first, and once we knew what we were doing, we just used to have small

ASKA Hemel Hempstead's very first kumite team
(Left to right: Dave Winfield, Tony Harwood, Me, Brian Harris and Kevin Leigh)

in-house competitions. We would supply small and not very expensive trophies and the youngsters especially would love winning these. I and a couple of others had to learn how to referee competition karate, especially kumite so that we could actually carry on properly with these small events. We attended some refereeing and judging courses in Southall and soon became reasonably adept at this side of our training as well.

We started to have a half-decent five-man kumite team, which included me as team captain. The team in those early days consisted of, Tony Harwood, Brian Harris, Kevin Leigh, Dave Winfield and yours truly. (See photo). Tony and Brian were already black belts locally in another style of karate, called Sankukai and were both decent fighters. They had both joined our club and enjoyed training in Shotokan. Tony especially was a great kicker and Brian was a strong fighter, so we didn't have too bad a team with three black belts and two brown belts.

Most of the tournaments we entered in those very early days were around the London area but soon we started to spread our wings and compete on a more national basis. We entered the ASKA National Championships annually and had started to pick up a few medals. My first personal medal was for our team kata. I led the team out as captain with our rendition of Bassai-Dai kata. We took the bronze medal and were chuffed to bits. We used to win the odd match with our kumite team but on the whole were beaten by much better opposition. Opposition that had trained in this side of karate for many years, but we put up a good show each time and the team was full of spirit. Our team may have been full of spirit but my mouth was most certainly not full of teeth. On the right hand side of my mouth I have lost two of my upper back teeth in kumite matches. One was after the referee had called yame (stop). I had scored with a chudan gyaku-zuki but had dropped my guard, knowing I had won the point. My opponent decided not to stop and even after the referee had called the match to a halt, decided to rearrange my face. The tooth was cut off level with my gum and so I spat the tooth itself out but the roots were left in the gum. It was bloody agonizing. It was the worst night's sleep I think I have ever had. I was dosed up on heavy painkillers but nothing seemed to work. I visited my local dentist next day and painfully had the offending root dug out. The only good thing is that I did win the match but got knocked out in the next round. About a year later another bloody tooth got knocked out in the dojo in kumite. It was right next to the first one I lost and after telling one of my sensei about these incidents, he just stated that I should learn to block that side of my head a little better! What wonderful sympathy!

It was around this time we decided to have a karate club holiday and booked ourselves into a small holiday camp at St. Margaret's Bay, near the white cliffs of Dover in Kent. It was cheap and cheerful and we had a lot of fun. We trained out on the grass on most days and were very proud to show off our art. Tracey and I shared one room and a couple of our friends and students of mine at that time, Chris Parkins and Jane Colin shared another. The rest of the club shared chalets,

either with their friends or their families. Chris was a very good guitarist and played in a local band in Hemel Hempstead. His main instrument was the bass guitar but he could also play a mean six string guitar. At that time I had two very nice instruments, a six string and a twelve string, both of which were acoustic Yamaha guitars. I took them both so Chris and I could have the odd jamming session

Chris and Malcolm (eat your heart out Simon and Garfunkel!)

when we felt like it. The holiday was going really well, when the camp announced there would be a talent contest on one of the nights in the main bar. Chris and I fancied our chances and so practiced a couple of numbers for the contest. On the night in question there were many different acts. There were ventriloquists, singers, comedians and you name it and it was there. The winner would be the act which received the best applause from the audience. We obviously stood a great chance as we had a large number of followers from the karate club and their families alone. We just called ourselves, Chris and Malcolm and eventually we were asked to take the stage. We had decided on two numbers, one an instrumental boogie, where Chris would play lead and I would play rhythm guitar. The other number we had decided on was, *Nights in White Satin*, the Moody Blues great hit. I was chosen to sing and again play rhythm guitar whilst Chris again played the lead. He was brilliant and where this wonderful song bursts into a flute instrumental, Chris had worked it out on his guitar. I have to say, and not wanting to boast or seem big-headed but it went very smoothly and we were by far the best and most professional act on the night. We finished and received a huge applause with lots of yelling and screaming from the karate club. We just had to win, didn't we? The karate club and its entourage decided that the rest of the acts were very poor and extremely amateur and didn't stand a chance, and as there was a Rock 'n' Roll night going on in the main ballroom, that's where they would head. Left in the bar were just Chris, me and our two ladies, Jane and Tracey. Eventually, with all the acts completed, the compére made his way on to the stage and announced that the voting would now commence. What? We thought we had already won! It turned out that the applause voting would be at the bloody end when all the acts had finished. We panicked and we didn't have enough time to round up the karate club again. The names of the various acts were called out and received their applause. Finally, our names were called out, 'Chris and Malcolm.' We stood and took a bow and received a decent applause but nowhere like what it would've been had the karate club and its trusty followers been present. To cut a long story short, we came third. We were beaten by the ventriloquist and an old lady singing fucking *Nellie Dean*! How bloody embarrassing. We bowed our heads in shame and congratulated the winners. We then beat a hasty retreat to the ballroom to give a severe bollocking to the karate club. But it was good fun and we all had a good laugh as we all got pissed. We had seen fantastic double acts such as, Eric and Ernie, Pete and Dud, Simon and Garfunkel, Abbot and Costello, Laurel and Hardy and even Benson and Hedges but there were none like Chris and Malcolm! (See photo of our wonderful double act!)

The next couple of years saw a huge growth in our local Hemel Hempstead dojo and with the opening of the St. Albans College dojo we were beginning to be a force to be reckoned with. Thanks to my wonderful boss at my last job, I could now concentrate on the clubs full time. We started to take trophies on a much larger stage and were receiving excellent coverage in the martial arts magazines of the day and indeed our local press. But a nasty shock was just around the corner. It was time for me to take my second dan grading and again I made my way to Featherstone School, Southall for the big event. This time quite a few of my students accompanied me to the grading and I felt as ready as I ever could. The panel of Blanti, Jack Warner, Jujhar Gill and Dan Bradley sat on the long table that was set up on the school stage. Alongside these four was a martial arts legend, Jim Elkin who was a genuine master in Aikido and held the rank of sixth dan in Tomiki Aikido and fourth dan in Judo. He was a martial artist that was respected highly throughout the world including Japan. He also held one of the top positions in the Martial Arts Commission in England. Jim was a huge man and a real gentleman and was just a guest of the panel and sat quietly on the end of the table and just watched. He was also very highly qualified in first aid thankfully, as this was not to be my lucky day.

All had gone really well until the jiyu-ippon kumite (semi-free one step sparring). Even this wasn't going too badly until my partner attacked me with ushiro-geri (back kick). He whipped around so fast and hit me square in the solar plexus. I went down like the proverbial sack of spuds! Jim Elkin witnessed this and literally jumped up and off the stage and came to my rescue. He felt my ribs and this general area for any breaks and slowly brought me back to life! It seemed like I was winded for an eternity and was in quite a bad way. Jim suggested to the panel, that as the grading was nearly over that I should retire and not take any more part in the exam. I was gutted, very nearly bloody literally, but there was nothing I could do about it. I felt really rough and sat miserably on a chair with a cold wet towel on the offending part with my gi top open, watching the other participants as they finished their grading. Of course, when the results were finally read out, I was not one of the lucky ones. Jack and Blanti said they were sorry but as I couldn't actually finish the grading there was nothing they could do.

So very near and yet so very far! The chap who kicked me came over and apologised and I told him not to worry, as it was an absolutely brilliant kick and certainly wasn't his fault. If I ever needed to know if karate would work on the street, then this was the living proof. I never even saw it coming and I prided myself on my jiyu-ippon kumite. Fuck it! Wrong again. Back to the drawing board! Sadly, big Jim Elkin passed away in 1983 and was a huge loss, not only to Aikido but to the martial arts world in general.

I trained extremely hard for the next three months determined to pass this grade the very next time. I certainly improved my blocking of bloody back kicks. This was the first grade I had really failed and it hurt my pride more than anything. Being the sensei of two very large and now quite successful clubs and having to come back to these clubs and state that you failed your grading can be very hard to take. This time the grading was at the Furzebank Centre in Walsall in the West Midlands and was the dojo of Bill Lloyd who was a third dan and one of the senior instructors in ASKA at that time. The actual date was the 25th October 1980. I am pleased to say that this time everything went extremely well and at the end of the exam was told that I had passed. I felt much better about myself now and could lift my head up again in front of my students. Of course they weren't in the least bit bothered when I had failed, but they were absolutely over the moon when I passed. Now that's what I call loyalty! My ego had taken a battering but now all was well and what was even better, there were no more bloody gradings for three years. I know it may sound like a bit of old rope, but it was probably a good thing that I did actually fail. First of all, it stopped me from becoming big-headed and secondly, and much more importantly, I now knew how students felt when they didn't pass a grading themselves. I never liked the term, failed, as the only people who actually fail at karate are those that give up and stop training. You do not fail just because you don't pass an exam. You march on until you pass the damn thing! I have always likened this to the driving test. Ask how many people failed the first time and you will see that there are many. But they kept on taking the test until they passed it. This is because the driving of a vehicle meant so much to them, that they carried on until they did pass. Karate students, I personally believe, should have this same attitude. Karate must be extremely important in your life if you wish to succeed at it and you do not fail at it just because you don't pass a bloody belt or two!

Wedding No. 2 (Left to right: Bridesmaid, Dave Winfield, my mum, the happy couple, Tracey's dad and mum, Diane Coen and another bridesmaid)

In 1981 I passed my refereeing exam in ASKA and although still competing myself also enjoyed this side of competition karate. And it was in those early 1980's that my clubs would become a real force to contend with on the competition mat. Considering we were late starters on this side of karate, we were doing extremely well. Many people jealously stated that we were only a competition outfit but this was not the case as our students were of a very high Shotokan standard as well.

Of course, I had already met Tracey and we had been going out for a while, when we decided to tie the knot. I knew her parents were not totally happy with this, as there was a large age gap of twenty-one years between us. Tracey was seventeen and I was thirty-eight but we eventually talked them round and they could see that we were very much in love. And so after a brief spell of engagement, we tied the knot on 19th September 1981 at the All Saints Church in Shrublands Road in Berkhamsted. The minister was the Reverend Cox, who I remember was a lovely man. This obviously was the highlight for me in 1981 but again there was a sad side to this year when my wonderful grandad passed away at the age of 92. He died earlier in that year and so sadly he missed our wedding in September. He used to make me laugh as he couldn't really understand the whole idea of karate and he thought I had made a gigantic mistake in leaving my very good job in London and taking up karate as a profession. He thought that karate wouldn't last and was only some type of Japanese fad. His actual words were, 'When are you going to get a proper job again?' I used to tell him that I was doing extremely well thank you and was now earning more money than I had been in London, but he would just smile and have none of it. He was a really lovely man who had devoted his working life to Rolls Royce as one of their top car mechanics and had fought in both world wars. I do miss our wonderful chats together, where he would give me the history of his life over and over again but it was always entertaining and never boring.

Another great karate love of mine at around this time was tameshiwari (breaking techniques). Any chance I got I used to smash my way through tiles and bricks and I must've been a builder's bloody nightmare. I remember one demonstration we performed at Cavendish School in Hemel Hempstead. One of my brown belts worked on a building site and supplied the materials for this demo. There were tiles, bricks and breeze blocks everywhere and the school gym looked like a bloody building site. The PE staff started to panic and insisted we did the breaking techniques on a huge groundsheet, therefore not ruining their lovely, shiny gymnasium

Tameshiwari! This time with ears in tact!

floor. So out came a gigantic groundsheet and off we went with the demonstration. Just about everyone in the club had a go and after about half an hour the crowd were getting a bit bored. So we decided to do some more flashy techniques using headbutts and elbows, instead of the more usual breaking techniques with fists and feet. I decided to be really flash and headbutt three roof tiles whilst someone held them at head height. I got ready and stood close to the tiles, preparing to give them a good solid *Glasgow Kiss*. Then, bang! My head disappeared into the first tile and went through all three tiles like butter. The crowd applauded but two or three of my students were frantically pointing to my ears. I looked down onto the shoulders of my gi and there were small pools of blood appearing. My forehead had gone through the tiles okay but then the tiles slid effortlessly along my unprotected ears and had caused them to bleed quite profusely. A lady from the audience came to my rescue with a heap of tissues for both ears but I felt such a prat. I quickly bowed to the audience and very swiftly disappeared into the loo. The first aid box quickly followed me in with one of my students and I left the toilet with two heavily padded ears. The crowd cheered on my return. I meekly bowed and wound up the demonstration quickly. What a wally!

It was also around this time that I first trained with the legendary Enoeda sensei. We had been invited as guests to train on a course at Hatfield Polytechnic (now Hertfordshire University) with the great man. There must've been around ten of us that went along to the senior grade session and the dojo was absolutely packed with black and brown belts from the mighty KUGB. One of the senior instructors informed us that when we lined-up, to sit absolutely still whilst sensei entered the dojo. This we did and behind me I heard the gymnasium doors open and quietly shut. Nobody moved. Then the great man appeared at the senior end of the lines and took his place at the front of the dojo. What a presence. The man had an aura about him that is hard to explain unless you were lucky enough to have ever trained with him. We bowed and the class started with the most senior black belt taking the exercise routine and then the lesson with Enoeda sensei began. He was everything I hoped he would be and better. I remember in this first session, sensei wanted us to drive forward with an oi-zuki (lunge punch) then quickly heel step with the back leg and then deliver a jodan mawashi-geri (roundhouse kick to the upper area) off of the front leg. A lot of us struggled to get this right and so sensei demonstrated on the biggest guy in the dojo. I think I let out a gasp as sensei drove the punch in and then threw up the fastest mawashi-geri I had ever seen in my life, hitting this chap square on the temple. It made a heck of a slap and I was just waiting for the big guy to fall down but to my utter amazement he wasn't hurt at all. What a technique!

In the afternoon session sensei concentrated on the kata, Bassai-Dai. Again a brilliant session but one bit did make me laugh, not in the dojo but afterwards. The class was performing the ryo sho tsukami uke (grasping block with both hands) just before the migi gedan kekomi (right lower level side thrust kick) and indeed the first kiai. We all stood in the double handed blocking position whilst sensei walked round putting everybody right. I was in the front line with three of my top ladies, Tracey Phipps, Val Henry and Diane Coen. Two of these were England international fighters and Diane was on the England 'B' squad at the time. Sensei came up to each one of these ladies in turn and gently put them right, moving their hips and hands into the correct posture and stating, 'Good!' He then got to me and thoroughly whacked me about until I got into a position he was happy with. I felt really uncomfortable both physically and mentally and when he had finished, he stepped back, looked me up and down, grunted and said, 'Better!'

There was only one downside to the whole course and that was in the break, when we sat outside drinking and eating any lunch that we taken to the dojo. A black belted idiot from the KUGB came up to my group and indeed to me personally, looked at my badge, which of course was the ASKA emblem, grabbed it, shook it and said, 'Who the fuck, are you lot?' The sensei who had invited us in the first place came to our rescue and told this wanker, that we were his guests and therefore the guests of the KUGB. This idiot did no more than snigger, stating that he had never heard of such a group and walked away. I wouldn't have minded normally but this cretin was in his forties and should've known better. The instructor that invited us apologised for this disgraceful behaviour and informed us that this idiot was one in a million.

The last part of the course was to be kumite and indeed circle training. I was a second dan at the time and found myself in one of the first and second dan circles. There was one higher graded circle which contained the third and fourth dans and one that I was glad not to be in, especially as our wanker friend was in this group. Sod's law immediately took over. There were too many students in our circle and so Enoeda sensei transferred some of our second dans into the higher group. You guessed it. I was one of these. The most senior fourth dan invited me, as the guest, to go into the centre of the circle first. Grief, I nearly shit myself. The attack was to be jodan and at Enoeda sensei's command, off we jolly well went. I held my own on most of the attacks but one or two did get through but these guys had brilliant control and although hitting me square in the head, it hadn't hurt. Then it was the turn of wanker. You could tell just by his facial expression that he was out to get yours truly. One of my favourite kumite techniques of all time is to use tai sabaki (body shifting) side stepping the punch quickly and then with a fast, fluent motion sweep the moving leg before it could land. He hit the deck like a sack of shit and I quickly followed up with a gedan gyaku-zuki to my crestfallen opponent. He got up and glared at me, so I glared back. The only trouble with the wonderful warm feeling I had inside when my time in the middle was finished, was that it would be his go in the middle in a few minutes. But in all honesty all he did to my attack was age-uke and gyaku-zuki and although his chudan counter attack was very hard, I was ready for it.

But overall what a brilliant course and afterwards I was so captivated with Enoeda sensei, I made a point of thanking him personally and obtained his autograph,

1983 Welsh Open Champions

which I still proudly own to this day. Later in my karate life I trained with him on a few occasions and another absolutely brilliant course was in Trowbridge, Wiltshire where we were the guests of Peter Bull, the local sensei. The instructors on this course were, Enoeda sensei, Tanaka sensei and Ohta sensei. It was meant to have been Osaka sensei as well but he had to return quickly to Japan, where I believe one of his close family was either very ill or indeed had passed away and so Ohta sensei took his place. This was another wonderful course and I know my group came away with so much knowledge from all three sessions. One thing I do remember from this course though, was coming away with my ankles absolutely killing me, as Tanaka sensei's session for us black belts was nearly all in neko ashi-dachi (cat stance)! I would've liked to have trained with Enoeda sensei more in my karate life but we were from the Kanazawa sensei faction and so this was nigh impossible due to that wonderful karate thing called politics! But I am so glad I had the opportunity to train a few times with this great man before he sadly passed away in 2003. A huge loss, not only to British karate but to the karate world in general. My group still train twice yearly in my local dojo with one of his great protégés and close friend, Dave Hazard and they don't come any better than Dave, who is a living testament to the wonderful memory of Enoeda sensei.

Anyway, Tracey started to win junior grade medals very quickly and it was quite obvious that there was a lot of talent in her just waiting to be tapped. It was when she was a yellow belt that she started to come across to the St. Albans College dojo for extra training. This club was just taking off and had over fifty students within a couple of months. Some of these would become very well known in the karate world and indeed two of them would become full English internationals with Ticky Donovan's England team. Indeed one of them would eventually become the 1992 World Champion in the men's kumite under 70 kilos division and his name of course was Willie Thomas. The other was a lady who became the over 60 kilos ladies English kumite champion and her name was Val Henry. There was a strong and healthy battle brewing between my two clubs and this started to produce a host of excellent male and female competitors. The St. Albans College dojo had some excellent competitors with the likes of Ivan and Joe Pletersky, Lawrence Baptiste, Chris Lewis, Diane Coen, Rick Crowhurst, Ravi and Nish Khanna and of course Val and Willie. And it wasn't long before we started to really fire on all cylinders. Willie and Val started their karate lives in my dojo and I took Willie to second dan and 1986 European champion and Val Henry also to black belt and English champion. This was just the St. Albans club. The Hemel Hempstead dojo also had its share of great competitors but Tracey stood head and shoulders above most of them and became British and English champion and fought for the English team on ten occasions. On one international tournament all three fought for the England team at the same time and I was so very proud of them.

This was around the period when Tracey, who was then a brown belt, and I would become television stars! A lady who worked with St. Albans College, Judy Holpin, who was working with an older group called, *The Women's League of Health and Beauty*, asked me if I would conduct a self-defence session for these retired people. I said of course I would and the next thing I know is that ITV were going to feature one of our sessions on, *Michael Aspel's Six O'Clock Show*. The day eventually arrived and we were very excited and waited nervously outside the St. Albans Conservative Association's building for one of the presenters on the show, Janet Street-Porter. She eventually arrived with the film crew and I couldn't believe how extremely tall she was. The funny thing though, was of all the cars she probably could've owned she peeled herself out of a bloody mini! We introduced ourselves to her and off we went. I conducted a self-defence lesson for these wonderful old people and then I was interviewed personally, as were a few of the older people by Janet Street- Porter. It all went really well but I was glad when it was over. I was drenched with nervous perspiration but was very pleased we had done it. It went on air the following Friday evening and Tracey and I were in the audience as guests of ITV. After the show we met the presenters in the hospitality guest suite and these included, Michael Aspel, Shaw Taylor and of course Janet Street-Porter.

It wasn't long before we would star on the small screen again and this time it was on *Thames News* with the late Andrew Gardner. This time the interviewer was Simon Westcott. It was on this show that these wonderful old pensioners were nicknamed, *The Kung Fu Grannies*! The late, great Spike Milligan and the Arsenal footballer, Alan Sunderland, were also on the same show. Obviously mixing with all the right people then! Next up was Mary Parkinson's show, *Afternoon Plus*, where again the idea of teaching old people to defend themselves was discussed. The police chief for Hertfordshire wasn't too amused about old people learning self-defence but the oldies told him that they were old enough and wise enough to decide for themselves and so a small six week course ensued. Articles in national newspapers followed our success and we had good pieces and photos in *The Guardian* and the *Daily Mail* papers.

ASKA had never produced any full international competitors before and this made me extremely proud, especially producing three nearly all at the same time. This may sound a little big-headed but in all fairness it was ASKA who gave us the ammunition and indeed the ability in the very first place and we just took it from there. When our two clubs combined to make an ASKA Hertfordshire team we were really powerful. 1983, 1984 and 1985 I think were our very best years in those early days. We used to travel all over the country competing. We used to enter the very popular CHP (Cliff Hepburn Promotions) tournaments throughout the land and of course any tournaments that ASKA would host and indeed the English Championships at Crystal Palace.

In 1983 we travelled to the Rhydycar Sports Centre in Merthyr Tydfil in South Wales to enter the Welsh Open Championships. We hired a 52-seater coach and it was full to the brim with competitors and spectators alike. We had attended the same event the year before in 1982 where Tracey had picked up the gold medal in the ladies kumite event and we also picked up a few other placed trophies. But what a difference a year makes.

I remember opening the sports centre doors at the 1983 event and I had never seen so many competitors in my life before. It was absolutely packed. But it was to be a brilliant day and one of the best in our history. This time Tracey was beaten in the final by a very good Welsh girl and came second in the ladies kumite. Willie won the male youth kumite title and we won a host of trophies throughout the day's proceedings. But the best was yet to come. Our men's five-man kumite team of, Dave Haworth, Lawrence Baptiste, Ivan Pletersky, Joe Pletersky and Chris Lewis were doing extremely well and fighting at their very best. I remember there were twenty-six teams in this event and we battled our way through the rounds and semi-final. Eventually, we reached the final and were to be against the very powerful KUGB Swansea team. They were most definitely the favourites but we had been fighting very well. The final was the very last event of the day and took place at a quarter to midnight! Many people had gone home by this time but there was still a huge crowd around the area for this final. Of course most of them were cheering for the Welsh team but we still had our coach-load of spectators and competitiors screaming for us. It showed the strength of our men's team in those days, as Willie Thomas was only the substitute and on the day wasn't actually needed. Both teams had won one fight each and there had been two draws. So it was down to the very last fight. We had Ivan Pletersky and the Welsh team had one of their very best fighters going out last. It went one way then the other with both competitors scoring with a gyaku-zuki for waza-ari (half point). Then our guy got hit extremely hard in the nose and it started to bleed quite profusely. The first aid team stopped the flow of blood and the match continued. The Welsh lad was warned about his lack of control. Time was running out and the thirty-second bell had gone. The crowd screamed for the winning point. Again the two fighters clashed and again Ivan took a hell of a crack to his nose and he bled like a pig. I thought that it must be broken but luckily enough it wasn't. There was nothing the refereeing panel could do but to disqualify the Welsh competitor and awarded the fight to Ivan. It wasn't exactly the way I wanted to win the match, but that's life. He had hit Ivan twice extremely hard in the face and Ivan's face was a mess. Rules are rules I guess and I wasn't going to complain. The Welsh team took the defeat very well and congratulated us on our win, which I thought was in the true spirit of karatedo.

I couldn't believe we had won one of the biggest competitions in the land. We were the 1983 Welsh Open champions (See photo). We were all leaping around like idiots. The whole squad got hold of me and threw me into the air many times and thankfully caught me on the way down. We were absolutely elated. The coach ride home was amazing. There was much singing in the Welsh valleys that night and it was all coming from an English coach!

It was the middle of the night and we sang all the way back to Hertfordshire. I felt so very chuffed as the whole coach sang, 'For he's a jolly good fellow', to me. This was followed by bouts of spontaneous clapping and cheering. Bloody wonderful! I had never felt so important and the bug had truly got a hold. We eventually arrived back in Hemel Hempstead at around five o'clock in the morning with the dawn breaking and the birds singing. As the competition was held on a Sunday, it was now Monday morning and people had to go to work, school and college but who cared. We were the champions! I'm pretty sure there were a few empty desks and chairs at the workplace, schools and colleges on that wonderful day.

The very next weekend arrived all too quickly and it was on to the next tournament and this again was huge. It was the Capital

Tracey scores Ippon!

Open Championships and these were being held at Picketts Lock in Edmonton, London. We were still a little battered and bruised from the previous week's experience but off we went again. Tracey this time won the ladies kumite event in real style and in one of the earlier rounds knocked out (not literally) the excellent Molly Samuels. This fight lasted less than twenty seconds as Tracey's roundhouse kick to the head hit home with such speed and accuracy for the ippon, that even Molly was stunned. This would be the only time that Tracey would actually beat Molly though. They met on two other occasions and both just went to Molly by the smallest of margins. Of course, Molly went on to become World and European champion on a number of occasions and was one of the best female fighters around at that time. But again it was to be the men's five-man team kumite that drew the crowds. This time there were no less than forty-two teams in this division and again round after round we came out on top.

Our line-up was the same as the previous week and once again the guys fought their hearts out. We eventually reached the final but this time the tables were turned and we just lost out to a very good team from London the, British American Karate Association. This was a very strong team that was led by a couple of great fighters from those days, Joe Johal and Greg Wallace. But I was extremely proud of our competitors as they had given their very all two weeks in a row.

Next up was an event that was held by Ticky Donovan on his home patch in East London. The event was called the 1983 Champions of the Future and was held at the Barking Assembly Hall. Again, Tracey had an absolute field day and won all of her matches in real style using her brilliant roundhouse kicking techniques to great effect. This was a really tough competition as just about everyone was there but she went on to win the trophy in the ladies event. The men's trophy went to the very dynamic Elwyn Hall and these two were just a joy to watch as they both fought in such an exciting way. They went onto the stage to receive their winner's trophies and Ticky promoted them both onto the England 'A' squad. Was I pleased or was I pleased? This was our very first student to land up on the England 'A' squad but thankfully not the last. Tracey was presented with the England gi badge, which she sewed on immediately and wore with pride in our dojos.

The last big thing for me personally in 1983 was my third dan exam. Again, this was to be at Featherstone School in Southall. As before, we trained in the morning for a couple of hours and then had a couple of hours break for lunch. In the afternoon, the main feature, the grading itself. I had trained so hard for this belt and didn't want a repeat of my second dan upset. The students taking their first and second dans were up first and then it was our turn. There were four of us in line and we went through the usual kihon (basics) and shitei (designated) katas. Then one at a time we did our tokui kata (kata of choice). I had chosen Gojushiho Sho, as it was a kata I was competing with at the time and it went really well. Then came the jiyu-ippon kumite and I was extremely pleased that this too went pretty well and I kept a special eye out for the ushiro-geri (back kick) attacks! Finally, came the sparring.

This time I was much more up for this as we had worked very hard on this side of our training, as indeed our competition results were showing. Eventually, it was all over and our names were called out one at a time. I was told that I had passed and I was absolutely over the moon. It had been a tough grading and only two out of the four had passed. This is a very physical and mentally demanding exam and I was physically shattered but mentally I was on cloud nine. Malcolm Phipps 3rd Dan – it looked good and by golly it felt good!

Anyway, things just got better and better. Next up were the 1984 English Championships at Crystal Palace in London and again the place was packed and buzzing. The earlier rounds had gone really well for Tracey and Val and both found themselves in their respective finals. Tracey was a middleweight and fought in the under sixty kilos division and Val was one division higher in the over sixty kilos division. These finals in the evening would be on the centre mat with all eyes on this one arena.

I was allowed on the area as the girl's coach and first up was to be Tracey. She was fighting an excellent fighter from the Higashi group, Annette Bailey. The match was so close but Tracey just came out on top, winning by two half points to one. I hadn't got time to celebrate as Val was up next against one of England's top lady international fighters, Yvette Bryan. Val caught Yvette early on with a very powerful front kick that made Yvette wince. As the fight went on it was Yvette's turn to score and she drilled Val with a cracking reverse punch to the stomach. The match was drawing to a close and Yvette had already stepped out of the area once and received a private warning for this. She was obviously very wary of Val's front kick and kept backing off every time Val threatened to throw it. After a brief affray with no score, Val came back to her mark. I told her to concentrate on pretending to throw the fearsome front kick, therefore getting Yvette to the edge of the area. Then with one big feint or indeed the kick itself, this might just do the trick. It was one of my very best pieces of coaching in those early days, as this is exactly what Val did. Yvette was right on the edge of the area, and Val let out a scream as she feigned another middle section

Tracey Phipps and Val Henry - 1984 English Kumite Champions with their very proud coach!

front kick. Sure enough, Yvette stepped out of the area and the referee stopped the fight. In the rules in those days you lost half a point for going out of the area a second time and this is exactly what happened. Val couldn't have timed it any better as there were only about five seconds to go in the whole match and she just moved around stealthily for this short period of time, and then the magic bell went for time. She had also won by two half points to one and I just couldn't contain myself. Not one English champion, but two on the very same day. I was so very proud and Ticky, like the gentleman he is came down and congratulated me personally and my two wonderful champions. I was on cloud nine. Goodness knows what cloud the girls were on!

1984 was also Tracey's biggest year on the international scene. After an England 'A' squad training session she was chosen to represent England at the European championships in Rome. We went and purchased the navy blue blazer, grey skirt and white blouse and the rest of the paraphernalia. She was given her England blazer badge, which was immediately sewn on and worn with pride. It was a great event which was held in the indoor Olympic arena in Rome. Eventually, it was Tracey's turn to fight and she lined-up against a very good Swiss girl. It was Tracey's first international performance but sadly not her best, as she was so very nervous. The Swiss girl won by a couple of points and so that was the end of Tracey's first England outing. I was watching from the seats and she came back to me with her head in her hands. I was so very proud of her and tried to console her. When she eventually did lift up her head she was in tears. Ticky was standing close by and came over to her and put his arm around her. He asked if she was crying

1984 English Ladies team and the English Junior Men's team in the Olympic Stadium in Rome

because she felt sorry for herself or because she had let her country down. She stated that it was the latter, to which Ticky replied that that was the right answer and casually walked away. I wasn't angry and nor was Tracey, as here was a man who was English through and through and the best competition kumite coach in the world.

Next up was a trip to Oslo in Norway. This was with the EKF (English Karate Federation) team as opposed to the EKC (English Karate Council) team in Rome. It was nearly the same ladies who represented both bodies but this time the coach was Eddie Daniels from Birmingham. It was a superb trip in a very pretty country and this time Tracey redeemed herself, as she was part of the ladies team that won the gold medal. One thing I do remember from this trip is the price of drinks. They had such a high cost of living in Norway you needed a bloody mortgage to get a round of drinks in!

Then it was the big one, the 1984 World Championships, which were held in Maastricht in Holland. This time it would be a Great Britain team that represented us, as this was always the case in those days for the World Championships. In the European Championships the home nations were all split into their separate countries, England, Scotland, Wales and Northern Ireland. This was one of the best Great Britain teams that had ever left these shores, men and women alike. The men's team included great fighters such as, Vic Charles, Jeoff Thompson, Pat McKay, Jerome Atkinson, Mick Sailsman, Mervyn Etienne, Gerry Fleming and

1984 Men's World Kumite Champions (left to right: back row, Jeoff Thompson, Jerome Atkinson, Ticky Donovan, Gerry Fleming, Mervyn Etienne. Front row, Pat McKay Vic Charles, Mick Sailsman)

Jimmy Collins, with the ladies team consisting of Tracey, Beverley Morris, Janice Argyle, Yvette Bryan, Lou Pauly and Shirley Graham, two in each weight category. Even to this day this had to be the most exciting championships I personally as a spectator and indeed video cameraman for the team had ever witnessed. It was superb. I had never seen so many competitors in my life. The GB team was just brilliant and the men won the team kumite trophy in real style. I think the most exciting match was the final of the middleweight division of the men's kumite between Pat McKay and Otti Roethoff of Holland. Pat was just phenomenal and if I had a favourite fighter of all time it would be him. The best lady fighter I have ever witnessed was the Dutch lady, Guus van Mourik, who won the world title three times in a row and goodness knows how many Europeans. In the final she beat Great Britain's Yvette Bryan.

Tracey's first match was the very first match of the whole tournament and she beat a Mexican girl six to nil. Next up was a girl from the USA and sadly Tracey just lost by half a point. In this match though she had been hit very hard in the face and her nose was bleeding quite badly. I thought the girl from the States would be disqualified but she just received a private warning and went on to win by three points to two. But it was a brilliant experience for Tracey, and as this was one of her earlier experiences, to make the last sixteen in the world was no mean feat.

Not long after this four day trip to Holland came a wonderful trip to the USA. Neither of us had ever been to the States before and the trip would be for ten days visiting and competing in Chicago and Stevens Point, Wisconsin. It was to be Chicago first stop and we stayed in the suburb of Schaumburg. The hotel we stayed at was a magnificent, five star hotel and was just over the road from the biggest Mall in the world at that time, the Woodfield Mall.

The match itself was to be in Chicago at the Harper College. There were posters everywhere in Chicago stating that this event was the 'Karate Olympics' and that the USA team would be taking on the current world champions, England. This of course wasn't absolutely true, as the world champions were Great Britain and not just England. But who cared! Again this was an EKF team with Eddie Daniels in charge and many of the men's world championship team from Maastricht were sadly missing. One reason was that this was an English team and so the Scots lads weren't present. But there was still a powerful squad and they just took the USA teams apart.

After a couple of warm up matches against different State teams, it was time for the big one. There would be fifteen bouts in the men's category and nine bouts in the ladies. The winners would be decided on who had won the most matches. The college was absolutely packed with spectators and you were lucky to get a seat. Every time a point was scored by a USA competitor, a drummer let out a huge drum roll and the crowd cheered and screamed loudly. First up were the men and to cut a long story short England wiped them out by fourteen wins to their one. Even the one match the USA team did get was for Livi White being disqualified for excessive contact. Then it was the ladies turn and the English team won by seven wins to two and Tracey won her match against a good USA girl. The USA teams were actually captained by the Chief Instructor for Illinois Shotokan, John DiPasquale and he and the USA group were the perfect hosts. Not only did we have a brilliant hotel but they took us everywhere. We went to a packed Wrigley Field, the home of the Chicago Cubs to watch the last baseball match of the season between the Chicago Cubs and the Los Angeles Dodgers. Whoever won this match actually won the league and it was so exciting. The Cubs won in extra time and the stadium just took off! We were also taken to the Six Flags Great America funfair and again had a brilliant day out. One evening they took us to a nightclub in the centre of Chicago. There was a brilliant rock band playing in the corner of the club and the music was excellent. But the highlight of the evening for our men's team was that a whole group of Chicago Cub's cheerleaders were also having a night out. This made the English lad's day as these stunningly beautiful eighteen to twenty-year olds, although not in their cheerleaders kit were still pretty scantily clad. Every time I casually gazed at one of them, I could feel Tracey's eyes burning a hole in the back of my head.

And then it was off to Wisconsin. We caught a small plane from O'Hare International Airport in Chicago to Steven's Point, Wisconsin. Again, we had another wonderful hotel and the USA people couldn't do enough for us. We all felt like royalty. The actual result in the competition was much the same though with the English men's team winning by thirteen wins to two and the English ladies team winning by eight to one. Tracey again won her match. But what an overall experience and Tracey and I thoroughly enjoyed our first trip to the States. This trip lifted Tracey's spirits after the Maastricht and Rome results, with two gold medals now to her name from this trip alone, plus of course the one from Norway and not forgetting she was the English kumite champion.

There were two more slightly smaller international events in 1984 and Tracey featured in them both. First up was a match between the Scottish men and women and the English teams in Cumbernauld, near Glasgow where both Val Henry and Tracey represented the England ladies team. The other international was against the Australian team, who were touring Europe and this match was held on Ticky's home patch at the Barking Assembly Hall. Again, like the Scottish match, the England ladies won both their events relatively comfortably and in both of these internationals, Tracey had won both of her individual matches and so it was a couple more gold medals to add to her growing international collection.

In 1984, Tracey was the only woman to

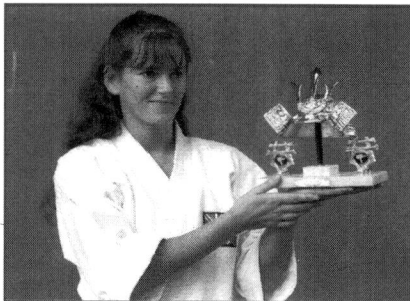

Tracey with yet another title!

125

1985 British Championships
(left to right: Me/Steve Blaney/Nish Khanna/Ravi Khanna/
Willie Thomas/Vicky Henderson/Lawrence Baptiste)

compete in every International event for the GB & England teams in Rome, Oslo, Chicago, Steven's Point, Maastricht, Glasgow and London and I was lucky enough to have attended every single one. I was a very proud man.

But 1984 would also see a huge change in our local clubs as we changed from ASKA to Seishinkai Shotokan Karate. It was something that was becoming unavoidable, as we as a group veered more and more to the ways of Nakayama sensei and the JKA style of Shotokan. I never wanted to go it alone as such, but this move was pretty much forced upon us. There had been one or two antics at the higher end of ASKA in the Southern region and this was a real shame. One senior instructor had a serious drink problem and on one dan grading two out of the three on the panel actually fell asleep whilst people were grading. Enough was enough and I sent in our resignation to Dan Bradley the secretary of ASKA who's actual comments were, 'I'm surprised you haven't done it earlier.' This was a sad day, as we had a great time in ASKA and we had learned one heck of a lot but it was time to move on. We put it to the vote to all our one hundred and fifty members and the vote was one hundred percent for leaving and going it on our own. As we were not big enough to totally go it alone, we had to join the EKF, which allowed smaller groups to join under their banner. And so in the November of 1984, Seishinkai Shotokan Karate was born. The international bit of our current title would come at a later date.

And so it was on to 1985, and another huge success for us personally was at the 1985 British Championships which were also held at Crystal Palace in South London. Yet again the National Sports Centre was absolutely packed and again we had one of our really good days. Willie Thomas won the young men's (18-21yrs) kumite title in fantastic style and one of our young girls, Vicky Henderson won the under sixteen's senior kata title. In the men's senior kumite another of my top fighters of the day, Lawrence Baptiste took the third place trophy, only losing out to the ex-world champion Vic Charles in the semi-final. The one hiccup of the day came in the men's team kata event. We had an absolutely excellent team of, Ravi Khanna, Nish Khanna and Steve Blaney. Their kata was Nijushiho and they performed this in a really novel way. They all stood back to back in a sort of a triangle and performed the kata. Their timing was immaculate and the kata was a joy to watch and brought the house down. They won the event all hands down – but had they? Ticky went over to the chief referee and you could see that something was not right. The chief referee then called all the judges over and demoted us into second place. The crowd did not like this one bit and booed and stamped their feet. When I asked the referee what was wrong with our kata he explained that somewhere in the bloody rules it stated that all three competitors of the team should be facing the front of the area. Ticky, who knew the rules upside down and backwards had very cleverly picked up on this and sadly we were demoted into second place. Guess who now came first? Ishinryu of course! I just wonder if Ticky would've complained as much had his Ishinryu team not been in second place.

Well, we had obviously learnt the hard way and never performed the kata like that again, only in demonstrations. So we came away from the British Championships with two winners, one second place and one third. Not too bad, considering there were only about one hundred and fifty students in our local clubs in total. (See photo). Again at Crystal Palace in 1985, Willie won the English championship kumite title with Tracey and Val taking minor medals this time, so all in all it had been a pretty good year.

Another big tournament in 1985 was the Champion of Champions event, which was held at the Granby Halls in Leicester. This was a CHP (Cliff Hepburn Promotions) tournament for those that had taken medals in the many CHP events that were held throughout the year in the UK. The ladies senior kumite event saw Tracey and Val both win all of their matches to find themselves in the final against each other that evening. Again our men's team powered its way to the final, where we would meet one of the favourites, the Toxteth club from Liverpool. They wore red karate suits and were excellent fighters. But this was one of the biggest controversies I had ever witnessed at a karate tournament. The match kicked off and both teams had won two fights apiece and so it was all down to the last fighters. These matches were one whole point (ippon) matches and both competitors were very wary of each other. The winner would be a hero and the loser would feel as though they had let their side down. No pressure then! Our guy, Jon Collier who came from our Winchester club dodged an attack from the Toxteth lad and scored with a superb roundhouse kick to the face. It was a perfect kick, which hit the Liverpool lad on the right cheek and the referee's hand shot up for an ippon. We were absolutely elated, as our team was the Champion of Champions. But hang on, were we? The Toxteth team surrounded the referee and complained that the technique hadn't scored and if it had it should've only merited a half point. This was absolutely pathetic as the Liverpool lad had a slight red mark on his cheek from the brilliant kick. All hell let loose. The mirror referee, who I caught winking and smiling at the Toxteth captain, and who was more senior than the actual referee, literally talked the referee round in to changing his decision to a waza-ari. The referee, who was an out-and-out wimp, had been well and truly badgered by the Liverpool team and the cheating judge. This referee just hadn't got the courage of his convictions and changed his decision and now only gave half a point. We were furious and the legendary Steve Cattle came over to me and said, 'Malcolm, you've been very badly seen off!' How right he was. The fight finished at one apiece and so the whole match was a draw. Then of course their top fighter came out against ours and won. Sod's bloody law! He was an excellent fighter and deserved the match but as a five-man team we were better. The place was in uproar and everybody was on our side. Willie Thomas was totally disgusted to say the least and asked the organiser and the refereeing panel, if they had ever actually trained in bloody karate! We had a quick meeting and decided we would leave the tournament. I went over to Cliff Hepburn and told him that we would be leaving and the reason why. He stated, 'That's life Malcolm!' And that there was nothing he could or would do about it.

I told him we would never be back to one of his tournaments again and in the long run it would be his loss and indeed we kept to our word. I told him that we wouldn't give him the satisfaction of watching my two brilliant English lady champions battle it out in the ladies kumite final and went over to the trophy table and took the first and second place trophies. We then as a group stomped home. Tracey and Val shared the title and indeed the trophies. There is nothing worse in karate than bloody cheating. The Toxteth lads came over to console us and I told them if it meant that bloody much to them, we would've given them the poxy trophy in the first place. Steve Cattle shook his head as we left and said he was totally disgusted with the disgraceful decision and the disgusting performance of the refereeing team for this match and that he had never seen anything like it before in his whole karate career. He said that we had done the right thing in leaving.

One even more seedy side to this story is that the mirror referee, who shall remain nameless but was a senior KUGB member, didn't like me very much from a tournament we had entered earlier in the year. Every now and then I got asked to referee or judge. This I didn't mind, and at the East of England championships, which were held at the Kelsey Kerridge Sports Centre in Cambridge, I found myself in such a situation. I was one of the kata judges for the ladies senior kata event. This chap's girlfriend was competing and indeed was one of the favourites to win. She came out in the final and performed the Shotokan kata, Chinte. About halfway through the kata she missed a whole sequence out of four movements but she covered this up very well. It could have been very easily missed by a judge who didn't actually know this kata too well, or indeed one that was half asleep. The main referee for this event was our friend. He blew the whistle for the scores and I gave her a pretty low mark. The other judge had also obviously seen these mistakes and gave a mediocre mark as well. Our friend gave her a massive mark. There were only three judges for this event, so all three scores counted. The main referee blew his whistle. He called the other judge and myself over and asked us why we gave such low scores. I told him there were four moves missing and told him exactly where these mistakes were in the kata. It was a quick sequence and he said to me that he had seen it but it should only be considered as one mistake. This was total bollocks! Of course with the score she now had, she wasn't going to get a medal and rightly so. Our friend asked us to go back to our chairs and give the scores again. He blew his whistle once more. I wasn't going to change my score as there were most definitely four moves missed. He obviously swayed the other judge who upped his score by a couple of points. So with the new scores she sneaked into third place. But it was obvious that our friend wasn't too happy with me and walked off in a huff once the event was over.

My good friend and World Champion, Jeoff Thompson and me

Sadly, on this day of Champion of Champions he got his own back. If he can live with cheating, so be it. Some people will do anything for the win but I have always made sure that my students play the game fairly. *With the freedom to do what you like, be sure you like what you do!*

Also in 1985 the world champion, Jeoff Thompson joined Seishinkai and this gave a huge boost to our squad. Jeoff was with us for two years and in that time won the gold medal in the European Team Championships in Oslo, the World Games Championship individual gold medal at Crystal Palace and the Karate Commonwealth Games title in Guernsey. He became a good friend and I was extremely pleased when a few years later he received the MBE from the queen at Buckingham Palace. Jeoff married the World Games Champion and England international fighter, Janice Argyle, who was a colleague and a friend of Tracey.

After the huge successes of 1983, 1984 and 1985, I was personally rewarded for my coaching successes nationally and internationally. At a reasonably posh function in our local sports centre, I was awarded the 1985 'Sports Personality of the Year' for the West Hertfordshire/Dacorum division. I received a nice cup, which I had to return after my year was up, and also a certificate, which I could keep. I was chuffed to bits, as I was only the second martial artist to receive this accolade. A few years earlier a judo chappie had also won this award.

1986 was yet another excellent year for us and in one international match where the English men's and ladies teams took on the Scottish teams in London, all three of my international fighters, Val, Willie and Tracey all fought in the same match for

My three English international fighters, all picked for the same tournament

the first and only time. On quite a few occasions two of them would go away with the England team together but this was indeed the only time that all three would compete for England in the same tournament. The match itself was a close run thing but both the English men's and ladies teams came out on top. Also in this year, Jeoff Thompson who was still with us at this point in time was a part of the Great Britain men's kumite team that won the world title in Sydney, Australia. And this was also the year that I personally passed my NCF (National Coaching Foundation) coaches award.

Next up were the ladies European championships and the junior European championships for the under twenty-one year old men. This was held in Sion in Switzerland and was a stunningly beautiful destination, surrounded by the Swiss Alps. The air was fresh and clean, as indeed was the town. We stayed at a lovely hotel and the championships were held over a long weekend. Tracey, who was in the individual kumite event was also picked for the England ladies kumite team and in a match against the Italian team, twisted badly on her support leg. She finished her fight but sadly lost, as the England team were narrowly beaten by two matches to one. They were placed fourth in the final analysis but the worst thing was Tracey's knee. It was very swollen and she was fighting in the individual tournament the very next day. They iced it for hours and the swelling did decrease a little but after an awful night's sleep the knee was very swollen again. The English medical team, which included Doctor Jim Canney did their very best and tightly bandaged the injured joint. Tracey fought her heart out but her main weapons were her legs and those extremely fast roundhouse kicks. In these matches she just couldn't kick at all but still won a couple of fights but sadly lost the third. As with the team result she came fourth, just missing out on the medals, which was totally amazing considering the injury. I know I am biased but I sincerely believe she would've won the title if she hadn't suffered the serious injury the day before. To crown it all, she was punched badly in the eye in one of the individual matches and she landed up with one of the best black eyes any of us had ever seen. So out came the sunglasses. Doctor Canney actually took a photograph of the offending eye and stated that it was one of the best he had ever seen, indeed a real beauty and that he would use the photograph in his lectures on sporting injuries in the future.

Willie was also excellent and helped the team to the silver medal winning all of his fights and in the individual event took the bronze. Ticky was well pleased with both of the Seishinkai fighters and in the hotel afterwards told me so.

Even I came home with a bloody injury and I was only a spectator. There was a beautiful private dojo in Sion and was run and part owned by the Swiss karate team captain of a few years previous, Jean-Claude Knupfer. At this tournament, also as a spectator was the legendary karate fighter, Dominique Valera, who was also, I believe, a part owner of the dojo. I was introduced to him by Ticky and he seemed a really great guy. Jeoff Thompson was also in attendance at this tournament, accompanying his girlfriend and wife-to-be, Janice Argyle. Jeoff knew the Swiss chap who part owned the private dojo and asked if we could work out for a while. I obviously hadn't got a gi with me and nor had Jeoff, so we worked out in tracksuits. Jeoff gave me a pair of focus mitts and instructed me how to use them for his training regime.

Tracey was on the stopwatch and the rounds were for three minutes duration. I had to move around like a competitor and at any set time place the pads in a special way for Jeoff to either punch or kick them, or indeed complete a combination technique on them. On the third round I was absolutely knackered and was sweating like a fucking horse. I put one of the pads out in front of me for Jeoff to hit with a reverse punch but for the first time in the whole three rounds he missed and punched me hard in the ribs. I thought I was going to die. I was badly winded and my ribs felt as though they were cracked. Jeoff dutifully apologised and I hobbled back to the hotel for an ice pack. If any traditional idiot thinks that competitors can't punch, then all I can say is try fighting some of them and I think you might change your blinkered mind. I have been hit by many competitors in my day but this was the hardest of all and I couldn't sleep on that side of my body for bloody weeks. Cheers Jeoff!

Ticky was obviously extremely pleased with Willie's performance in Sion, so much so that he picked him for the senior European championships, which were to be held in Madrid, Spain later the same year. I remember I was busily teaching at one of our clubs in Hemel Hempstead when I was rudely interrupted. It was at the St. Albert the Great School dojo in Bennetts End and halfway through the lesson one of Willie's friends, Paul Tate, who was one of my St. Albans brown belts burst through the dojo door in jeans and a jumper and shouted, 'He's won!' I was going to tell Paul off for bursting into the dojo without any etiquette whatsoever and asked him what the hell he was talking about. He then explained that Willie had only gone and won the senior European championships and had just phoned Paul up, so as to tell me. We stopped the class and everyone just cheered and

Willie Thomas,
1986 European Champion
(was I chuffed or what?)

clapped and danced around like idiots. Who cared, I was over the moon. One of my students was now the 1986 European Champion. I was so proud of him and it also turned out, as a small bonus, that at that time he was the youngest man to win this prestigious title. In the final he had beaten Scotland's Bunny Burns in a very close encounter but had eventually emerged the winner. This put my ugly mug back on the television screens as, *Anglia Sport* did a piece on Willie winning the Europeans with me as his successful coach. *BBC Radio Bedford* also did an interview with us both and these were really nice extras at the time.

The final international tournament of 1986 and indeed sadly Tracey's last outing for England was held in Swansea in South Wales. Tracey had decided it was time to retire from the international scene and they made her captain of the ladies team, as this was to be her final match for her country. I thought this was a really lovely touch and I know it meant a lot to her. The England ladies were much too powerful for the Welsh team and again Tracey had won all her fights and led the team to the gold medal.

There was a comical side to this tournament though. The English referee hadn't turned up for some reason and the Welsh wanted an English referee to balance out the odds. I had refereed quite a few big tournaments by now and indeed had helped Ticky on many occasions on the England squad training sessions, acting as a mirror referee to him in many of the playoffs for the team. But at this event I was a spectator and hadn't got the correct apparel for the job. Everyone was pointing at me and asking me to do it and what a fine job I would do if I accepted. Bullshit! I truthfully didn't want to be thrown to the wolves and declined on the premise that I hadn't got the right clothes. They then had a quick whip round and somehow managed to come up with the whole bloody set! The only trouble was the trousers were much too long and the blazer landed up around my knees! A lady in the audience came on to the area with some pins and pinned the trousers up. The only things that fitted were the shirt and tie.

The chief referee was Chico Mbakwe from Wales and he couldn't stop bloody smiling. I told him I couldn't wear the jacket but he insisted that I must for the bowing in ceremonies and national anthems. He said I could remove it when the matches actually started. Bloody wonderful! I stood there for the anthems looking like fucking Frankenstein's mate, Igor. I only needed a bloody hunched back. Anyway, after this embarrassing moment was over I quickly removed the jacket and placed the offending article over a chair. The fucking chair disappeared in a haze of navy blue. To this very day I still haven't got a bloody clue

Malcolm the referee
(this time in bloody clothes that fit!)

whose jacket it was but it was so big that I certainly wouldn't want to argue with its owner. Halfway through one of the matches the bloody pins came loose on one of my trouser legs and I tripped over the offending material which was now over my toes. This caused much mirth in the audience and bloody Chico nearly burst his sides fucking laughing. On rushed the 'trouser lady' and dutifully pinned my trousers up again and off we went. Most tournaments call for first aid for injured competitors. Here in Swansea we didn't need first aid but a bloody tailor!

The final accolade for Tracey in the year of 1986 was that she won the 'Sports Personality of the Year' for the town of St. Albans and this was a fitting tribute to her excellent international career.

The late eighties were also reasonably successful but we couldn't quite match the mid-eighties. In 1987 Willie won the team bronze medal in the England team at the European championships, which were held in Glasgow. He also went on to win team gold for the English team in a three-way match against Italy and Spain. This event was actually held in Italy. Two of our Haringey club members won gold medals in the 1987 British Championships at Crystal Palace. Trevor Justin won the 16-18 years kumite and Robert Talbott took the 12-16 years kumite title. Both were taught by their sensei at the Haringey club in North London, Clive Needham.

Another highlight for me personally, was that I was awarded my 4th Dan Certificate and received a wonderful letter from the English Karate Council, signed by Dan Bradley. It stated that I was to be specially awarded my 4th Dan by the World Union of Karate Organisations (WUKO) and the English Karate Council (EKC) for services to karate nationally and internationally. I still have the letter and was very tempted to frame it. Big-headed bastard!

In 1988 at the English Championships, Sonia Evelyn, also from the powerful Haringey club of Clive Needham, won the kumite, under 60 kilos English title at Crystal Palace and in the same event Willie also took the kumite gold medal in his weight category.

But in a somewhat sad way this was the year that we would lose Willie Thomas. Willie wanted to further his competition kumite career and not so much his Shotokan one, and joined Vic Charles', British Sport Karate Association. He had started his karate journey with me as a young lad of fourteen and was now into his early twenties. He had started with me as a beginner and I had taken him to 2nd Dan and to European, English and British champion. The transition was done properly, with Vic sending me a nice letter asking if I was happy with this situation. Of course I didn't want to lose Willie, who not only was an excellent fighter but also a good friend. But I knew Willie had many international friends in Vic's new group and so I knew he would be very happy there and I wouldn't stand in his way. His new found Association over the next few years became extremely successful and won many gold medals at national and international level. The biggest highlight for

Willie personally, was when he went on to actually win the WUKO world title in Spain in 1992 and I was so very proud of him and phoned him up on his return home. He had obviously made the right choice of Association for himself personally but I honestly think he would've won it anyway had he stayed with Seishinkai. Another reason for this change was that Seishinkai was veering more and more to the JKA teaching of Nakayama sensei and this took up all of our time, and our competition successes started to dwindle a little. But looking back it was definitely the right way to go and I have no regrets whatsoever. Seishinkai, although not as successful as we were in those 1980's, is indeed much better technically now and we are still producing competitors of a very high standard. We have no current international competitors but this is not down to us, it is down to the bloody state of English karate in general, thanks to poor politics and huge bloody egos.

Jeoff Thompson also finished his two-year stint with Seishinkai and thanked us for giving him a happy karate home for this very successful time for both him and for us. Jeoff, and one of his students, Knoxley Greaves were the only two students to date, who were not actually Shotokan stylists. Both were from the Wado-ryu style of karate.

Also, with Tracey and Val both retiring and losing Willie, our international stardom had come to an abrupt halt. Val had decided to retire at about the same time as Tracey and all three had done us so very proud and helped put Seishinkai on the map. I was a very happy man to have been their coach and instructor from the very start. Over those years in the mid-eighties we entered so many minor and major competitions it would need another book to describe them all but we did excellently well in all of them and everyone knew the tracksuit of ASKA Herts!

I was also asked, two years in a row, 1988 and 1989 to be a guest instructor on the very popular annual course held in Butlin's Somerwest World in Minehead, Somerset. The other instructors were, Dave Hooper from Japan, John Cheetham the editor of *SKM* and the organiser, Steve Hyland. These seminars were very well

Seishinkai students on the Minehead Course (Instructors in the front line, left to right: Me, Steve Hyland, John Cheetham and Dave Hooper)

attended and I have to say the instruction was of the very highest level. There were many, many sessions over the long Bank Holiday weekend of both years and when we weren't actually teaching we would jump in and participate in the other instructor's classes, especially Dave Hooper's, as these were absolutely excellent and straight from the JKA in Japan where Dave was now residing and I believe has done ever since. I made lots of good friends on these courses, people like Terry Oliver and Linden Huckle and many, many more.

Here are some of the quotes from these seminars from *Shotokan Karate Magazine*, Issue No. 18 (Page 14):
'Brilliant, truly enjoyable and instructive' D. Brown - SKGB
'Excellent, has boosted my enthusiasm for karate' T. Page - SSK
'Great atmosphere, I learnt a great deal' T. Sylvester - TASK
'Best course I've attended. So much information' D. Guy - NASKO
'Absolutely fantastic, real quality instruction' C. Harrop - KODOKAI
'Really friendly course, lots of new friends' M. Walker - KUGB
'Incredible course, detailed instruction of the highest standards' T. Oliver - SEKU

Over this period of time Tracey and I were ecstatically happy. We had moved from my little bedsit in Larchwood Road to our first home together in Crawley Drive in the Grovehill part of Hemel Hempstead. It was here that we made two of the best purchases we would ever make. We bought, on separate occasions our wonderful two Red Setters, Bill and Ben. Benjie was to be our first puppy and then about eighteen months later we decided he needed a buddy and so purchased Billy. Benjie came from Langley near Slough and Billy from Letchworth in Hertfordshire and both had decent pedigrees. Personally, we couldn't care less about pedigrees and the like, as these were pets and part of the family and not for showing at those bloody awful dog shows. They were absolutely magnificent and I was so proud to walk out with these beautiful animals on their leads. I have never owned anything so precious in my whole life as these two Irish Setters. Their personalities were

Bill and Ben!

Tracey and me in our posh frocks!

magnificent and extremely comical and as one breeder once stated, 'Irish Setters are one hundred percent heart and one percent brain!' Couldn't have put it better myself, as these two were certainly one hundred percent heart but actually they weren't that daft either. They became our family and you couldn't have asked for a better and a more loyal one.

In those days our clubs had really expanded, mainly due to our amazing competition successes and indeed the hard work of both me and Tracey. Tracey had an excellent Watford dojo at the Watford Girl's Grammar School which is just off of Vicarage Road in Watford, which of course is the home of Watford FC. The Hemel Hempstead and St. Albans dojos were extremely successful and were my personal clubs. Bill Burgar one of my Hemel Hempstead black belts at that time, opened up the Reading University club where he was studying and Julian Burton started the Welwyn Garden City dojo. John Beasley and Mike Meredith, who were two of my ex-St. Albans black belts, opened up the Cambridge dojo after moving into this area. Other clubs that joined us in that period were, Haringey in North London with Clive Needham sensei, Winchester with Simon Budden sensei, St. Ives in Cornwall with Julian Berry sensei, Croydon with Rod de Silva sensei and for a while we also had clubs in Bexhill-on-Sea, Battersea and Upminster. The Association expanded beyond our wildest dreams and with this amazing success and our home life with Bill and Ben, life just couldn't get any better.

For the first time in my life and indeed in Tracey's we really started to earn an excellent wage. Our house in Crawley Drive was a council house and they gave us the option to buy, which we jumped at immediately. This meant we would have to stay put at Crawley Drive for another three years, as this was the council's ruling but that wouldn't bother us in the least, as this was a comfortable house and perfect for the setters.

Our favourite dojo to actually visit was St. Ives in Cornwall. This had absolutely nothing to do with the students, just the beautiful part of the world it was set in. The club itself was situated in a school in the Carbis Bay area of the town and we would go down and do a small course, which was followed by the three monthly grading. This would take up one day but we would go down to Cornwall for a week at a time. These trips became our holidays and meant that we would visit Cornwall four times annually and in all the different seasons of the year. It very quickly became my favourite place in the whole world and still is to this very day. The pace of life is so much more relaxed there and we found the sea air so wonderfully refreshing. We used to take Bill and Ben in our car, which at first only Tracey could drive, as I still hadn't passed my test. We owned a maroon Ford Sierra Estate in those early days and again it was our pride and joy, as it was our very first car. Again, with good money coming in we updated this car to another Ford Sierra Estate but this time it was brand spanking new and indeed the top of the range, blue Ghia model. It wasn't very long before I also had passed my test and so we used to share those long three hundred and twenty-mile journeys from Hemel Hempstead to St. Ives. We always stopped around halfway at the same service station on the M5. This was Taunton Deane and it was one hundred and fifty-one miles exactly on the car milometer from our home in Hemel Hempstead. The main reason for this stop was that it had a nice grass verge and Bill and Ben could get out and stretch their legs and have a pee and of course we would fill the car up with petrol and ourselves with coffee. The dogs always instinctively knew, that when we packed our cases and made them comfortable in the back of the car, that they were going on a week's holiday to that wonderful place with sand and sea and fantastic new smells and walks. We used to hire two different cottages at different times that were way out in the country, halfway between St. Ives and Penzance. The village itself was called Newmill and the two cottages were Bay of Biscay and Kitty Noys. They were perfect as they were set in their own spacious grounds and the dogs could go mad if they wished without having to worry about any traffic. I have never walked so far or so much in my whole life. But it was great fun walking with these two characters and my lovely wife and I could've spent the rest of my days doing this and I would've been a very happy man. If you have two Irish Setters you certainly don't need a television. The antics these two got up to was just unbelievable and in the main absolutely hilarious and certainly kept you on your toes. But they were also very loving and great fun and I now miss them like crazy. I would give up more or less anything to have those two characters back again in my life and indeed those wonderful, wonderful times but of course this is sadly impossible. Let's hope we meet again one day as they were most definitely soulmates. Each day we would literally walk all day, either in the country, or along the seashore, or indeed along the brilliant Cornish cliff path and down into all the little coves and bays. Then we would go back to our cottage in the late afternoon and feed the dogs. This was followed by forty winks and then a bath or shower to prepare for the evening. The dogs would be totally shattered and always fell asleep straight after their meal and would be totally out for the count! In the early evening Tracey and I would drive into St. Ives and try out all the different restaurants. We would share a bottle or two of our favourite claret, Mouton Cadet 1982, and eventually make our way back to the cottage. Once there we would be met by our two boys, who after saying their mad and very enthusiastic hallos, would run around the vast grounds for about half an hour, chasing anything that moved! What a way to spend your life, absolutely idyllic. I loved my home in Hemel Hempstead and of course my karate clubs but it was always a heartfelt push to leave St. Ives. Even the dogs seemed miserable and the long journey home was never as happy as the one down to Cornwall and indeed seemed twice as bloody long.

Our love of nature became a totally natural thing and both of us got excited when seeing the slightly more unusual creatures from this part of the world, such as

The Birdman of Hemel Hempstead!

In my dreams! (Sadly, this was not Tracey's Porsche)

buzzards, peregrine falcons, dolphins, seals and adders. Creatures we wouldn't normally see at home. I purchased, and indeed started to carry a good Nikon camera around wherever we went and shot some really decent photographs. We always carried a pair of binoculars with us and were ready for the unexpected, and all four of us just seemed so at one with the world.

I remember a couple of instances with adders. The first one was as we were driving to our cottage on a beautiful summer's day, when suddenly on the road up ahead was an adult adder crossing the bloody road. Had Tracey not stopped immediately we would've killed the creature. I dashed out of the car with camera at the ready and very carefully took a couple of great photos. Another time we were just coming up out of a bay at Nanjizal Cove, near Lands End. I had just reached the top of the steep climb and was about to put my right hand onto the ground to pull myself up that last bit, when I suddenly stopped dead. There, hidden amongst the thorns and small stones and fantastically camouflaged was another adder. I would've put my hand right on it but luckily enough all I did was take a couple of photos of it. I showed it to Tracey and told her to keep the dogs away just in case they got bitten.

The three years went by so fast at Grovehill and before we knew it, it was time to move house. Thanks to the council, we made a tidy sum on the deal, as we only paid approximately £16,000 for Crawley Drive and sold it for just over £65,000. Not a bad return, I think you'll agree, for three years happiness and now we were on the property ladder. We moved into another part of Hemel Hempstead and into a town house in Garland Close. This was a house with three floors and again we would be extremely happy there, with the clubs doing so well and the dogs loving life to the full. We had also moved up the car ladder and Tracey now owned a black Porsche and I had a silver Range Rover. She had started with a cheaper version, the 924 that was white, but now had this beautiful black, sleek machine, which was her pride and joy. I also eventually changed my silver Range Rover for a more up market and newer green version, which of course was perfect for the dogs. We also both had private car number plates. Tracey's were her initials and mine was A1 SSK. Posers or what! But life was good and we could have no complaints.

We had been ecstatically happy at Crawley Drive, all except for one really bad incident, which I am eternally ashamed of. It was an accident and I never meant to do it but even so it did happen and I feel I should write the truth about this horrible incident. It would've been very easy to have left this bit out of my story but this is an autobiography and I feel it should tell the truth about the bad times as well as the good. Anyway, I had got absolutely paralytic one evening on red wine and Tracey had gone to bed a little earlier. I just about remember going to bed and as I rolled over in the bed with my back to Tracey, she came to cuddle me and say goodnight. I didn't want to know and shrugged her off, raising my left elbow and telling her to leave me alone. Then I fell into a bloody coma. Next morning and on awaking, Tracey had a black eye. I asked her whatever had happened and she told me, that when I lifted my elbow to push her away and told her to leave me alone, my bloody elbow had smacked her straight in the eye. I couldn't believe this had happened, as this was the last person on the whole planet that I would want to hurt. She wore sunglasses for the next few weeks and we made up a cock and bull story of her falling over but till this very day, I am so ashamed. She forgave me and I promised sincerely never to do anything like that again and immediately went teetotal. Fancy hurting the one you loved so much. But I know it was an accident but this is no excuse, as I shouldn't have been that drunk in the first place. I have always really detested violence of all kinds, whether it is against other humans or indeed animals, and I knew that this was just not in my personality. But too much drink or drugs can turn us from a peace loving Dr. Jekyll, very quickly into a very nasty Mr. Hyde, but I'm glad to say that this never happened again. Of course we would still have some fierce arguments, as we were both karateka with hot tempers but never again would this horrible kind of event repeat itself.

But life itself was grand. Our trips to St. Ives continued for many years and we were very happy in our new home. The clubs were doing well and the dogs were fine until one fateful day when we noticed a small lump in Billy's top gum. If you peeled back his soft mouth flap and looked just above his top teeth, you could see a small lump appearing. We immediately took him to our vets who took a small biopsy and sent it away to be analysed. A week later and the news couldn't have been any worse. It was a malignant cancerous tumour and it needed removing immediately. And so about a week later and the vet had removed the lump but poor little Billy's face looked a little strange to say the least. They had to shave one side of his face for the operation and so on one side he was a beautiful red, copper colour and on the other side he was pink. (See photo). In himself though he seemed very happy and life continued as normal. But sadly, around ten months later the tumour

Billy, after his cancer operation

reappeared. Again, we took him immediately to the vets who told us that this did happen quite often as the cancer was an aggressive kind called sickle cell cancer. This time we had to take Billy to Cambridge University where they have a cancer unit for animals. They were marvellous and poor little Billy had to undergo another operation to remove this new tumour. This was followed up by a burst of radiation, which we could witness from the waiting room on a small black and white television monitor. He looked very forlorn as he lay there, still as the night. But again in a couple of hours he was back in the waiting room with us wagging his tail as though nothing had happened. We took him about three times to the unit in Cambridge for radiation treatment and each time he had to have an anaesthetic to put him to sleep and each time he would come out of it a little groggy but still very happy to see us. This treatment gave him the best part of a year of good quality life but sadly the tumour got so big, there was nothing else they could do for him and suggested that we really should put him to sleep immediately. We telephoned the local vet who came round to our house one morning at around ten o'clock. Before he arrived we gave Billy one more walk with his brother Benjie at the local park and I cannot explain the sadness I felt on this walk, knowing it would be his last on this planet. Eventually, the vet came round and administered the fatal dose, as an injection into one of Billy's front legs. It took about two or three seconds to work and Billy's little tongue lolled out of his mouth and he was gone. Tracey and I just broke down. We had lost a very close family member and indeed a great friend and a huge hole had appeared in our lives. Benjie for months couldn't understand where his brother had gone and he was really depressed and it took him a really long time to get over this huge gap in his life. We placed a photograph of little Billy in our bedroom and every night before going to sleep we would light a small candle by the photo and say a small prayer, asking the good Lord to keep him safe. This may sound a little sentimental but it was most definitely the right thing to do and people who have never owned a dog that was a close friend, may not quite understand how we felt.

Another of the reasons that our dogs meant so much to us is that they were indeed our family. We could have no other family as such, as very stupidly back in 1985 I had a vasectomy. It seemed like the right thing to do at the time, whilst Tracey was in her international prime and with the quite large age gap as well. After much discussion we decided to go ahead with the procedure. We had already had one big scare in our lives on this subject and I didn't want Tracey to go through any more similar traumas. The surgeon who carried out the operation was a Mr. Nicholls and he gave me every chance to pull out, right up until the snip itself. But I was adamant and so the operation went ahead under local anaesthetic at our local hospital in Hemel Hempstead. The slightly comical thing though, was that the nurse who stood by my head and talked to me throughout the operation, obviously to take my mind off of what was happening to my lower parts, was the wife of one of my bloody brown belts, Tom Nyman. She was sworn to secrecy but even so I really didn't enjoy showing my private parts to someone I actually knew. How bloody embarrassing. Anyway, after the usual sperm tests, which were carried out over the next few weeks by the pathology department, I was pronounced all clear and it was now apparent that I could no longer have any children. Of course, the bloody inevitable happened. After Tracey's competition career was over she had started to get a little broody, which of course is totally natural. But it was too late, the damage had been done. This was one of the reasons for our downfall a little later in our lives and I would most definitely not have had it done, had I

The brilliant Kawasoe sensei and yours truly after a session in Kent

known the final outcome. They say that hindsight is a wonderful thing and I had twenty, twenty bloody vision in mine. Tracey still competed for a little while into the early 1990's and indeed won the FEKO (Federation of English Karate Organisations) ladies kata title in Sheffield in 1990. Overall she won both the Seishinkai national kata and kumite titles five times in her career and indeed her last win in these championships was in 1991, where again she took both titles. It was after this final success that she decided to call it a day. She had competed non-stop for approximately nine years and had been wonderfully successful in this busy period of her life.

But life was still good and we still had our beloved Benjie and again the clubs weren't doing too badly. Another group had joined us from North Hertfordshire that had clubs in Baldock, Letchworth, Ware and Oaklands but they only lasted less than a couple of years. A few others had vanished, as is the case with certain karate clubs and their instructors, and the main reason for this was that we weren't competing as much as we had done in the eighties and we were working much more on our JKA Shotokan karate. We had many guest instructors in the early 1990's, teachers such as, Sadashige Kato, Terry O'Neill, Dave Hooper and John Cheetham. A handful of us trained a few times with Kawasoe sensei in Kent and made trips to Waltham Abbey to train with Kato sensei. This was the way in which we chose to go, and although still competing in more minor tournaments and of course internally, were not involved in any international events in this period.

One seminar, which was held at my Hemel Hempstead School dojo in the May of 1992, really topped the rest. Kato sensei asked me if I would host a seminar with the great Kagawa sensei in my dojo. Kagawa sensei and his family were visiting Europe on holiday and Kato sensei thought it would be a nice idea if he visited my dojo to teach. I had been present at Crowtree Leisure Centre in Sunderland in 1990 and watched this great man perform, as he won the 1990 World Shoto Cup. He was phenomenal in both kata and kumite events and so this invitation from Kato sensei was a great honour indeed but I was only given about five days to arrange it. I phoned around in panic trying to get students to the dojo but I needn't have worried as on the day 120 students turned up for this course. My dojo at the

Tracey and I receiving an after Course kicking lesson from Kato sensei!

school gym will only take around 60 students and even then it is packed to the brim. We all started off in the gym and had a kicking session with the great man, who can kick a bit to say the least! I was stuck in a corner, partnering Dave Perrett 5th Dan and instructor to the Waltham Abbey club. We were practicing jodan mawashi-geri with our partners but there just wasn't enough room in the dojo for 120 people to do this technique safely. Luckily enough though, the school hall wasn't being used and we split the class into two groups with Kato sensei taking the other group. The groups swapped instructors halfway through the evening and so everyone trained with both of the sensei. The course was phenomenal and everyone thoroughly enjoyed the experience. After the course was over Kato sensei said that Kagawa sensei would like to have a drink with the senior instructors of SSKI. This was a very nice gesture and so we made our way to, 'The Steam Coach' pub in Boxmoor, which was only a couple of minutes from the dojo. Kagawa sensei had his wife and two children with him and asked if we would all like a drink? There were around four or five SSKI instructors present, as Kagawa sensei went to the bar with Kato sensei to order a round of drinks. Kagawa sensei was most definitely dressed for summer in a very colourful Hawaiian shirt and shorts. Luckily enough, the weather was very pleasant and we all sat outside the pub in the early summer sunshine.

Kagawa sensei winning the 1990 World Shoto Cup in Sunderland (Photo permission of Sylvio L. Dokov)

One of my instructors smiled, as Kagawa sensei ordered the drinks in his very broken English helped along by Kato sensei and commented that could you imagine if some local hard man took the piss out of Kagawa sensei's clothing! Most definitely not a man to argue with!

My love for football was heightened, when at my St. Albans club and unbeknown to me a top professional footballer joined. His name was John Byrne. He literally lived in the house next door to the school dojo at Fleetville Infants School and came along to the dojo for the first time with his wife's sister, who had trained in Shotokan karate in Finland. I didn't know who he was at first but this would soon become clear at his first grading. We used to make a whole weekend of gradings in those days with a course on the Saturday and the grading on the Sunday. John apologised that he couldn't make the Saturday, as he just couldn't have the time off work. So on the Sunday he turned up at the Watford dojo with his licence and fee for the grading. As he left the desk I opened his licence and there on the first page was a very posh, black and white professional photograph of John in a football kit. I went over and joked to him and asked him who he played for? His reply knocked me back a bit, and at first I thought he was joking. His answer was, Queens Park Rangers! I said something like, yeah righto, pull the other one! But he was sincere and then told me the reason he couldn't make the course the previous day, was that he was playing for QPR at Old Trafford against the mighty Manchester United. I couldn't believe my ears as QPR were the top London club in the top division at that time. Not only was John a top league striker but also a bloody international and eventually played for Jack Charlton's, Republic of Ireland team on 23 occasions. John actually came from Manchester and was English through and through but his grandmother or great grandmother, or some similar distant relative was Irish and so he was allowed to play for their national team. John and his family became really good friends and on home matches he used to take me along and I used to sit in the posh seats at Loftus Road amongst famous politicians, television stars and authors. I would meet some of the players before the match and be given a free programme and then watch the match in style. After the match, I would be shown into the hospitality suite and meet both the home and away team's players. Tracey wasn't that interested in football and actually only came to one game, which of course turned out to be the most boring match on bloody record and a nil, nil draw. This just confirmed what she already believed, that football was highly overrated. I disagreed intensely and enjoyed every minute of this new found part of my lifestyle and John and his family were lovely people. His beautiful wife Anna came from Finland and she was so pretty. John had met her in Finland on a QPR tour and it wasn't too long before they were married. On one home game she came to watch the match with their first child, Thomas. After the pre-match hospitality bit, we were shown to our seats amongst the rich and famous. I was in heaven. I was sat next to one of the prettiest women I had ever seen in my life and had this little boy on my lap, who wasn't interested in the match at all but just wanted to play games with his new found friend, yours truly.

In karate, John had reached the yellow belt level and was doing very well. He loved it and said it gave him an extra fitness and had helped his balance and strength for his football career. In Seishinkai we had made him president and he was over the moon at this. But sadly, all good things must come to an end and it wasn't long before he was transferred. This wouldn't have been so bad had it been in England but he was sold to the French club, Le Havre for about half a million pounds. I missed going to these matches and hearing the crowd shouting his nickname, 'Budgie'. After a while he did come back to England and played for Brighton and Hove Albion and Sunderland. When he was with Sunderland he actually played in the 1992 Cup Final at the old Wembley. Sadly they lost 2-0 to Liverpool but what an experience. We eventually lost touch after that but still send the odd Christmas card. The last I heard they were living in Shoreham-by-Sea in West Sussex, which of course was convenient for his Brighton and Hove Albion career.

I personally had started to write my first book. In all truthfulness I had started it many years before when I worked in London and before I had even started karate training. But after a few chapters and many grandiose ideas, I put it to bed and didn't really pick it up again until the early nineties. It would be a comedy novel that originally was going to be set in the Royal Navy but the publishers thought that it might be a better idea if the book was set in Civvy Street. The world had already had the brilliant, *Virgin Soldiers* by Leslie Thomas and the publishers thought that the world wasn't ready for another book starring the HM Forces.

So I had to transpose all the stories from places like Malta, Gibraltar and Naples to somewhere in the UK. The place needed to be by the sea and the only place I knew really well and might fit the bill was St. Ives. And so I set about changing all the stories from my Mediterranean cruise with Grimble and Doc' on HMS Aisne to a period of mayhem in Cornwall. I still used Grimble and his personality, as he was the central theme of the book and after about a year I had it finished. The book eventually was published in hardback in 1992 by 'The Book Guild' and the title was, *Wild Oats in Cornwall*. I was obviously over the moon at seeing my name in print and the book on bookshelves but my greatest accolade was being asked to do a signing session at one of our local bookstores in Hemel Hempstead.

On one of our many trips to Cornwall, Tracey and I visited Lands End and as we entered the souvenir shop, lo and behold there was my book displayed as Book of the Month. There was no stopping me now and I immediately put pen to paper again and started to write a karate story, which was also published in 1992 and the title of this little book was, *Uchi Deshi and the Master*. This book was also published in Germany, where the title became, *Uchi Deshi und der Meister*. Both books were relatively successful and would be templates for later works.

Another highlight at this time, was that I was interviewed on *BBC Radio* by the *ex-Blue Peter* presenter, Simon Groom about my karate life and my first novel, *Wild Oats in Cornwall*.

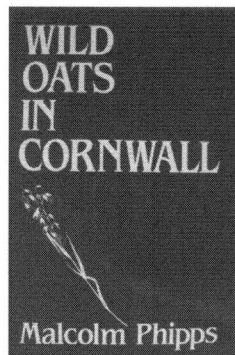

Wild Oats in Cornwall (the masterpiece!)

Uchi Deshi and the Master (the second masterpiece!)

Uchi Deshi und der Meister (The German publication of the English masterpiece!)

I was extremely nervous and Tracey sat in the waiting room and listened to the interview on a loudspeaker system. Again, it seemed to go really well and I was extremely pleased to be now called an author, amongst many other things! I also had a poem published in the *St. Ives Times and Echo* newspaper. It was a wordplay on the many, funny street names in St. Ives, such as, The Stennack, Wheal Dream, Downlong, The Digey, Teetotal Street, Clodgy View, Salubrious Terrace, The Wharf, Bunkers Hill, Fore Street, Virgin Street, Court Cocking. These names always made me laugh and I just thought I would put a poem together about them. I never expected it to be published and this was certainly another string to my bow. Perhaps one day Poet Laureate, who knows? Here is the poem as it was published anyway.

SUMMER IN ST. IVES by Malcolm Phipps (1994)

They're shuffling down The Stennack,
Advancing through Wheal Dream,
Downlong The Digey,
To Porthminster Beach they stream.

They're drinking in Teetotal Street,
At Clodgy, there's a View,
There's a Terrace that's Salubrious,
With a Cornish tea for two.

Dad's promenading along The Wharf,
On his arm, old Auntie Lill,
Mum's busy looking for a loo,
Somewhere near Bunkers Hill.

Now Uncle Fred's in Fore Street,
And finds the prices shocking,
Young Mavis is in Virgin Street,
Little Johnny in Court Cocking.

And round the back there stands The Tate,
For cultured and for purist,
Whilst the Atlantic rolls in on Porthmeor Beach,
For your more average tourist.

Every summer it's the same,
With children, men and wives,
Pouring in to the little streets,
That constitute St. Ives.

Not Alfred Lord Tennyson or Sir John Betjeman I think you'll agree but it was fun to do all the same. I did write a handful more poems but never sent them anywhere. Tracey did a few as well and I thought hers were really profound. She was also a very good artist and did some stunning drawings and paintings and was a lady of many talents. An excellent artist, both martial and otherwise.

Here are some of our poems from those halcyon days:

NEW ENCOUNTER by Tracey Phipps (1993)

I long for the cool touch of granite under hand,
To feel the undulating surface worn by tide and time.

I long to sit on springy grass and stand on tide uncovered stone,
To feel your elements rush over me anew.
To reach out and know He is still and always will be with me as I am to be with you.

In loss I feel apart, the latest stitches in an ancient tapestry that is Kernow.
Life, love and death entwined in every vision of your land.

I long to return yet fear prevails, have life and death changed our bond?
We face uncharted times.
How will it be? Will our spirits be once more as one when on your shores again I will stand?

Have life's sorrows enriched our union, founded now on every emotion? Life and death the circle complete, no more trials to endure. The finest, the lowest, all have been experienced.

HEAVEN ON EARTH by Malcolm Phipps (1994)

Heaven on earth is different for some,
But for me it is most simple,
The sound of the sea, the rustle of trees,
And a pair of red setters so nimble.

My love and I watch the buzzards soar,
On the cliff path to Porthgwarra,
We stand to one side as the setters rush by,
The path at this point is so narrow.

And far up ahead, two trusty red heads,
Peer hopefully at mistress and master,
'Will they proceed and carry on walking?
To turn back now – a disaster'.

Many's the time we four trod this path,
Each occasion full of great joy,
The sea to our left, the fields to our right,
A man, a wife and two boys.

And back at the cottage we rested our bones,
The walk made us feel so much better,
An armchair for you, a sofa for me,
And a floor full of red setters.

Those days are now past, well for now anyway,
Those wondrous times full of joy,
But we'll all meet again on that cliff path someday,
A man, his wife and two boys.

FOUR LITTLE LIGHTS by Malcolm Phipps (1994)

Four little living lights,
Dancing through the trees,
Little Billy went to heaven,
And then there were three.

Three little living lights,
Missing Billy so,
One popped off, to even things out,
Two up and two to go.

Now there's only two living lights,
Dwelling 'neath the sun,
Sadly one rainy day,
There'll only be one.

One little living light,
Living on its own,
With three up in heaven,
Preparing the welcome home.

Four little spiritual lights,
Dancing on springy grass,
Happy to be together once more,
And never again to part.

For this is the promise,
From our Lord above,
Who answers all our genuine prayers,
And surrounds us with His love.

MY LOVE FOR YOU by Tracey Phipps (1994)

When the last leaf has fallen from the last tree,
When the sun has set for the final time,
When mankind has made its ultimate mistake,
My love will still be with you.

As the moon ceases to light up the night sky,
And the stars vanish one by one,
As the final forlorn cries from the animals dies away,
My soul will be with yours.

In eternal heaven we will walk side by side,
Never looking back,
Always striding forward with our heads held high,
Our arms around each other, knowing our love will last forever.

As you can see we were head over heels in love with each other and those years were easily the best of my whole life, constantly visiting the St. Ives area of Cornwall with our pair of beautiful red setter's, Bill and Ben. Incidentally, Kernow is the Cornish name for Cornwall and the springy grass is a cliff top place we used to visit with Bill and Ben that is situated between Porthminster Beach in St. Ives itself and Carbis Bay, where the grass is amazingly springy and soft and we used to roll around with the dogs until we were crying with laughter. Genuine fun that had Tracey and me in absolute convulsions and it never cost a penny! The dogs just loved it as we wrestled and fought and chased each other around this beautiful area until we were all well and truly knackered!

It was at this time that I became joint editor for *Dojo Magazine*. We already had a decent Association magazine and thought that we would try and go national with this new idea. The other editor was one of my students, Bill Burgar and whose father let us use his house and computer equipment for the editing and publishing of the magazine. Tracey would be the editor for the kid's pages and Nina Khanna would in turn be the graphic designer. At first it went really well and was a quarterly magazine that could be bought by subscription only, a little like John Cheetham's, *Shotokan Karate Magazine*. In actual fact, John helped us on our way a little bit right at the very start. We would put articles together and get other people to do similar. It was fun but very hard work and sadly for not much financial gain. I believe it ran for five issues and then we just had to call it a day. The first cover had Gichin Funakoshi on it and the second cover featured Masatoshi Nakayama. Issue number three had Enoeda sensei on the cover and we had to ask his permission to use this photograph, to which he kindly agreed. There is a picture of the cover of this magazine in Rod Butler's book, *Keinosuke Enoeda – Tiger of Shotokan Karate* (page 154). Issue number four had Kanazawa sensei on the cover and finally issue number five, my first instructor, John Van Weenen.

But eventually it was just too much hard work and started slowly but surely to interfere with our training regime. All four of us were training hard in our karate lives and this was now just getting in the way. I could now see the hard work that John Cheetham and his staff must put in to produce the exceptional, *Shotokan Karate Magazine*. Our magazine did actually carry on but only as an Association magazine again. Many years later in 2003, Bill Burgar had an excellent book published, *Five Years, One Kata*, and presented me with a nice signed, first edition copy as his first instructor.

Those early 1990's went by extremely quickly and Tracey and I decided that with our newly found wealth it was time to move house again. This time we wanted to move out of Hemel

First edition of Dojo Magazine

Hempstead and more into the country. Obviously not too far away because of our dojos and so the lucky town was to be Tring. Tring is approximately ten miles from Hemel Hempstead, and a new road, the A41 had been built that by-passed the town of Berkhamsted, which made the journey much easier and much quicker. We purchased a beautiful three-bedroomed, fully detached house in a plush area of Tring in Station Road. The house itself was sold to us by a doctor and had everything we could ever need. To start with, all three of us were very happy in our new surroundings and Benjie enjoyed the new walks and smells. But Tracey was still naturally very broody and wanted a child and we discussed, 'in vitro fertilisation' treatment (IVF) and all similar sorts of options. We even had a good friend who was willing to donate his sperm for this procedure but I think that would've been even worse, actually knowing who the father was. Rather comically though, he did actually support Wolverhampton Wanderers, so I was sorely tempted. But no, I'm only joking. He was indeed a Wolves supporter but I just didn't want this, as I just couldn't get to grips with her having someone else's child. Other than our friend, I knew I would never know who the real father was but somehow it just didn't seem right. I realise now that this was a rather selfish attitude to take and one that sowed the seeds (or didn't in this case) for trouble ahead.

On actually moving into our house in Tring, Tracey made a very shrewd gesture and literally took all her hard won trophies to the local dump and threw them bodily into a large skip. There were bloody hundreds of them and all shapes and sizes. There were small ones, big ones, metal ones, wooden ones, plastic ones and a few cheap and nasty ones. The only trophies she kept were her international honours and her British and English titles. She said they were only dust traps and that these were not what true karate was all about. Extremely philosophical and I could see where she was coming from. Later I realised we should've kept them and reused them in our internal tournaments. All we had to do was take the little engraved metal tag off of the trophies, replacing them with new ones and they could've been used all over again. Recycling trophies - now there's a thought! There's that bloody twenty, twenty hindsight again! Tracey had a whole carload of the damned things. You could've got mine in a fucking carrier bag! I remember coming fourth for three years in a row at the ASKA National Championships in the men's senior kata division and used to give the excuse, that I hadn't washed my hair that morning and didn't want to be in the photograph for first, second and third! On the karate front I was now a 5th Dan and had been awarded the EKGB coaching award and was duly authorised as an EKGB Assessor as the chief instructor of Seishinkai. An assessor, Wow! Whatever would be next? The answer to this question was most definitely on the very near horizon.

They say pride comes before a fall and I was about to make the biggest mistake of my whole life and my gigantic *faux pas* is a warning sign for all middle-aged men. As a reasonably successful karate instructor who had had a good deal of success and indeed was running a very good karate Association and now had been lucky enough to have had a couple of books published, I suppose I was a target for any young lady. I don't mean this to sound big-headed in anyway but it was just the truth. I was very flattered at first when young Allison Kay, one of my 1st Dan black belts showed a growing interest in me and of course the inevitable happened. I say the inevitable, not for most men perhaps, but for someone with his bloody brains in his pants, I just couldn't resist the temptation. And so an affair ensued. It started relatively innocently but then it wasn't long before it turned into the real thing. We kept it quiet for quite a long time but Tracey wasn't daft and started to suspect that something wasn't right in our marriage. I think the IVF thing helped the situation along a bit but this was no excuse for the inexcusable. It got so bad that Tracey decided enough was enough and went back to live with her parents in Hemel Hempstead. I don't think at this time that she was one hundred percent sure that I was having an affair but she had a pretty good idea. And so I now lived alone in a big house in a very well respected part of town. Well, not quite alone as I still had Benjie but even he was now really showing signs of his age. He also knew that something was amiss and of course pined for Tracey. With all this self-inflicted pressure I decided to start to drink again, not heavily but more for company than for anything else, as obviously with Allison being so young and still living with her parents, I couldn't see that much of her. I became a regular at the pub at the end of my road, the 'Robin Hood Inn'. The pub itself was a Fuller's pub and managed by a fantastic couple, John Robinson and his lovely wife Chris. We got on straight away and I told them of my current situation and they were extremely supportive. He was something big in one of the local lodges of Freemasons and had the freedom of the City of London for all his excellent work for charity. There was an excellent certificate stating this fact displayed proudly in the pub. John was an ex-boxer and a really down to earth Cockney who seemed to know everyone worth knowing, villains and good guys alike. I believe he was invited to one of the Kray brother's funerals but I can't remember if he actually attended. Probably be silly not to!

Tracey got so suspicious and very nearly caught me at it one evening. Well in fact she did catch me but had the decency not to pursue it on the evening in question. Allison and I decided it would now be relatively safe to spend some time in my house in Tring, as up until then we had steered clear of this, obviously not wishing to get caught. We were fed up with the back of the car in Ashridge forest and so took a gamble. We were lying in bed in the spare bedroom, as I would not use my marital bed or bedroom, as that didn't seem at all right. A little hypocritical to say the least and I suppose a small spark of decency in a highly indecent situation. All of a sudden the deep throbbing sound of a sports car drove into the driveway below the bedroom window.

Allison stated that it sounded like Tracey's Porsche and so I peeked through the curtains. Blimey, she was right! I panicked and didn't know what to do and so started to throw on some clothing. Tracey of course had her own key and she had let herself in. I met her halfway up the stairs and apologised for the bedraggled state I was in. I told her I had just got out of bed and that I didn't feel very well and thought I might be coming down with flu. She said she was sorry to hear this but there was a small grin on her face. I asked her what she was doing back at the house and she answered that she had come to get some more clothes. She took an eternity to pack a suitcase with her clothing and all the time smiled that sickly smile that said, I know what you're doing. After a good half an hour she eventually finished and started to walk slowly down the stairs. She then asked the inevitable. 'Who have you got in the spare bedroom, Malcolm?' I told her nobody but of course she didn't believe me. She then said, 'You won't mind if I have a little look then?' On hearing this statement of course I panicked. I said okay you win, there is a female from the pub in there but I didn't want to embarrass the lady in question. Tracey smiled and left the house, slamming the door. I heard the Porsche door slam and the engine start up and then it drove away. I made for the spare bedroom and quickly opened the door. There was nothing, just an empty bed but no sign of any life. I looked under the bed but nothing. I looked out of the window but the window hadn't been opened. All of a sudden I heard a small noise from the airing cupboard which was actually in this room. I opened the door and there, totally stark naked was an extremely compressed Allison!. The airing cupboard had the usual hot water tank at the bottom with a wooden board above it for the storage of clothing. Allison had naturally panicked and climbed up on to this shelf and scrunched up in what could only be called a foetal position. Now the coast was clear, she climbed gingerly out but couldn't straighten up. Although she was only sixteen and as fit as a fiddle, she had been in this ridiculous position for over half an hour and it took her forever to be able to stand up straight again. This whole episode was a warning not to try and be too clever and one I would dearly pay for in the very near future. Tracey wasn't daft, she knew all along who was in the bedroom but had the decency not to pursue the matter any further on the night in question.

The next thing I knew was that I was served with divorce papers from Tracey's solicitors. She wasn't citing me for adultery but for a general breakdown in the marriage and us not being compatible anymore. The solicitors stated that it could be a very quick process if I didn't actually contest it and so this is what I decided would be the best option. But the solicitors had one more trick up their sleeve and this one would hurt financially. After the airing cupboard episode, Tracey, unbeknown to me had asked a good friend of hers to film Allison and me in the house together. I hadn't got a clue about this and the next thing I knew was that the solicitors informed me of the existence of this videotape. There was nothing very damaging on the tape, as it just showed me and Allison in the kitchen making a cup of tea and then disappearing and switching the light off. The next light to go on was upstairs in the bedroom and that was the total footage on the tape. We were dressed in dressing gowns though and so this was the total sum of the evidence against us. The solicitors informed me that I hadn't got a leg to stand on and therefore most of the estate would go to Tracey. The house alone was worth a lot of money and indeed everything in it but I lost the lot. I was given around a six thousand pounds pay out and the rest would go to Tracey. Now I was in trouble, as Tracey demanded and rightly so, that I immediately move out. I had nowhere to go and started to panic. But true friends came to the rescue from the most unlikely source. I had told my tale of woe to John and Chris Robinson at the 'Robin Hood Inn' and they just told me, not to worry and that they would arrange everything. There was a good friend in the pub called Roger and he hadn't long lost his mum. He was living alone in a three-bedroom house in Morefields in Tring and said that he would be very happy for me to move in with him, as it would be company for him and obviously a huge favour to me. John and Chris at the pub also helped out and said I could store anything I liked in their outhouse-cum-cellar in the backyard of the pub. And so I packed everything in cardboard boxes and moved the whole lot into this outhouse. There was all my personal belongings and the Association's gear all boxed up and standing amongst the Budweiser and Guinness crates. I took what I needed to live on a day-to-day basis up to Roger's place and a whole new life started for me.

The net seemed to be closing in on Allison and myself and we weren't quite sure what to do. Then all of a sudden an amazing array of events all happened at once. Just before my actual move into Roger's house, one of the saddest days of my life was about to unfold. My beloved Benjie passed away. He had seemed very quiet for a few days and I just put this down to missing Tracey again but on the very last day of his life he wouldn't eat or drink and didn't want to go anywhere, not even for a walk which was extremely unusual for him. That night he waddled out into the garden for a wee and just couldn't walk back in to the house. It was only a few yards but he just lay on the concrete patio floor and wouldn't budge. In the first instance I thought he was just being obstinate and I shouted at him to get up and get back in the house but he just wouldn't move. I even gave him a small smack on his backside to get him to move but he was totally adamant. And so I half carried and half dragged him the few yards back indoors. I tried to get him to eat something he really liked and opened a tin of tuna for him, which I know he adored. But he only sniffed at it and so I helped him into his bed, which was in the kitchen where we were. I thought to myself that I would get up early and take him immediately to the vets. I went to bed and on awaking went straight down into the kitchen. To my horror, there was my beloved Benjie lying on the kitchen floor, dead. Rigor mortis had set in and he was as stiff as a board. I didn't know what to do next and phoned the vet. They told me to bring him in and they would dispose of his body. And so I placed my dear friend into a large cardboard box and lifted him into the back of the Range Rover and drove him to the vets in Tring. They took him from me and told me to go home and not to worry. I was totally devastated. Not only from losing a dear friend but on how I had treated him on that last evening. It is something that has stayed with me and will do for the rest of my life. He was such a great friend and we had had such wonderful times together. I just sincerely pray that we will meet again one day, therefore giving me the chance to apologise to him personally for that very sad last day. This may sound mushy to some but we were the greatest of friends and inseparable for many, many years.

Eventually, the divorce papers came through. First the decree nisi and then a few weeks later the decree absolute was served on the 24th May 1995. I was single yet again and had now moved out of Station Road and into Roger's place in Morefields. But still things were not right with the situation between Allison and myself, as obviously Allison's parents forbid us from seeing each other. Of course, when I look back I can now see that they were right and I was very wrong. Still we met furtively when we could and we both decided that there was only one option open to us and that was to get secretly married. I had arranged the wedding ceremony in Gretna Green but not the hotel arrangements, thinking that the less people who knew about our elopement the better, and so we just waited for the day to arrive. The reason for choosing this destination is that you can get married at sixteen years of age in Scotland and without your parent's consent, and so this was absolutely perfect for us. A couple of my close friends at the 'Robin Hood Inn' knew and my top instructors at the karate club had agreed to take over the club until my return. They didn't actually know why I was going away and just thought I was holidaying in Scotland for a few weeks. So as not to be recognised anywhere, I even sold my beloved Range Rover and its private number plate and purchased a green fastback Rover.

The day eventually arrived and I met Allison in the garages close to her house. She had a couple of medium sized holdalls, a vanity case and a furry Bugs Bunny which I had given her a few weeks before. I personally just had a large suitcase and my guitar. As she arrived at the garages she stumbled and dropped her cases and smashed a bottle of Lucozade all over poor old Bugs and one of the cases. Luckily enough, only Bugs really suffered and so off we drove. Allison had left a letter for her parents with a good friend of hers, Krisha Lief. Krisha was not, under any circumstances, to take the note to her parents until later that same evening, therefore giving us precious time for the long trip to Scotland and the ceremony.

Her dad, Dave was in the police force and worked for the Metropolitan Police in North London. Her mum, Tina worked for a local computer software company and so this would give us time to elope and drive to Scotland. The drive took forever but eventually we arrived at a hotel in Gretna Green, 'The Garden House Hotel', and asked for a room. They asked if we were to be married and we said yes. The receptionist said that the bridal suite was available, and so with it being a very special occasion, we booked this for a couple of days. The actual wedding was in the afternoon and we had already booked a couple of professional witnesses, Emma and Joan from the Scottish Tourist Board a few days earlier on the telephone. And so we made our way to the Registry Office in Central Avenue, Gretna at 4pm on the 16th June 1995. Emma and Joan arrived and we were all ushered into the beautiful room specifically set aside for just this purpose. After taking our vows and the signing of the official documents, at 4.10pm we were man and wife. The cost of the whole wedding was exactly £67.00. Emma and Joan even gave us a card wishing us a happy life together and they were absolutely wonderful people and wouldn't accept a penny for their services. I promised them both that when I returned back home I would send them signed copies of my book, *Wild Oats in Cornwall* and on our return this is exactly what I did along with a sincere note of thanks. Blimey, I had been a confirmed bachelor for all of three bloody weeks!

Wedding No. 3 - Allison and me with our two witnesses, Emma and Joan

We were both very happy and Allison joked that I was quickly catching up with one of our countries famous or infamous monarchs. In England, we had experienced the six wives of Henry the Eighth and now we had the three wives of Malcolm the First! At least I wouldn't be beheading any of mine, well not for a while anyway! The next stop was to the famous, 'Old Blacksmith's Shop', which has made Gretna Green famous for many years, since 1753 in fact. Here we would be married all over again and after a tour of the premises and its history, were married by an older chappie called John over the famous anvil. John had done this for donkey's years and after the tour told us both to place our hands on the famous anvil and he would bring down a large hammer and hit the anvil, just missing our hands by bloody inches. This ceremony is not official in any way, shape or form these days but it was fun and we were given a certificate to say that we had undergone this procedure. So now we had two wedding certificates, one official and one not. After the ceremonies were all over we made our way back to our hotel. There was still one huge scare for us that evening. We were sat in the restaurant of the hotel having a wonderful three course meal and a bottle of champagne, when all of a sudden a whole host of sirens interrupted our meal. We both nigh wet ourselves, as we thought it might be the police looking for us. But just then and stomping through the restaurant doors came a load of firemen. Thankfully for us there had been an emergency call to the hotel's kitchens and the last thing on their minds was us. It turned out to be nothing serious but this put us on our guard though, and our hearts were in our mouths, and so we decided that very next day it would be time to move on to another and hopefully safer destination. Allison telephoned her parents that evening and of course they were absolutely devastated and threatened all sorts of things. Her mum was in tears and this was the first time that I felt bad about the whole thing. Although we hadn't done anything really legally wrong, it was morally wrong and I hadn't really wanted to hurt anyone, but we were put in such a position, it just felt like we had no choice. With her dad Dave being a policeman, we both thought of all sorts of horrible things that might happen to us and started to look at the worst case scenarios. So we thought it best to disappear for a while. And so, next morning we quickly packed and off we went to Edinburgh. Here we stayed at the 'Post House Hotel', which again was very comfortable. We stayed here for a couple of days and visited the zoo and had a lot of laughs but my biggest memory of Edinburgh is getting six points on my driving licence and a hefty fine for going through a poxy red light in Princes Street in the town centre. I didn't find this out until I got back home to Tring and was eventually shown the photograph from the camera and it had been red for 5.3 seconds. What a pain!

Allison started a scrapbook of our travels and when I now look back at this time in Scotland, I see what a lot of fun and how exciting it was at the time. One entry still makes me laugh. We were having our dinner in the hotel restaurant, when we were approached by the restaurant manager. He asked the usual questions and asked if we were enjoying our stay at the hotel and was the food okay? Sadly for us, I was wearing a polo shirt that had a karate logo on it and he picked up on this and never stopped talking throughout the whole bloody meal. Allison's entry into her scrapbook states:

Next stop Edinburgh. Here we stayed at the Post House - We met the restaurant manager. 'I'm a prat, I've done karate, I'm an 'ard man, now I'm gonna talk to you all the way through your meal.'

Another entry on the same page stated:

Bad boy Malcolm, you go through a red light. Get caught on camera. 5.3 seconds and then tell police, 'I was on honeymoon and I'm very sorry.'

As you can see she certainly had a sense of humour.

Over the next couple of weeks we would visit many places in Scotland. We next went to Stirling and then on to Dundee. Our most northerly stop was Aberdeen and we had great times in all of these places. I think our favourite place was Dundee, where we had a really excellent time and indeed stayed the longest at the 'Carlton Hotel' just down the road from Broughty Ferry. Allison would phone home every evening to let her parents know that everything was okay and not to worry and that we would be back home soon. Something we were obviously dreading.

But eventually it was time to go home. Allison had to face her parents, I had to face my mum and I needed to get back to the dojo to earn some cash, as things were getting a little tight. We drove down the east coast of England and stayed at Scarborough for a night and breaking up the long journey home. And then it was non-stop to Tring. I would like to say that everything was tickety-boo but it wasn't. We arrived back at Roger's house in Morefields and unpacked. Allison went to see her parents and I went to see my mum. Obviously Allison's parents wanted to kill me but I think they could see that we were in love with each other and so let us get on with our lives. Allison's mum, Tina eventually became a good friend and accompanied us on two of our wonderful holidays in The Maldives and the Dominican Republic. Sadly, her and Allison's dad Dave parted company and were eventually divorced but this had nothing at all to do with our marriage. My mum thought I was a bloody idiot but again could see that we loved each other and became quite happy with the situation. In actual fact, she really liked Allison and enjoyed her down to earth attitude to life.

The biggest hiccup was yet to come though. On arriving at the Hemel Hempstead dojo for the first time, we were greeted by one student. I asked this young lad where everyone was and he told me that Tracey had placed a notice on the dojo door, that sensei Malcolm would not be coming back to Hemel Hempstead and so therefore the club was now closed down. I panicked and started ringing around the instructors that I had entrusted this club to. They had all listened to Tracey's side of the story and had done the cowardly thing of bloody vanishing! So I started to ring up a few of my more loyal students and they just confirmed what I had already been told about the notice on the dojo door. In fact one of them had torn it down and later showed it to me. Nothing more dangerous than a woman scorned! And so in a nutshell, I had to start all over again.

Eventually, students started to arrive back at the dojo but it was a slow and painful process. Certain club instructors took Tracey's side and in an instant the Association was halved in size. Tracey then formed her own Association, the Traditional Shotokan Karate Union (TSKU). I fought for all I was worth but there was still more trouble on the near horizon. The whole matter was put before a meeting of the English Karate Governing Body (EKGB) and they decided to look into this further and to have a disciplinary meeting. This was to be held in a hotel at the 'Barbican Centre' in central London. Allison and I both had to attend, as did her parents and Tracey. There were three cases on the day in question and ours was the last to be heard. After a very long wait in the hotel's foyer, we all started to file into the room one at a time to put forward our side of the story. They wouldn't let Allison in as she was under eighteen, which of course was extremely unfair as this heaped up the odds in favour of our opposition. Finally, I was called in. The head of the disciplinary committee was Rob Curtis and along with two others started to ask me questions. In the corner and hidden behind a huge tape recorder was the administrator to the EKGB, Brian Porch. He had the wonderful job of taping the proceedings. He was a really lovely man and sadly has since passed away.

I was extremely belligerent and would hardly discuss the matter, as I didn't think it had anything to do with them what I did with my private life. After all, we were legally married. Before the meeting had actually started a large television and video recorder had been wheeled into the room on a stand and I could guess what their next move might be. And I was right. They stated that they had got video evidence of Allison and me in my house in Tring before we had actually married and whilst I was still married to Tracey. This of course was the same video that the solicitors used a few months previous. They said that they would now show this to me. I replied that they needn't bother, as I knew exactly what was on the tape and indeed it was me that was in the starring role! This didn't go down to well but the funny thing was that Brian Porch had ducked down behind the tape recorder and I could see his shoulders moving up and down with laughter. I thought fuck'em and obviously gave this impression and they could see it was no use continuing with the discussion and so I was dismissed.

Anyway, to cut a long story short I was thrown out of the EKGB at the very next meeting. I know many people stuck up for me, wonderful karate people such as, Ticky Donovan, Bob Poynton, Dave Hazard, Mick Dewey and Aidan Trimble. Ticky thought the whole thing was a bloody farce and told the meeting so. Dave actually apologized to me and I said whatever for? He said that when they asked for a show of hands to form the disciplinary committee, all my above friends opted out as they didn't want anything to do with it. Of course, had these wonderful people actually been on the committee, I would've probably only got my wrist slapped. This committee was made up of people that were just out for blood and this is what they got. Sadly mine!

The weekend after this farce, Dave and his girlfriend Paula White invited Allison and me down for the weekend to his flat in Hove near Brighton. We had an absolutely brilliant time, eating in great restaurants and getting well pissed on red wine and vodka. We went back to Dave's place and had some great fun watching old video footage of Dave and Paula in action. Paula was then a 3rd Dan and one of the very top Karate Union of Great Britain (KUGB) ladies in kata and kumite competition. Anyway, over the weekend I discussed the case with Dave and told him that I was a little worried about the future of Seishinkai and more importantly my student's welfare. He told me not to worry and that it wouldn't make one bit of difference in the long run. He told me that I was an excellent instructor with a great record and that it would be their bloody loss, not mine. How right he was, as the EKGB didn't last for much longer and soon was disbanded with splinter groups all over the bloody place. English karate politics at its very best again!

My very first instructor, John Van Weenen, in his excellent autobiography, *In Funakoshi's Footsteps*, wrote this nice piece about me in the biography part of his book:

Malcolm Phipps 6th Dan - a dedicated Chief Instructor who has made a sizeable contribution to British Karate, but not without having to parry the arrows at one time from those within the profession who sought his downfall.

Luckily enough for Seishinkai and indeed yours truly, a group had been formed called the English Traditional Karate Board (ETKB) and the administrator was my good friend, Bob Poynton. This group was headed by, Andy Sherry, Steve Arneil, Walter Seaton and Leo Lipinski. This was excellent, as there was one very senior instructor from four of the major styles of karate and all the ETKB wanted was like-minded groups that were not interested in karate politics and just wanted to get on with training in traditional karate. Also, there was no money involved which made a welcome change. Bob asked if Seishinkai would like to join and we immediately took up the offer. We stayed in this group right up until Karate England (KE) was formed and then joined this new body under our own steam. Surprise, surprise, as this new group lasted all of a year!

After my marriage to Allison and after I had got the Association running properly again, we decided that it was time to go international. Tracey hadn't wanted to go down this route, as she stated that it would be a lot of hard work for very little reward. In the early days she was right but looking back it was the right move. We placed an advert in, *Shotokan Karate Magazine* stating our international intent and

USA Instructors at Kyle Long's shodan grading
(Left to right: Ed Cox, me, Kyle Long, Randy Bodey, Jan Meyer and Jeff Sanders)

within months had received a few enquiries from abroad. The first to actually properly join was my good friend in the USA, Ed Cox. We hit it off straight away and he wanted a decent group to follow, as he stated that there wasn't much traditional Shotokan karate in the vicinity where he lived in Ohio. He lived and taught in a small town named, St. Paris which is about a forty-five minute drive from the capital, Columbus. He was a very likeable guy and his request was a genuine one. Unlike many we had from the certain Asian countries that just wanted a home and pay absolutely nothing for it and of course with their instructor jumping up the dan grade ladder a grade or two. Of course, we turned this sort of group away but there were one or two real enquiries from this part of the world. We had a group from India join and another from Pakistan. One of my instructors, Terry Churchill and his family from Luton had decided to emigrate to Australia and set up a small group near Adelaide. Another of my instructors, Stephen Jones also emigrated, this time to New Zealand and he also set up a group in Auckland. But in time most of them went their own way, especially as it is rather a long way to the other side of the planet and therefore extremely hard to control. Might as well have a club on fucking Jupiter!

Eventually, and to this day we just landed up with, England, USA, Hungary and Kazakhstan and all of these are excellent groups with genuine instructors and are properly structured and are in SSKI for all the right reasons. In the USA, as mentioned a little earlier the Chief Instructor is Ed Cox 6th Dan, who runs the Urbana dojo (which took over from the St. Paris dojo) and the Montessori School dojo. The Springfield dojo is run by three 2nd Dans and these are, Randy Bodey, Jeff Sanders and Jan Meyer. In Budapest, Hungary the Chief Instructor is Zohner Szilard 5th Dan and our man in Kazakhstan is Tuleukhan Iskakov who is currently a 2nd Dan.

And so life was back on track. I took over a small club in Wigmore, Luton, that had originally been run by Jamie and Yvonne Harrison of SEKU but they moved down to Ivybridge in Devon and asked if I would take it over. Sadly, they left it a little late and when I eventually did take it over, most of the students had vanished and there were only around three or four students left. One of these was the young Adam Cockfield, who I believe was a third kyu at the time and who has gone from strength to strength. Adam, who is now a fourth dan is our London sensei and Association coach and is indeed one of the most prominent Shotokan competitors in the country today. The club at Wigmore consequently folded due to lack of students and joined forces with the Luton club which was run by Terry Churchill and was held at Ashcroft High School. When Terry and his family emigrated to Australia, I took the club for a while but eventually passed it on to Allison, where she became the sensei for this club and indeed its sister club at Slip End.

Allison eventually passed her driving test and we traded in the huge, green fastback Rover for a much smaller, red Renault Clio. Allison had also got a job working at the same place as her mum and with two wages now coming in we decided to purchase our own little home. We liked the Tring area and eventually decided on a lovely two-bedroomed, terraced property in the nearby village of Pitstone. Number 31 Old Farm was on the market at £62,500 and we purchased it for a decent £60,000. And so another mortgage ensued. After fully furnishing the new house we decided it would be really nice to have a dog.

And so we searched different publications and eventually came across what we wanted. We had decided on an Old English Sheepdog and we just couldn't have been luckier. We drove to a small village near Shrewsbury on the Welsh border and after Allison and I had been thoroughly vetted, we were allowed to eventually purchase the puppy we wanted. The puppies all lived in a disused stable with their parents and when the owner opened the stable doors, out charged about fourteen dogs! They raced over to Allison and myself and jumped all over us. It was a beautiful summer's day, so we both quickly sat down on the grass before we were knocked down. There were bloody dogs everywhere! After a short while and after the very physical reception we received, most of the dogs decided enough was enough and went off in all directions chasing smells and just about anything that moved. But one puppy stayed with us and just wanted to play. We both agreed immediately that this was the one for us. We hadn't so much as chosen the puppy, the puppy had chosen us! We had already decided to have a little girl and had also decided on the name we would give to our new family member, Beenie. Whilst filling in certain Kennel Club documentation, Beenie's mum Lucy appeared at the window and looked in at the situation before her. She gave us both a look that said, look after her. It was really uncanny. After the filling in of a few more forms and a general discussion on looking after Beenie with the owner and of course the paying of the fee, off we drove with our new little friend asleep in the back of the car.

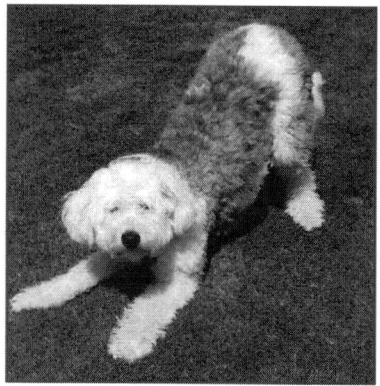

Beenie, wanting to play!

We told the lady owner that Beenie would be a pet and not be shown, although she had a magnificent pedigree and was directly in the same family line as one of the famous 'Dulux' dogs. Beenie turned out to be an absolutely wonderful pet that became a massive part of our family and a great and trusted pal. I have been very lucky with the three dogs that I have owned Benjie, Billy and Beenie and I would trust these more than I would trust most humans. Their love is totally honest and unconditional and there is no side to them. The character of these three dogs was just unbelievable and they were much more than pets, they were very close friends. If you have never owned a dog that you have been really close to, then you might find all this a little over the top and sentimental but if you have been lucky to have had a great dog then you know exactly how I felt. If you ever watched the film, *Marley and Me*, then you have a good idea of what I'm talking about.

At the end of 1996 I was promoted to the dizzy height of sixth dan, and so life was good again. On the home front we had the usual rows you find in most marriages and our life had its ups and downs but generally everything was back on track and going well. After living in Pitstone for a couple of years we decided that it would be a good idea to move back to Hemel Hempstead. After all, this is where our main dojo was situated and where Allison worked and it seemed a little silly to keep driving backwards and forwards the ten or eleven miles to teach and work. And so we purchased our next home in Tattershall Drive, which is in the Woodhall Farm part of Hemel Hempstead. It was a much bigger end of terrace house and had three bedrooms, as opposed to Pitstone being terraced with only the two bedrooms. We were very happy at Woodhall Farm and it suited our purpose brilliantly. The Association was doing well again and we were picking up a lot of excellent titles and trophies.

On the writing front I had three more books published in 1999. *The Ah So! Stories* and the *Conequest* were published by the, St. Ives Publishing and Printing Co. in Cornwall. Both books did really well. *The Ah So! Stories* became a karate bestseller and the *Conequest* was being looked into by the BBC for an animated children's television series. The third book I principally created for the Association,

The Ah So! Stories

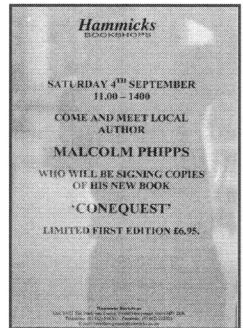

Signing session notice in
Hammick's window.
Fame at last!

The day of the signing session for the Conequest.
Note the length of the bloody queue!

which was titled, *The Little Book of Seishinkai*. This book included the syllabus, a large karate glossary and the history of Shotokan karate, plus a history of the Association. This was always going to be a bestseller as people needed this information when they joined and were given a copy when they actually licensed.

I did two signing sessions in Hammicks, a large bookstore in the mall in Hemel Hempstead that is now owned by Waterstones. The first one was for the *Conequest* and the second session was for *The Ah So! Stories*. These were great fun and made me feel extremely important at the time. One of my black belts, Sue Carson made up two fantastic papier mâché cones of two of the characters from the book and these were superb and on show at the signing. One was of Conefucius and the other was of the Conejuror .

It was in the April of 1999 that I took a squad to our Ohio group in the USA to train and to compete at the Highland Nationals, which were held in Hillsboro in Ohio. It was an open competition that had just about every martial art under the bloody sun competing and probably a few from another universe, looking at some of the weapons and clothing that adorned the dojo. I remember taking a very young Adam Cockfield, Emma Norman, Paul Monks, Paul Shannon and Carly Sinclair on this trip and all of them did extremely well and along with Ed Cox's USA SSKI group we took most of the medals. Ed was presented with a silver tray for the most supportive school, which he very nicely presented to me as a reminder of the competition. We won many trophies but the highest accolade was young Paul Monks winning the title of 'Grand Champion' in the kata event with Empi kata, beating the local favourite in the final. On this very enjoyable trip we stayed at different student's houses in the USA and were made very welcome. The trip was for approximately two weeks and we trained at Ed's dojo regularly, and generally all had a lot of fun on our first trip to Ohio as a group.

My wonderful mum

But sadly, as the millennium approached my wonderful mum was diagnosed with lung cancer. She had been suffering pains in her back and chest for sometime but they couldn't find anything wrong. Eventually, after a stay in our local hospital the diagnosis was made. She put up a gallant fight but finally, as in many cases the cancer won. She spent her last few days in St. Francis Hospice in Berkhamsted and passed away at around 4pm on the 2nd May 1999. She was 79 years old. I was by her bedside and actually holding her hand as she drew her last breath on this earth. Allison was with me and her husband of a few weeks, Roy.

Roy Haldane had been her boyfriend for a few years and lived with her in the beautiful village of Little Gaddesden. Mum had been the warden of some old people's bungalows in this picturesque Hertfordshire village and on retirement was given one of these lovely bungalows to live in for the rest of her days. Once mum knew she only had a few months to live (which turned out to be a few weeks), she actually married Roy, so he could stay on in the bungalow when she had gone with no arguments from the local council. Personally, I didn't really get on with Roy and nor did Allison but he made my mum happy and that was all that mattered.

And so mum died, Hilda Haldane. She was cremated and her ashes were buried in the church that she so much loved and indeed was one of the churches bell-ringers. The church was literally at the end of her road and you could see it from her bungalow's front garden. As you can imagine, I was devastated. She was the best mum anyone could ever have and a wonderful shoulder to cry on. She would tell me off when I had done wrong, even as an adult but she was always there for me when it really mattered.

I dedicated my children's book, the *Conequest*, to her and the wonderful nurses, doctors and staff at the Hospice and actually gave them a pile of books to sell at the Hospice, with the monies from the sale of the books going to their funds. Just a small token gesture to say thank you for looking after my very special mum in her final days on this planet. Now, nearly all of my family had passed on. My brother Martin, my dad, my mum, my nan and my granddad. Even my beautiful Irish Setters Bill and Ben had long since gone. I started to feel very vulnerable and very much alone but at this time and luckily enough for me, I still had Allison and Beenie. The big question though, was for how much longer?

Then in the year 2000, I suppose the obvious struck. Allison also became broody and naturally wanted children and I had had the dreaded vasectomy in 1985. She said her biological body clock was ticking! I thought to myself that it was a good job she wasn't of Middle Eastern appearance, as the police firearms unit would've probably fucking shot her! But seriously, we looked into the matter of a reversal vasectomy quite deeply and our doctor thought that it might just be possible. Allison was with BUPA through her work and I was also a member through this scheme, being her husband. So our doctor put us in touch with BUPA Harpenden and a consultation was set up with the consultant urologist. His name was Mr. Pancharatnam (who I would come to know even better later in my life, thanks to my prostate operations).

He said he thought it could be done and described in detail how he would go about it. He explained that the only trouble he could foresee was that it might not actually work, as it was fifteen years since the vasectomy and my age also had to be taken into consideration. He said there was only a thirty percent chance of it working. Anyway, I went ahead with the operation, which is a lot nastier than the actual vasectomy itself. This operation is carried out under general anaesthetic, which was followed by a three to four day stay in hospital. After the operation was over and after I had regained consciousness I had a quick look at my nether regions. Bloody hell, my testicles were the size of two medium sized apples and there was a drain coming out of my scrotum, which drained any excess blood from the wound. I was told the operation had taken over three hours to perform. After a day in bed I was encouraged to get up and slowly walk around. Slowly being the operative word. They gave me a walking stick and I walked up and down the hospital corridor very tentatively and very bow-legged. After a day or two of this agony and having the dreaded drain changed on a daily basis, I started to feel a little better and on my many walks down the corridor started to wave the stick around and give the nurses my Charlie Chaplin impression. One of the head nurses at the hospital, Jane Carden was a great friend of mine, as her son, Sam Carden was one of my black belts. I actually heard her say to Mr. Pancharatnam one day, to look after me as I was a very special person. What a lovely comment from a really lovely lady.

Fleetwood instructors
(left to right: Ronnie Christopher, Cyril Cummins, me, Yoshinobu Ohta)

Ashi barai, gyaku-zuki!

I remember one time when the drain had to be changed and they brought in a very pretty student nurse to learn how to take the drain out and replace it. She was a blonde and stunningly pretty and on the command of the head nurse she slowly and very carefully removed the pipe from my scrotum. At any other time Mr. Pecker would've popped up to say hallo but sadly on this occasion not even a flutter! He looked very sad as he limply sat on top of the two fucking rugby balls that filled up my scrotum! To digress slightly, about a year after this slightly embarrassing situation, I attended Jane Carden's birthday party which was held in a local village hall and guess who should be one of the guests? You guessed it, our pretty blonde nurse. I don't know who blushed the most but this time Mr. Pecker did at least have the decency to have the slightest of flutters and not a bloody rugby ball in sight!

With the operation now over, eventually it was time to go home and I was told I could not teach karate for at least a month to six weeks. I think if I threw anything that even looked like a kick something would've definitely fallen off! The hospital said they would recall me in for further sperm tests to see whether the operation had been successful or not. Time passed slowly and I had to sit and watch the karate lessons for about a month. In this four week period I had undergone the sperm tests and was eventually called back in to see Mr. Pancharatnam. Sadly, he told me the bad news that the operation hadn't been a success and that my sperm count was zero. All that pain and discomfort for nothing but at least I gave it a try. The other painful thing is that the operation cost nearly £3000, as it was deemed to be a cosmetic operation and one that was not life threatening. Ouch! Personally, cosmetic wasn't the word I would've used!

It was also in this year (2000) that one of my 14-year-old black belts, Emma Norman was awarded the 'Diana, Princess of Wales Memorial Award for Young People'. It was a well-deserved accolade and I was really very pleased for her.

The prestigious Funakoshi Cup

Kerry Gillard (Luton's 2002 Young Sportswoman of the year)

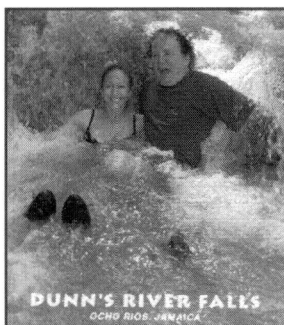

Allison and me splashing down in Jamaica!

It was in these early years of the new millennium, when I was asked by Cyril Cummins if I would like to be one of the instructors on his annual Shotokan Course, which was held in the Cala Gran Caravan Park, in Fleetwood, near Blackpool. I said that I would be most honoured and took a good sized squad from SSKI to each visit. Instructors on these courses, other than myself were, Yoshinobu Ohta, Ronnie Christopher, Cyril Cummins and Jim Wood. Everyone seemed to have a good time and I felt very privileged at being asked and thoroughly enjoyed teaching on these courses and at £65 for adults and £40 for children, which included the caravan and all the training for the whole weekend, had to be a really good deal.

And so it was on to 2001. This was the year that I was personally inducted into the 'Combat Hall of Fame' at Aston Villa's football ground in the October and the same year was also awarded the runners-up certificate for 'Sports Personality of the Year' in the Dacorum/West Herts region. In 2002 I was highly commended for my 'Service to Sport' in the same region and if I received any more certificates I could probably decorate the bloody living room with them!

In 2001 and 2002 we entered the World Traditional Karate Organization's world championships which were both held in Staten Island, New York. We did extremely well picking up many titles with Emma Norman and Gareth Hains winning gold medals in both years. Kerry Gillard and Alexis Raymen took gold medals in the 2002 event. The first time we visited New York in 2001, the twin towers of the World Trade Centre were still standing and the second year in 2002 they no longer existed and were just rubble and now had the sad title of 'Ground Zero'. On both years we visited this site with quite a few of the squad going to the top of one of the towers in 2001 and as a squad we visited the devastation in 2002. Everyone was in tears on this last visit and you just had to see it to believe it. Unbelievable what man can do to his fellow man in the name of religion! Also on these trips, we trained with Richard Amos sensei in his Manhattan dojo and also John Mullin sensei in his Staten Island dojo and were made to feel very welcome at both venues. Neither sensei would take a penny for the wonderful and very informative sessions.

SSKI HQ (3, The Copse with Range Rover and its posy number plate, F1PPS)

In the 2002 English national championships for the under eighteens, which were held in Milton Keynes, Toni York, Gareth Hains, Alexis Raymen and Keanu Mayhew all won this prestigious title in their respective events with the SSKI boy's kumite team, the SSKI girl's kumite team and the youngster's kata team all taking the gold medals in their respective categories as well. Three team events and three golds and it wasn't surprising that SSKI was awarded the 'Funakoshi Cup' for the most medals taken at the tournament, a trophy I am very proud of and still have on display in my dining room to this very day. In the English Championships of 2001 which were held in Nottingham, Gareth Hains and Toni York again took well deserved gold medals. 2002 also saw young Kerry Gillard, who was fifteen years old, picking up the very prestigious,' Young Sportswoman of the Year' award for her home town of Luton and was presented with the trophy by the then Luton Town FC player, Emerson Boyce. I was in attendance at the presentation with her family and was extremely proud of her. It was a great time again with the Association back on track and life in general was excellent.

And so we decided to move up the housing market yet again and after five good years at Woodhall Farm we moved to a really lovely part of Hemel Hempstead. Our new home was in The Copse and was situated in the Fields End part of the town. The mortgage would be a bit of a struggle at first but we were both bringing in decent wages and it wasn't long before we found we could afford the new home relatively easily. It was everything we could ever want. It was fully detached and had four bedrooms and a decent sized garden for Beenie. At around this time we were also having some wonderful holidays and spent some great times in, Ocho

With the legendary Fumio Demura sensei
after training session in Dallas

Nunchaku - weapon of choice
(well, Okinawan one!)

Rios in Jamaica, the island of Kuredu in The Maldives and finally at Bavaro Beach in the Dominican Republic. On two of these holidays in The Maldives and the Dominican Republic, Allison's mum Tina accompanied us. As I stated earlier in this book, she had gone through a nasty divorce and had come to accept our marriage and indeed became a good friend. These holidays were absolutely fantastic and made a wonderful break from the constant karate teaching and training and Allison's job.

We were very happy at The Copse and had wonderful neighbours, Ken and Pam Jarrett at number five and Sarah and Colin Sparrow at number one. And so it was on to 2003. This was the year that I was inducted into the 'United States Martial Arts Hall of Fame' in Dallas, Texas. At the banquet and all dressed up in my tuxedo, with Allison looking very beautiful in a red dress she had specifically purchased for the occasion, I received a lovely wall plaque and a certificate but the highlight for me personally was training with the legendary, Fumio Demura sensei. It was a fantastic session and Allison and I sweated our socks off. For one exercise he picked me out personally to demonstrate how action was faster than reaction. He used his number two, who had the wonderful name of Kevin Suzuki. He had to punch me in the stomach ten times and all I had to do was to touch his arm with either of my hands and stop him. Dead easy I thought. My hands were placed on my hips and I stood ready. There was no set timing and Suzuki sensei stood before me totally poker-faced in front stance. To cut a long story short, he hit me ten times out of ten with excellent speed and accuracy. Demura sensei laughed as he witnessed my frustration. He told me not to worry, as he could hit Suzuki sensei also ten times out of ten, to which Suzuki sensei nodded and totally agreed. He got his message across superbly and I have used this exercise many times in my dojo to prove this point to my students. Outside the dojo he signed one of his books for me and showed Allison and myself his photograph album of the Hollywood stars he had worked with and of which he was most proud. There were pictures of him with, Arnold Schwarzenegger, Tom Cruise, Wesley Snipes, Sean Connery and many others, all who he had helped in the fighting scenes from their famous films, which included the excellent, *Red Sun* and *The Last Samurai*. I approached him about me starting a traditional nunchaku group in England and he thought this would be an excellent idea. And so the English Traditional Nunchaku Association

USA Hall of Fame
(Jeff Sanders, Ed Cox, Allison and me)

(ETNA) was born. When I arrived home I put a small book together giving a proper syllabus and a structured belt system for the nunchaku, a weapon which I had practiced for many years and was the one Okinawan weapon I really enjoyed. I had dabbled with the sai, bo and tonfa but the nunchaku was for me. I liked the dynamics and speed of the weapon and still train to this very day.

On the major competition side of 2003 and in the English under sixteen's championships, which were held in Dudley, we won both the boy's team kumite and the girl's team kumite events. Ross Carson won an individual kumite gold at the same event. And finally in this year, at the SSKI National Championships on the third of November, I was awarded my seventh dan grade and was given an excellent certificate to mark the occasion. The grade had been ratified by the World Traditional Karate Organization (WTKO) and the English Traditional Karate Body (ETKB). I received a wonderful congratulatory letter from John Mullin sensei, the Executive Chairman of the WTKO, which stated that he had now made me Joint Chairman of the WTKO Advisory Panel. This was the icing on the cake and a wonderful personal finale to yet another excellent year for me and SSKI in general.

In comparison 2004 was a very quiet year for SSKI as an Association but not for me personally. I believe the reason it was so very quiet on the karate front, was that Allison totally surprised me and left me in the February. I just couldn't get my mind around this astonishing decision and had no notion whatsoever that it was about to happen. We seemed to be very happy and wanted for nothing. She had a good job where she was now an Accounts Manager for an IT firm in Borehamwood and the karate clubs were doing really well. When I look back I can now see certain signs but at the time it was a total shock. Her timing couldn't have been any worse either. She came home early from work on the Friday and told me she was leaving me and going to live with her mum. She packed a few things together and off she went. The very next day I had Terry O'Neill sensei coming to my house and dojo for the weekend to take an Association course. I just didn't know if I was coming or going. Terry turned up at my dojo and I told him the sad news. He couldn't believe it. The course was about to start when he told me not to train as I wasn't in the right mindset for karate training. He was probably right, as one minute I felt as though I would breakdown in tears and then the next minute I felt like decking someone! The course seemed to take an eternity on the Saturday as I sat outside the dojo door watching the proceedings. My mind was on other things though and I just wanted to get back home. Eventually, the course finished and we said our goodbyes to the students and told them we would see them the next day. On arriving back at my home there was a note from Allison. She still had a key and had let herself in. The note just said, that she hoped the course went well and that she had taken Beenie for the weekend so she wouldn't be on her own. It was signed, *Love Allison*. Terry was a little bemused at the signing off of the letter and said something like she should make her fucking mind up. Anyway, that evening we went for a curry and both got drunk on whiskey and coke. The next morning though, things were even worse as there was now a massive hangover to contend with. We had a small breakfast and went back to the dojo for the second day of the course. Once more, Terry said he didn't want me training, which was just as well with the bloody huge hangover I was nursing. When the course was finished, we said our goodbyes to the students and made our way back to The Copse. Again we had a few drinks and Terry was wonderful and said he wouldn't go straight home but stay for most of the evening to keep me company. He rang his wife Bernie and told her the situation and kept to his word and didn't leave for Liverpool until quite late that evening. He was absolutely wonderful and told me to keep my chin up and if there was anything he could do, just ask. Once more it was time to set out on the next part of my journey throughout this life as a single man again. I now knew how Jan and Tracey must have felt when I left them. They say what goes around, comes around. How bloody true but it still hurt. I was determined to stay living at The Copse but knew it would be hard to afford.

A good friend in a time of need (Terry O'Neill and me at the Hemel Hempstead dojo)

And so I tried to put my life back together again. Eventually, it turned out that Allison had met somebody else and it wasn't long after our divorce that she married this chap. The decree nisi was served on the 7th September and the decree absolute came through on the 21st October, basically on the grounds of incompatibility. Although the divorce was no fault of my own, I still lost quite a bit of money on the deal and had to take it on the chin and add it to my mortgage. My solicitors said I could fight the case but it could take up to two years for a settlement to be made. They thought the outcome would probably go in my favour, as the innocent party but I wouldn't be much better off after paying solicitor's fees and court costs and the like for these two years. I couldn't be bothered with all the hassle and after all it was only bloody money!

But financially I was now really stretched but if I tightened my belt and was sensible with my life I could probably just afford to stay on at The Copse. I started to visit the USA a little more to teach my group in Ohio and so it was agreed that Allison and her new husband would have Beenie. I didn't want to part with her but if I didn't it just meant that I would keep on seeing Allison on a weekly basis and I just wanted to cut myself off from this situation completely. And so now I was really alone. When these things happen it makes you realise how lonely it can be being a sensei and even more so a Chief Instructor. I call it the, *Loneliness of the Long Distance Sensei*, which is loosely based on an article by Joyce Meyer.

In the dojo the relationship between a sensei and their students is pretty much the same as an employer/employee relationship. There may be one or two exceptions but on the whole it is not an operable situation for the sensei to become extremely close to those under his or her authority. Sometimes students do not realise this fact and think that their sensei separates himself/herself from them because he/she thinks he/she is better than they are. The truth of the matter is, if a sensei tries to be really friendly with his or her students, they can develop a spirit of familiarity that causes them to take liberties with him or her that they should not take, or to assume things about their relationship they should not assume. Through many years of experience I have personally learned that I simply cannot become close friends with most of my students because it inevitably causes problems. I can think of a few cases in particular where this has led to a parting of the waves. When you are in a position of leadership, students tend to look up to you. They may even develop expectations of you that are not realistic. They know you are only human, as they are, but they really do not want to see your human flaws or weaknesses. And so it can be pretty lonely at the top trying constantly to become someone that people can look up to, not just in the dojo but in life in general. I have been lucky on this score and have a handful of real friends in the Association

Allison, with an excellent mawashi-geri

and a few outside of our group and of course many colleagues and acquaintances but I do find it hard to get really close to people again after this huge kick in the teeth.

One of my instructors Peter Welch and his partner Sarah gave a really good reply to the article above and I thought it was most intense and definitely worth printing, so here goes:

'I thought your article 'Loneliness of the Long Distance Sensei' was poignant and very well observed and put. I would say that the employer/employee relationship between students and yourself as head of the Association generates an inevitable paradox that in most cases may never alter. This is probably true for other Chief Instructors and higher Dan grades. In fact it would seem that forming a close friendship with most or dare I say all students may in time lead to certain unhealthy traits of character from them. Over familiarity leading to loss of respect is to be avoided and of course contrived friendships for personal gain or promotion, is as ugly as it gets.

On the other hand, perhaps students of integrity are acutely aware of this student/instructor paradox and hold back from a deeper friendship in the knowledge that this too could be perceived as divisive or unhealthy. I think this generates an uncomfortable situation for both parties when dwelt upon. All I can offer is that if both find unconditional happiness and joy in the company of each other then that defines a good and lasting friendship. I believe most of your Hemel Hempstead students including both of us experience this pleasure, a friendship that with sensitivity to the negative side can and will endure with introspection and self-truth.'

As for Allison's part, she eventually moved out of Hemel Hempstead to a village in Bedfordshire near Flitwick and gave birth to two children with her new husband. He, I believe was also a divorcee and already had a young daughter from his previous marriage, so they are now quite a family. I bear them no malice whatsoever and only wish them the very best in their new lives together. After all, no matter what happened, Allison and I had eight and a half pretty wonderful years together and many great adventures, especially in the beginning of our relationship. This was an integral part of my life and although it hurt when she left, there were still some great times to remember. She was also missed in the dojo, as when she left she had attained the grade of yondan (fourth dan) and was a very good instructor, especially with children and was the sensei of the Slip End dojo in Luton. She was also an excellent competitor and won the SSKI National Championships many times in both kata and kumite. She took an excellent bronze medal in kata at the WTKO World Championships in Staten Island, New York and trained a couple of times on the England kata squad, once with Ticky Donovan and Helen Raye and once with Dave Hazard but she never quite made the English team.

Anyway, to change the subject, later in the year there were a couple of television highlights, where the *BBC News 24* did a piece on young Aaron Gould and his excellent competition successes and the forthcoming IKA World Championships that he would be attending and I was interviewed by the reporter as his instructor. I was then given the prestigious title of, Martial Arts Adviser for the Carlton Television production of *Lloyd and Hill*. All I had to do really was set up a martial arts scene in a dojo for one of the episodes, but it was good fun mixing with one or two of the minor stars of the show.

In the August of this year I was made a Founding Fellow of the ISKS (International Shotokan-Ryu Karate-Do-Shihankai) and given the shogo (title) of kyoshi. One more certificate. That living room is now very nearly decorated! Not only a Founding Fellow but a Jolly Good Fellow to boot! That's the fun of writing your autobiography - you can bolster yourself up every now and then!

I seemed to be getting more bloody titles than the Queen. I know many people are into titles and certificates but in all honesty they mean very little. It's how you act and how you train and teach that matters. People will make up their own minds about your persona and it will not make one jot of difference how many ridiculous titles you give yourself or how many certificates you amass, or indeed what number dan grade you have after your name. True respect is earned and has nothing to do with self praise whatsoever. I believe it is what a student thinks of you in the car park after the lesson is over that really matters, not the respect you demanded in the dojo itself, strutting around like a prize wanker!

If 2004 had been a quiet year on the karate front, 2005 was totally the opposite. The competition side of the year started in the April, with the WTKO UK Championships, where I personally was the host. This tournament was held in my home dojo at Hemel Hempstead School and was a competition for WTKO members only and basically involved ourselves, Gerry Breeze sensei's group the FBSKUI, Charles Gidley's group the BSKI, a small squad from the WTKO in New York and also a small squad from John Cheetham's dojo in Altrincham. Guests of honour included, Richard Amos sensei, the Chief Instructor to the WTKO, John Mullin sensei, the Executive Chairman to the WTKO, Charles Gidley, Gerry Breeze, George Carruthers and Ged Moran of *Legend Productions* who videoed the whole event. The Chief Referee was SSKI's Steve Wilson who did a really excellent job on the day and along with the other referees and judges kept the event running smoothly. It was a great competition that started and finished on time and each event was well subscribed to and medals hard to come by. Adult competitor of the day went to Ross Young from the FBSKUI, with the under sixteen's competitor of the day going to Douglas Carson from SSKI. The gold medals were taken by, Ross Young, Alison Grundy, John Parnell, Clare Worth, Douglas Carson, Alexis Raymen, Oliver Rigby, Stacey Barton, Aaron Gould, with the BSKI winning the men's team kumite event, SSKI winning the boy's team kumite event, Altrincham SKC taking the adult's team kata title and BSKI winning the children's team kata event. This turned out to be a really good tournament and an excellent grounding for the two really big competitions that would take place a little later in the year.

Here are a couple of lovely emails about this tournament:

From: John Mullin WTKO
To: Malcolm Phipps
Sent: Friday May 6th
Dear Malcolm, I have posted a link to your excellent report of the WTKO English Championships on the WTKO website. I am still amazed at how many different groups attended and were able to put egos aside and cooperate for a successful event that we can all be proud of. Much of the success must go to you for such an outstanding job. I know that you have had a lot of praise for the job you did, but you deserve it. I am very proud to be associated with you and your fine organization. I think the future looks bright for us all and the WTKO. See you in Romania. Continued success Malcolm, Kindest regards, John.

and

From: Ged Moran (Legend Productions)
To: Malcolm Phipps
Sent: Saturday May 7th
Hi Malcolm, Many thanks for the very quick information. I haven't looked at the rushes yet, but I'm sure we'll be able to make a very exciting programme from the footage. I'm undecided as which format I'll use: very fast clips or full length. Whichever I decide on, it'll be a good programme because the overall standard was so good. Again I must compliment you on the very smooth running of the event (still can't believe it actually started and finished on time) and also your own students. Not only did they provide a level of Shotokan that's sadly rare these days, their attitude and behaviour was of the highest standard: they are indeed a credit to you. I'll keep you informed as to when the finished programme is likely to be available,
Sincerely, Ged Moran.

It was really lovely to receive these accolades and made my job even more worthwhile.

The first really big tournament of this year was in the May, where we attended the WTKO European Championships, which were held in Brasov in the Transylvania part of Romania. We took a few minor medals but only one gold medal and that was fifteen year old James Smith winning the kumite title in his age category in real style. Aaron Gould took a silver medal in the boy's senior kata event after a play-off for the gold medal with a Romanian and Emma Norman picked up a bronze in her kumite event.

This was an excellent trip though and we all enjoyed the training as well as the competition itself. Some of the refereeing left a lot to be desired, as I think about eighty percent of the referees and judges were from the host country and some of the decisions were extremely suspect to say the least. The actual host for these championships was Simion Tudorel sensei and the guest instructor for the seminar was Reuben Cernuda sensei from Spain. His sessions were excellent and very knackering in the immense heat of a dojo that had no air conditioning. Following this we all went on a trip to Bran Castle in Transylvania, which was reputed to be Dracula's castle and the most haunted place in the world. After a tour of the castle itself, one of my young students thought that Dracula was not a great host as he hadn't showed up when we visited. I didn't want to shatter her dreams and told her that he only came out at night. She asked if we could come back at night time and meet him, to which of course I declined. Mainly because it was about an hours drive from Brasov and our hotel, and secondly, just in case the worst case scenario might happen and he was fucking there! Outside of the

Dracula's country pad! Bran Castle in Transylvania

castle there was a market that sold just about everything to do with our friend, Dracula, or Vlad the Impaler, as I believe he was also known in these parts. There were masks, capes, false fangs, tee-shirts, mugs, baseball caps and even a bottle of Vampire Merlot wine. I had to purchase something and so came away with a bottle of red vampire wine. I still have it in my wine rack but should probably drink it before it fucking clots! Also in the grounds of the castle there was a place similar to the London Dungeons to visit and the youngsters just couldn't wait to go in. The students decided that sensei should go first, as he should really be the bravest. Ha bloody ha! We paid the fee and started to walk down this very dimly lit corridor, which was total wall on one side and sackcloth from floor to ceiling on the other side. Yours truly gingerly led the way and halfway down I nearly had a bloody heart attack. It was dead silent and then all of a sudden there was a huge and horrendous scream as the bloody sacking literally leapt out at me. My heart was going ten to the dozen. There was a person hidden behind the sacking, who every now and then, moved the sackcloth quickly towards its petrified victim. The kids screamed with delight as their sensei nearly shit himself! Typical youngsters – they found the castle and its history totally boring but the bloody haunted house of horror was the dog's bollocks and worth the whole visit. But all in all it was a decent trip and the squad now looked forward to the 12th IKA World Championships in Sardinia,

Vampire Merlot wine from Dracula's castle (drink it before it clots!)

Italy a little later in the July of this year.

The Sardinia trip was a most enjoyable one and indeed a very successful one for our squad. We stayed in a small town, a few miles from the island's capital, Cagliari called, Cittá di Quartu Sant 'Elena. We had a nice hotel and made friends very quickly, especially with the large Australian squad led by their instructor, Bill Wakefield sensei. The heads of the countries were all taken by car to meet the mayor and the officials of the town and this was a very nice gesture. We were all given a pennant to take home of the town's crest. The training sessions were with the legendary Soke Tak Kubota 10th Dan and his number two, Shihan Rod Kuratomi. The IKA Chief Instructor is Soke Tak Kubota and soke basically means founder of style. Soke Kubota's style is called, Gosoku Ryu and is very similar to Shotokan. These were good sessions but as with Romania extremely hot, as this dojo also was not air conditioned. In the competition itself we had three fantastic results, the best of which was Douglas Carson winning the cadet kumite division. He fought his heart out and won all his fights in superb fashion with his excellently timed punching combinations. He had six fights to win this prestigious title, beating a Russian, an Italian and an Armenian en route to the gold medal and in this category SSKI's James Smith came third. Next up was young Aaron Gould who took the youngster's gold medal in the senior kata division with club colleague Leah Hoey taking the bronze. Leah made up for it in the girl's kumite and took the gold medal. This division was very poorly attended and the girl Leah should've fought in the final decided that she didn't want to compete after all and so Leah won the title by default. She was upset at not being able to fight and said she didn't really deserve the medal. I told her this was rubbish and you can only beat what is put in front of you. Our boy's kumite team just lost out in the final by two matches to one against the very strong and much older Armenian team. Our guys were all around the fifteen and sixteen years of age, where their team was all nineteen year olds. It was a strange and very large age range for this event from fourteen to twenty-one years, but we gave them a run for their money and again Douglas Carson won every single match in the four rounds and also his match in the final itself.

So it was three IKA World Champions and I was very proud of them. They all received a winner's jacket, which was royal blue and embroidered with the

Soke Kubota and me,
discussing life in the Sardinian hotel's pool

championship's logo and stated that they were IKA World Champions. In total we took eight medals, with Adam Demetriou taking a silver medal and Charlie Want a bronze, so all in all it had been a great competition and a tournament that had around thirty countries competing for the spoils. A little after the medal ceremony, Soke Kubota sent a message over to me that he would like a photograph taken with the three successful English

Soke Tak Kubota with SSKI's IKA World Champions (Aaron Gould, Leah Hoey and Douglas Carson and a very proud coach)

gold medalists. He congratulated them all personally and told them that their standard was excellent. Of course I was chuffed to bits, especially when he asked me to be in the photo as well.

He was staying at the same hotel as our squad and on one swimming session in the outdoor pool he came over to me and we had a great chat as we bathed in the pool. He said he knew Terry O'Neill and remembered his famous magazine, *Fighting Arts International.* He asked me to say hallo next time I was in contact with him. He again congratulated me personally on the behaviour and etiquette of our successful squad, not just in the competition but in the hotel and in general. He was a really lovely man and very humble. We spoke about his great friend, Fumio Demura sensei, who I'd trained with in Dallas and both these great sensei have dojos in Los Angeles and Tak Kubota especially has been in countless films. After the competition was over there was a small party in the hotel for the organisers, referees and coaches, where the heads of delegation of the countries that participated all received a certificate of attendance signed personally by Soke Kubota and were also given a small statuette as a token of remembrance of the trip. Nice one!

On this final night and once the organiser's party was over we all got together with the Australian squad and got well and truly pissed. Soke Kubota and his American wife joined in the fun. It was a great night and we swapped tee-shirts and baseball caps and of course stories and anecdotes but it was a wonderful ending to a great trip.

In this year alone we topped the gold medal charts at the Legend Open, the Shobu-Ippon Open and the WTKO UK Championships. Not bad for an Association of only two hundred students! Strength in depth and good sportsmanship in adversity!

In the October and after all of these great successes of 2005, the BBC asked us if

we would appear on the longest running UK children's television programme ever, *Blue Peter*. *Blue Peter* has been constantly on our television sets since 1958 and of course I was delighted to be asked and got together a squad of children to participate in this show. The organisers wanted to mainly interview the two young IKA World Champions, Leah Hoey and Aaron Gould and whilst they did this there would be fourteen other youngsters free-fighting in the background. Sadly, Douglas Carson, our other world champion and indeed James Smith our European champion were both deemed too old and too tall for this children's programme. Both were over six feet tall and not really right for *Blue Peter*! I was asked to choreograph the event and am pleased to say it went really well. I felt very proud and extremely important, as I stood behind the camera and watched as Leah and Aaron performed Sochin kata as a team kata and then taught the two *Blue Peter* presenters, Gethin Jones and Liz Barker, Taikyoku Shodan or as it is also known, Kihon kata. They were then interviewed personally about their training and their success at the world championships. I was very proud of them all and the show went out a couple of weeks later and I have to say was absolutely brilliant. Stars in the making! The only sad thing really, was on the day we were actually being filmed at the studios, the great Ronnie Barker died and the news spread like wildfire throughout the BBC corridors. I thought he was an extremely funny man and a great loss to the nation.

2006 was another of those up and down years. On the competition front we did quite well again and it was whilst I was teaching in Ohio that our men's team had probably their best result for quite a few years. They won both the three-man team kumite and the adult team kata event at the mighty Shobu-Ippon Open

Championships. Both teams consisted of the same three men, Adam Cockfield, Daniel White and James Smith. I was a very proud man as I received an email at the Sanders family home in Ohio telling me the good news. Not only had we won these two gold medals but we took eight in total, with Aaron Gould, Leah Hoey, Alexis Raymen, Thomas Carson, Douglas Carson and our youngster's team kata of, Alexis Raymen, Aaron Gould and Ross McGirr making up the eight. The joke was made that I should go away more often. Charming!

Shobu Ippon Men's Team Kumite and Team Kata winners
(left to right: Daniel White, Adam Cockfield and James Smith)

But seriously, it was around this time that I had thought about stepping down from my role as the Association coach. It was most definitely time for a younger man to take over and there couldn't have been a better guy than Adam Cockfield. He was a great competitor and very well respected by the rest of the squad and I knew the team would be in safe hands. I would stay on as team manager and oversee the paperwork side of things and if and when we went abroad I would become the head of delegation. And so on my return this is what basically happened.

Whilst I was in the States on this visit, Ed Cox's wonderful wife, Terry was suffering badly from cancer. She hadn't long been diagnosed with this horrible disease but it had spread extremely quickly and as my visit was coming to an end, she really didn't look well at all. I said my goodbyes and returned back to England but sadly, this farewell would be the last time I would see Terry alive. I had only been back in England a couple of days when I received the terrible news that she had quietly and peacefully passed away. Ed and Terry had been friends of mine for many years and so I made very quick arrangements to return to Ohio, so as to attend the funeral service. Jeff Sanders and Randy Bodey, I believe, were the only two that actually knew that I was returning and this would be a shock to Ed but hopefully a nice one. I jumped back on a plane at Heathrow Airport and arrived back in Ohio for my second visit in less than a week. My poor old body didn't know which way to turn, as the jet lag kicked in quite badly. But I wouldn't have missed it for the world. We got out of the car outside the Atkins-Shively Funeral Home in St. Paris and Jeff and Randy went ahead as I basically hid behind them. Ed welcomed them both and then they parted like the waves and there I stood. Ed broke down, as tears welled-up in his eyes and he just couldn't believe what he was seeing. We hugged and I told him how sorry I was and that Terry was such a lovely lady. We had been really good friends and she had a great sense of humour and I would miss her very much. The coffin was an open one and there she lay, now at peace. I quietly said my final farewell. The cancer couldn't hurt her anymore now. Terry was eventually buried at the Terre Haute Cemetery near Urbana and the cavalcade of cars was absolutely amazing and seemed to stretch for miles. A well loved lady who would be very sadly missed.

Another sad event happened in 2006, as this was the year my friend and Assistant Chief Instructor and Chief Referee, Steve Wilson resigned from SSKI. We had a difference of opinion and after much thought, he left. This of course also meant that the Harlow club would leave with him and this was a shame as they had been an integral part of the Association for many years. But all good things must come to an end. Steve though, was one of the first to ring me up and ask how I was after my two prostate operations and although we don't see much of each other now, we stay good friends. He told me a couple of years ago now that he has stopped training totally and has handed the club over to his number two, Erik Thorpe. This is a real shame as Steve has a lot to give but I know he wanted to spend much more time with his growing family. The reins of both Steve's posts went naturally to the next most senior, Kevin Thurlow but this didn't last for long, as he left on bad feeling just after my prostate operations in 2007. Kevin was a nice enough fellow but just not right for the job. Soon after my operation was over and back in the Hemel Hempstead dojo, all my senior instructors came up to me and said that if the very worst had happened in hospital and I hadn't made it through, they would not have followed Kevin and they just thought I should know. This made me very sad, inasmuch that I wouldn't want to see the Association dissolve when I eventually shuffle off this mortal coil. So Kevin, who was already planning to resign from SSKI at the Association AGM anyway, was asked to leave. He now runs his own Association that is mainly based in Kent and I wish him all the best for the future. And so now Tony Bunting was my new number two and everyone seemed very happy with this. I also made preparations financially in my will for the Association to carry on after my days on this earth are over. So another rocky period was behind us, as the Association moved into less troubled waters. Whenever I'm around Tony though, I keep finding a lot of banana skins scattered around and I'm blessed if I know what for!

Richard Amos and me on the Course the day before the 2nd WTKO UK Championships

2006 would also see the running of the 2nd WTKO UK Championships, which again were held in my dojo at Hemel Hempstead School. The guest of honour was the Chief Instructor to the WTKO, Richard Amos sensei. The gold medals this time were taken by, Kayhan Sefat, Alexis Raymen with two, Leah Hoey, Lee Power, Douglas Carson, Jade Callan, Wadhah Saleh, Lucy Castle, Ferrari Faqiri, the FBSKUI Men's Kumite Team, the BSKI Boy's Kumite Team, the SSKI Adult Team Kata and the SSKI Children's Team Kata. It was another good tournament where again we topped the gold medal charts with seven gold medals out of the fourteen categories. Once more we were rewarded with many fine comments on how well the event had been run, especially starting and finishing on time again.

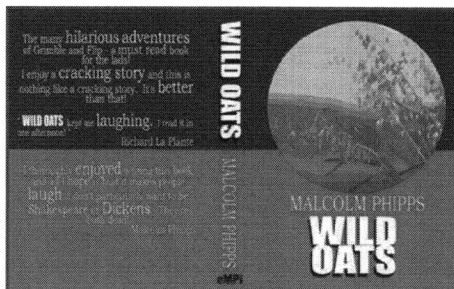

The final adventures: Wild Oats

This was also the year, *Wild Oats* was published, which was a compilation of two books, *Wild Oats in Cornwall* and *Wild Oats in Smoke* and concluded the adventures of Grimble and Flip.

In the August of 2007 I was inducted into the Global Martial Arts Hall of Fame in Indianapolis, Indiana in the USA and again this was a really nice touch and is very nice to be rewarded for one's work in any field. At the same time the 1980 world kumite champion, Tokey Hill was inducted and we talked about those old times and the competitors and coaches we both knew. Names like, Ticky Donovan, Jeoff Thompson, Vic Charles and the legendary Pat McKay, who Tokey had actually beaten to win his world title in 1980. Pat of course went on to win the world title in 1982 and 1984 and even to this day is the greatest competition fighter I have ever seen. My living room wall is now totally decorated! No more room for any more certificates or awards. Have to start on the dining room now! Sadly, 2007 turned out to be not such a nice year on a personal basis. After returning from Indianapolis and on a high, I was diagnosed with prostate cancer and went through a very nasty time in my life. I have devoted a chapter to this below, (The Final Battle) and so won't bore you again with all the details here.

And so the years rolled by. I was still on my own but comically enough started to enjoy this new found freedom. First of all, it was very lonely when Allison decided to leave and then of course Beenie, but after a couple of years I had become accustomed to my own company and basically could do what I liked with life. When I spoke about this to Dave Hazard, who at that time was in a similar situation, he said it

1980 World Kumite Champion, Tokey Hill and yours truly in Indianapolis

wasn't so bad, you could watch what television you liked, play what music you liked, get out of bed whenever you liked and fart whenever you liked! This is of course, very true but there are still the lonely times when I rattle around this big, beautiful house and wonder if I'll ever meet anyone again to share my life with. Dave has been very lucky and is now married to the lovely Saengjan and I know they are very happy together. One day perhaps...!

My life is interesting though and I have been given many gifts and talents. I enjoy writing, as I hope this book and my other books will testify and I love playing the guitar. I have played since those early days in the late 1960's in Bahrain and I am very lucky to have three brilliant guitars. My acoustic guitar is a Gibson *Hummingbird*, my semi-acoustic guitar is a Gibson *Chet Atkins SST* and my electric guitar is a Gibson *Custom Les Paul*. As you can see I love Gibson guitars. When I was about to purchase my first decent guitar, I confronted one of our students in the Radlett club which was run by Tony Bunting. This student was very famous in music circles and at the time was a fourth kyu (purple and white stripe belt) in Shotokan. His name was Mike Moran and he had written the music for the superb film, *The Time Bandits* and also the music for the extremely popular television series, *Taggart*, which included the hit, *No Mean City* sung by Maggie Bell.

The theme music from television's *New Tricks* is by Mike, as indeed is the catchy song, *It's Alright* sung by Dennis Waterman from this series. Mike also co-wrote with Freddie Mercury the theme song for the Barcelona Olympics aptly titled, *Barcelona* which was sung by Freddie Mercury and the female opera singer, Montserrat Caballé. He had worked with Freddie Mercury and Queen, David Bowie, Paul Simon, Stevie Wonder, George Harrison and Ozzy Osbourne to name but a few. Mike was a superb pianist and music producer and when I asked him what guitar I should buy he told me in no uncertain terms, the most expensive you can afford. He said it was no good buying a cheap instrument if you were going to be serious about playing the guitar properly. And so, with this new found knowledge and wisdom I purchased my first Gibson guitar, the *Chet Atkins SST*. He was so right, as it is just wonderful to play, as are the other two Gibson's that I purchased quite a bit later. Thanks Mike!

I like most kinds of music but I really love the old Mississippi Delta Blues and the music of the late 1950's through to the exciting 1960's, especially that of, Bob Dylan, Buddy Holly, The Animals,

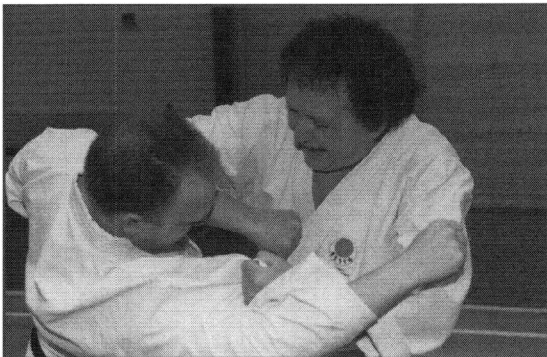

Hey Patrick, have you seen my tattoo?

The Who, The Kinks, The Hollies, Bob Marley and many others. I play with my friends, Maggie and Keith Martindale who live a few doors away, on a reasonably regular basis and we have a good old jamming session together. They play loads of instruments, guitar, mandolin, bass guitar to name but a few and their music of choice is Blue Grass. Also training in the Hemel Hempstead dojo we have another extremely professional and very talented singer, songwriter and pianist, Andy Fleet, whose CD, *The Night Falls Fast* is absolutely superb. You can hear songs from this wonderful album on, www.andyfleet.com and believe me it is certainly worth a listen.

And of course there is my karate training and teaching. At my tender age and if the truth be known, it is more teaching than training now but I do love passing on our wonderful art to other people. Don't get me wrong, I still have much to learn about our art and still enjoy the many challenges set before me in this side of my life and still train on all our courses with the guest instructors. My weekly teaching regime, as I write this book, is twice a week at the Hemel Hempstead honbu dojo and of course anything the weekend might throw at me, which of course is quite often. I like those immortal words: *Old senseis don't die, they just grade away!*

The Association is very strong at this moment in time and I believe we now have the best team we have ever had with Tony Bunting 6th Dan, by far the most competent Assistant Chief Instructor in our history of late. Adam Cockfield 4th Dan is an excellent coach to the squad and Jeff Carson a superb Chief Referee that has been highly praised by his peers. The club instructors are a great band of people who have all been mainly taught by me. Now this isn't meant to sound big-headed in anyway but it does create a solid and steady standard for the Association in general. After myself, Tony and Adam, there is Peter Welch, Nick Forgham, Paul Carvell, Daniel White and Gary Richards. I basically teach at the Hemel Hempstead club, whilst Tony teaches at Slip End in Luton. Adam has a very strong London dojo and Daniel White is the Berkhamsted sensei. Peter Welch teaches in the Old Basing, Lychpit and Hook clubs which are all situated in the Basingstoke and Hook areas of Hampshire. Nick Forgham is our instructor at the Winnersh dojo which is basically a suburb of Reading. Paul Carvell is the children's instructor at the Hemel Hempstead dojo and is ably helped by Stacey Barton and Gary Richards teaches at the Bovingdon club. As I write this book, assistant instructors to the Berkhamsted, Bovingdon and Slip End dojos are Jason Foxwell-Moss, Sam Richards and Aaron Gould respectively. Tony jumps in and takes the Hemel Hempstead club when I am teaching elsewhere.

I visit my clubs in Ohio in the USA three times a year and I really enjoy this and stay with my great friends the Sanders family (Jeff, Lisa, Mary-Rose, Bishop and AJ). I see a lot of lovely people whilst there, which include Randy Bodey and his good lady friend, Teresa and his two sons, Luke and Nathan and of course the Chief Instructor Ed Cox and his new wife, Diane who is also a black belt. There is also Jan Meyer, Jeannie Yates, Kyle Long, Dennis Huff, Vince Raska and his family, Frank Segreti, Corie and Theresa Fish and really just too many to name but I love them all. I have visited Budapest in Hungary a couple of times now and after the training sessions and gradings are over, have been shown around this beautiful city by the Chief Instructor for Hungary, Zohner Szilard sensei and his lovely wife Ildiko.

We have many actual large families training in the Hemel Hempstead dojo, which is a great advert for the club. We have the Carson Clan, where all five of the family (Jeff, Sue, Dougie, Ross and Thomas) are black belts. There is also the Richard's family, Gary and his youngest son Sam, who again are both black belts and Gary's brother, Mark and his son Danny also train regularly. Three of the Barton family train at the club, Stacey a very good 2nd Dan, her dad Phil and her brother Steven. I think the only Redford we don't have in the club is bloody Robert Redford, as Lorraine, Luke, Matthew and Bernadette Redford are all with us! We also have the three sisters of the Gower family training at the dojo, Amanda, Emma and Samantha. The Hemel Hempstead dojo is a big club with over seventy students and twenty-four of these are black belts, but it has been in operation since 1977.

Ed and Diane Cox's wedding (receiving the blessing from Jim Chess the minister with yours truly the best man looking on!)

I eat in great restaurants a couple of times a week, eating wonderful food and drinking excellent wine. The owners of these restaurants and many of the waiters have become good friends. My favourite Italian restaurant is 'Sinatra's' in Hemel Hempstead. The food there is absolutely wonderful and I have known Carlo the owner for many years. He is competently helped by Fernando, a real character from Lisbon in Portugal and whose dad actually played in goal for the Portuguese national football team in the late 1940's. Then there is the brilliant chef and of course Carlo's wife Caroline who often helps when it gets really busy.

I spent one brilliant evening in there a few years ago with Vinnie Jones and his wife Tanya talking about life and just about anything

The Carson Clan
(left to right: Dougie, Sue, Thomas, Jeff and Ross)

in general but mainly his footballing days and his films. I think we left the 'Casanova' restaurant (as it was then known) around 1.30am. Vinnie is a local Hemel Hempstead lad and for a while we drank in the same pub, 'The New Venture' in Adeyfield. Although Vinnie is a bit younger than me, I did go to school with one of his great friends, Johnny Watts. Another of his mates, Vince Needham, who then lived in Homefield Road, was also a good friend in those far distant school years. Both still live in the local area. I believe Vinnie now lives in Los Angeles. Where did we go wrong?

Another of Vinnie's friends was one of my top black belts, Peter York who sadly had to pack up karate training at the 3rd Dan level due to the injuries to his knees. Peter was and still is a carpet fitter and has been for donkey's years, but this has taken its toll on his knees. His wife Elaine and his daughter Toni were also very good black belts at my dojo but sadly no longer train. Hopefully they'll come back one day. Toni won many competitions in her young career in karate and they are all sadly missed in the Hemel Hempstead dojo. Pete makes up for it though in golf, where he is superb. I am told he now plays off of one, but has in his days been a scratch golfer. I know very little about golf but I do know that that is a bit good to say the very least. Back to the eating and drinking! I have two Indian restaurants that I frequent on a regular basis. There is 'Saffron' in the Old High Street of Hemel Hempstead and is owned by another good friend of mine, Ali. Two of his sons, Imran and Iqbal actually train at the karate dojo in Hemel Hempstead and are doing really well. His number one waiter Mohammed, better known as Mo' I have known for many years as well, and who sponsored the Association when he owned his own restaurant in the old town, aptly named 'Mo's Spice Inn'. And then there is Shah and Ahmed, two of the waiters that have been at 'Saffron' the longest. Shah is for ever playing jokes on me. Once I asked for a glass of red wine and he gave me a glass of blackcurrant juice. He found it absolutely hilarious as I wretched at the sweetness of the offending liquid. Another time he brought me the bill with the customary free little chocolate sweetie. Shah had bloody removed the chocolate very cleverly and carefully replaced the silver paper to make it look as though it still contained a chocolate. But in all seriousness they are really great.

The other Indian restaurant I frequent in Hemel Hempstead is the 'Bengal Spice' and is run by Tanvir and his family with his two trusty waiters, Noor (better known in the restaurant as Ahmed) and Shah. Again these have become good friends over the years that I have known them. Also great food! I normally take Dave Hazard to one of these restaurants when he visits, as the food is so good and he loves it.

So I can have no complaints and live a wonderful life and indeed keep myself busy, teaching, writing and playing guitar and as you can see eating and drinking rather splendidly as well. I'm a great believer in enjoying your life to the full, as nobody but nobody gets out alive! But if I'm really lucky, perhaps one day I'll meet the lady of my dreams, who knows? I wonder what Christina Aguilera's doing this evening!

Since the demise of my marriage to Allison, I'm actually getting really worried about my *Sex Appeal*. Not one bloody donation yet!

Even my hairdresser, Michael Jackson (no, not the dead singer), from Michael Anthony's Hair Salon in Grovehill in Hemel Hempstead always takes the piss and asks me every time if I would like to have my hair cut on the day they do the pensioner's hair, therefore giving me a chance to pull an oldie!

Over the many years of our history we have hosted some absolutely fantastic courses and seminars with some of the very best in Shotokan karate. In the Seishinkai dojos of Hemel Hempstead and Watford alone we have trained with, Dave Hazard, Aidan Trimble, Terry O'Neill, Sadashige Kato, Masao Kagawa, Graham Austin, Yoshinobu Ohta, Ronnie Christopher, Sean Roberts, Dave Hooper, Cyril Cummins, Richard Amos, John Mullin, Steve Ubl, Dennis Martin, Willie Thomas, Simon Oliver, John Cheetham, Tony Bunting, Adam Cockfield, Steve Wilson and of course, little old me! Dennis Martin and Willie Thomas are not actually Shotokan instructors but had a lot to give to our students about unarmed combat, edged weapon defence and competition kumite respectively. Not a bad batch of names, I think you'll agree but I have to say my favourite, and I know I speak for many others in SSKI, is my great friend Dave Hazard. He is just phenomenal and if you have never trained with this great gentleman make absolutely sure you do. You don't know what you are missing.

On the competition side we are still very strong. Although we do not have fighters

Adam Cockfield
2009 Shobu Ippon men's senior kata champion

as good as Tracey Phipps, Willie Thomas or Val Henry, we are probably now much stronger in depth. Adam Cockfield is probably our best male all-rounder ever, constantly winning individual gold medals in kata and kumite and also team gold medals in both team disciplines. Three times he has been awarded the male Competitor of the Day award at the Legend Open Championships, in 2005, 2006 and 2008. In 2004 he won the men's senior kata at the Legend Open and in 2005 he repeated this feat. In 2008 he won the men's kumite title 6-1 in an excellent and exciting final, beating one of the best fighters around at this time and indeed still to this very day, Dave Galloway of SEKU. In 2009 Adam won the Shobu-Ippon Shotokan Open kata title with his excellent rendition of kata

Unsu in the final. He has won so many team titles and minor medals it would need a few more pages to list them all. We have the best boy kata competitor around for many years in Shotokan, Aaron Gould who has won just about every competition he has ever entered and has featured on the television twice now, on *BBC News 24* and *Blue Peter*. Douglas Carson and his younger brother Thomas have won many competitions between them and Alexis Raymen also has taken many titles in her competition career. Daniel White and Paul Hazell have been an integral part of our men's kumite team for quite a few years now and Arthi Niranjan, Stacey Barton, Sam Richards, Danny Richards, Claire Cerins, Emily Blundell, Olivia Christodoulou and Cameron Lennon are always in the medals somewhere. Plus there are a lot of very good youngsters coming through at this time, which make the future look very rosy indeed. As I write this book we are top of the medal charts for the Shobu-Ippon Open Championships, the WTKO UK Open Championships and must be right up there somewhere in the Legend Open Championships and the Portsmouth Open Championships, so we must be doing something right!

We are now proud members of the Shotokan Alliance, which to me is the best thing that has happened in my personal karate experience, where like-minded instructors and their Associations have come together to support each other's events. As I write this book the member groups are, SEKU, TKI, FBSKUI and SSKI. There is a camaraderie which is second to none in my thirty-six years of Shotokan and I believe one of the reasons for this, is there are no egos on show or indeed financial problems within the group. There are no politics and no fees to join and we all just get on with what matters, the karate itself. We have made some wonderful friends along the way, the likes of, Shaun Banfield and Emma Robins who run the brilliant website, *The Shotokan Way*, Matt Powell, Dave Galloway, Keith Williams, Steve Hollister, Stacy Crowe, Terry Oliver, Shaun Eglinton, Paul Uren, Hannah Day, Tracey Corby, Simon Staples, Darren Jumnoodoo and of course, Mick Dewey, Gerry Breeze, Brian Smith, Colin Putt, Merv O'Donnell and many, many more. And one of the huge bonuses is that we all still fight in the good old traditional karate way, shobu ippon. One whole point and it's 'bye, 'bye time! Ikken hissatsu! To kill the enemy with one blow! Not to chase him round and round in bloody circles in an endless game of tag, boring the enemy and the public with a million and one blows!

Now I do not doubt the athleticism and skill of these sport karateka in any way but in my view it has very little to do with traditional karate and the martial arts. Katas are made to look prettier and more dynamic with very little idea of the bunkai or oyo and kumite has become a bit of a game and seems to have nothing at all to do with self-defence whatsoever. This of course is only my personal view but I know is also the view of many other good traditional karateka. The gap seems to be sadly widening between traditional and sport karate. The trouble with training for sport only, is that it teaches students that winning is the most important aspect of the art and in many cases winning at all costs. This I find can create an unhealthy arrogance found in many other sports but not really wanted in karate but sadly, too often seen. Hardly the philosophy of karate as handed down to us by the great masters of yesteryear, Gichin Funakoshi and Masatoshi Nakayama. With ability comes humility! Again on a personal note, I couldn't care less whether karate becomes an Olympic sport or not. To me it is a serious martial art and a way of life and not just a way to win poxy medals and titles. That which is seen is soon forgotten – that which is not seen is eternal.

The panel of instructors that basically head the Shotokan Alliance are, Mick Dewey, Gerry Breeze, Simon Staples, Darren Jumnoodoo, Brian Smith, Colin Putt and little old me, who they decided to make Chairman, only because nobody else wanted to bloody do it!

I have also been lucky enough to have been featured on the cover of a few karate magazines. I can be seen flying through the air with the greatest of ease at Tracey on the cover of *Shotokan Karate Magazine* (Issue No.8) and also again with Tracey on the cover of *Traditional Karate* (May 1991) performing the second move of Jitte kata. *Traditional Karate* (April 2001) featured yours truly on the cover and all of these three magazines had cover articles inside. The October/November 2007 cover of *Traditional Karate* starred my young student, Aaron Gould on the cover with again an article about his phenomenal successes inside. I haven't quite made the cover of *Playgirl* yet!

Follow Me

This chapter actually tracks back to 1975 but I thought it merited a chapter on its own. I think, somewhere at the back of my mind, I had always believed that there was a God. I hadn't any specific beliefs but had started to ask myself some serious questions about life and the Universe in general. My wife Jan had very similar feelings and so we started to attend church on a regular basis. Well, I say church but not in the gigantic, great monolithic building sense. We attended a small and very friendly group of people, who met weekly in what could only be described as a very small but longish type building, which was approximately a similar size to a small Boy Scout hut. It went by the name of Sunnyhill Christian Fellowship and was named after the road it was located in, in our home town of Hemel Hempstead. It was run by a married couple named Geoff and Lyn Bone. The meetings were very informal and were led by Geoff. There were no hymns as such, just choruses that were played on a myriad of instruments from guitars to penny whistles, recorders and all sorts of percussion instruments. I listened intently to the informal sermons and sang along with the catchy choruses but was still not totally convinced that what these people believed in was the answer that I was looking for but I was willing to give it a good try. In karate I was a purple belt and although I loved karate training and its philosophy to the hilt, it still didn't answer all of my spiritual questions.

On the many occasions of visiting my wife's family in Pembury, near Tunbridge Wells in Kent we visited the local Baptist Church, where again we were made most welcome.

Geoff Bone, the leader of Sunnyhill Fellowship, a few years previous had lost both his legs in a horrific train accident at Watford Junction Station. Both legs were severed above the knee and although he could walk on prosthetic legs, chose on many an occasion to sit in a chair with them removed. He still had an immense amount of pain in his legs and it was a welcome relief to rest them by removing the false limbs and just sitting on his torso. He was an amazing man who I came to respect greatly. His actual accident happened very early one morning when he was about to travel to Northern Ireland to lecture at a Christian conference. He arrived at Watford Junction Station very early in the morning to catch his train and fell asleep in the station waiting room. The next thing he heard were train doors slamming and a whistle being blown. He picked up his suitcase and ran out of the waiting room but the train was already moving. He managed to open the very last door of the last carriage but as he did so his case got wedged in the gap between the train and the platform. This threw him awkwardly and he fell under the last set of wheels of the train, which severed one leg completely and left the other one hanging off by the merest of shreds. Luckily enough for Geoff, (I'm not sure if luckily is the right word here), waiting in the station car park was an ambulance that was standing by for another passenger from another train. The ambulance men were alerted and they ran to Geoff's aid. I don't know all the medical terms but they eventually stopped the bleeding and rushed him to the closest hospital, where after being on death's door from shock and the loss of a huge amount of blood, he survived to tell his tale. The severed leg was found a few hundred yards down the track where the train had dragged the unattached limb! Sadly, they couldn't save the other leg either. I found this scenario absolutely horrific, as I had played sport all my life and now was heavily engaged in Shotokan karate and couldn't imagine what it would be like to have no legs whatsoever. I am still to this day amazed that he survived, as could you imagine the amount of blood loss there would have been with both femoral arteries being totally severed. His story was an absolutely amazing one and he said he felt at peace throughout the whole horrible scenario and that he felt that the Lord was with him every step of the way. Excuse the pun, but he said he felt at peace and not in pieces! What a man, and what a testament of faith.

Anyway, this story and my constant searching led me to what I could only describe as, nearly believing. If there was such a thing I was half-a-Christian! The day I was to become a whole Christian was fast approaching. Geoff and Lyn had become parents for the first time about two years previous, when Lyn gave birth to their daughter, Ruth.They were both due to attend a conference one evening a few miles away and asked Jan and I if we would babysit little Ruth. This we wholeheartedly agreed to do and were accompanied by our seven year old daughter Tracey for the evening.On the night in question, (which would turn out to be the greatest in my entire life), all three of us made our way round to their house, which was literally next door to the Fellowship building in Sunnyhill Road and within easy walking distance from our home. We were made comfortable and told where everything was situated. Their house was an older building and they had a fabulous big log fireplace with large armchairs on either side of it and Jan and I made ourselves comfortable for the evening. Ruth and Tracey were both upstairs asleep and Jan would pop up every now and then to see if they were all right. The one thing the Bones didn't have at that time and that was a television. Neither of them totally believed in this media tool and so it was down to reading and playing the old vinyl records for the evening.

After nearly an hour browsing through books and magazines I thought it would be nice to put on some music. I flicked through their collection hoping to find some of my hero, Bob Dylan but to no avail. The next best thing was Johnny Cash and I spotted a record I had never seen before called *The Gospel Road*. It also had Kris Kristofferson and June Carter on it, so I thought I would give it a try. I placed the record carefully on the turntable and started to listen to the record, which was in a story form of Jesus' life and was broken up by songs by these great stars. It was extremely lifelike, as you could hear people and animals going about their natural lives in the background in such places as, Jerusalem, the Sea of Galilee and the River Jordan. I listened intently to every word of Jesus' life and in all honesty have never listened to a recording so deeply before or indeed after this event. One of the main songs on the album is *Follow Me*, which was originally written and sung by John Denver. As the record approached the crucifixion scene, Jan popped upstairs to see how the two girls were doing. It turned out that Ruth was just slightly awake and so Jan stayed with her for about twenty minutes. During this time the horrific crucifixion of Jesus was played out on the record. The song *Follow Me* went slightly offbeat and very slow as you could hear the nails being driven into his hands and feet. People in the background were wailing, crying and some cheering as the painful cross was lifted into place. Something hit me deep inside. I just couldn't help myself, as I wept like I had never wept before and I just could not stop. My face was drenched with my tears and this went on for quite a time. Jan eventually appeared and looked a little worried at seeing hubby broken and in tears. She asked me, whatever was the matter? I could hardly speak. Eventually, I found my voice again and told her that throughout my life I had been such a sinner and that I now knew for certain that I was, most definitely one hundred percent a Christian. On hearing this news she started to cry in joy as she had become a Christian a few months before and unbeknown to me had been praying for me fervently. It may sound corny but I can tell you from my heart that I have never felt like that before or after the event. I know for a fact that the good Lord came in to my life that very evening and I can assure you most definitely, it was much more than just emotion. The date was the 15th August in the year 1975 and as I said earlier was the greatest day of my life.

The following April, Jan and I were baptised at Pembury Baptist Church and the year after my mum and dad were baptised at the Belmont Road Baptist Church in Hemel Hempstead. They had watched our progress intently and eventually had also taken this wonderful step. I do go to church a few times a year, mainly in the USA, where I attend the Urbana First Baptist Church with the Sanders family that I stay with. The church has a wonderful minister, Brian Wonn and a great congregation and I feel very much at home there. But I am not a regular church-goer but pray on a more personal daily basis. Someone once said, 'That going to church no more made you a Christian, than going to a garage made you a car!' The greatest thing I have ever read in my entire life is Jesus', *Sermon on the Mount* from the New Testament and is in the book of Matthew, chapters five, six and seven. As you read through this, my autobiography, you can see that my life is very far from perfect, even after becoming a Christian but every time I fall down, the good Lord picks me back up again, dusts me down and hopefully I proceed a better man. It is extremely hard to explain to non-believers these personal experiences but all I hope is that at some time in your life you can witness a similar event.

I know many other great karateka who have the same or similar beliefs, Stan Schmidt, Keith Geyer and Geoff Thompson, to name but three, all give thanks to the Lord for what they have achieved in their lives.There were no flashes of lightning, no visions, no one had twisted my arm or brainwashed me. It was by far, the most important day of my life and believe me I have had some other wonderful days as well. I am not a religious nut and if you know me, you know this to be true.

I do not go around condemning other people and saying what they should or should not do with their lives but I just sincerely hope they have a likewise experience one day. I do not know all the answers of the universe - I just know what is right for me. I do not look at myself through rose-coloured sunglasses and at others through a bloody magnifying glass!

I personally don't like the word religion, as it is a man-made word and under the heading of this word religion there have been many wars, terrorism, starvation and poverty throughout the ages. But this is all due to man's incessant greed and violent nature and who likes to blame God when things don't go in his favour. We were given freedom of choice by God and if we choose to pay eighty million pounds for a bloody footballer and a poxy fortune trying to get to other planets and calmly watch while half the world starves or dies from disease or lack of water, then I really think that the blame must lie squarely and uncomfortably in mankind's lap. What I am talking about is a spiritual and personal relationship and not a religious or man-made one as such. I believe there is a spark of God in all men's and women's hearts and what amazes me is that when us humans are in real trouble, you often find us praying. It was said that when the Titanic was sinking, you could hear the Lord's Prayer actually being chanted all over the doomed liner. Also, in the current worldwide climate of terrorism and religious fervour, I am very proud to call myself a Christian and refuse to take the middle ground and pretend I don't believe in anything. Bollocks to so-called political correctness!

And so finally, my spiritual life, my karate life and life in general were all on the right track at last. Not bad for someone who needs a satellite navigation system to climb a fucking ladder!

The Final Battle

The final battle; well, so far and at the time of writing!

My latest struggle and toughest yet was in September of 2007. I had been diagnosed with prostate cancer and had two operations to rid myself of this horrible disease. I'd been having my prostate checked for just about three years and the PSA test results were getting higher and higher, which is a sign that something is not right. First of all my prostate gland was diagnosed as being enlarged and so I went into BUPA Harpenden Hospital for three days for my first operation, which was called a Transurethral Resection of the Prostate or TURP for short. This is where they shave bits off of the prostate gland to bring it back to its normal size. I won't go into the gory details of how they do this, as it could make grown men quake. At the same time they took a biopsy of the prostate and sadly found out there was a cancerous tumour in the gland and so I had to go back into hospital a few weeks later to have the prostate totally removed. This procedure is called a Radical Prostatectomy.

This is not a nice operation and I was in hospital for twelve days with tubes coming out of nearly all orifices known to man. The word catheter is now a swear word in my book! I was a very lucky man to have the best urologist in the country, Mr Manoah Pancharatnam and a great bunch of nurses to help me pull through. I really felt like death warmed up though but also thanks to my daughter Tracie, grandson Christopher and to the many great friends who visited me in hospital, I slowly started to get through this very trying time. I had a string of wonderful visitors, the likes of, Tony Bunting, Adam Cockfield, Gary and Sam Richards, the Carson family, Nick Forgham and Michelle Gould, all who brought gifts but even more importantly, their friendship. This is when you find out who your true friends are. Dave Hazard rang me up nearly every day whilst I was in hospital and I nearly popped my many stitches laughing at his wicked jokes!
The nurses were absolutely amazed and couldn't believe how many friends I had and how many gifts and Get Well cards I had amassed. My bedside cabinet looked like a small branch of bloody Tescos! Eventually, I accumulated nearly forty Get Well cards. It was very touching in such an unpleasant situation. My next door neighbours at number five, Ken and Pam Jarrett looked after my house and garden whilst I was in hospital and picked up the mail. My dojos were taken over by some of my instructors, Tony Bunting, Adam Cockfield, Daniel White, Paul Carvell and Ross McGirr, and to these people I owe a great debt of gratitude. Tony especially was fantastic, as he took my Hemel Hempstead dojo for the next four and a half months, which is one heck of a long time.

After going back to hospital for a check-up, I was told that the lymph glands, which had also been removed from the area surrounding the prostate gland, had been sent to pathology and were found to be totally clear of cancerous cells. Also, after having an MRI scan and a bone scan they found that the cancer hadn't spread from the prostate, which was the best news so far and so I was given the all clear. It was then the long road back to full recovery but at least it was nearly all over. I sat and watched every single lesson in the honbu dojo in Hemel Hempstead and realised how much I missed actually being in a gi. I eventually got back training and teaching proper in January 2008, just over four months after the first operation. As my great friend Dave Hazard said at the beginning of this saga, 'You've met some tough opponents in your karate life but this is going to be the toughest and it's an opponent that just has to be beaten. You can do it!' These words and the love of many great people and my faith helped me through this very trying time.

One of the more annoying things about the aftermath of the main operation is that it leaves you incontinent for a few months. Of course Dave now had a wonderful nickname for me, 'Mr Pissy-pants', which he used for a couple of months every time we spoke on the telephone. All I can say is that all men over 45 years of age should get their prostate checked on an anal, sorry I mean annual basis, and try and avoid the worst. I had no symptoms whatsoever and was very lucky that the cancer was caught in time but this would not have been the case if I had not been having regular check-ups.

Whilst I was actually in hospital the second time, Dave Hazard's excellent autobiography, *Born Fighter* was published and after being home for a couple of days, Dave made the trek all the way down from Nottingham just to bring me a wonderful signed copy. When I told him he didn't have to come all that way just to give me the book, he replied that he hadn't come to give me the bloody book he had come to see how I was recovering and if there was anything he could do for me. My daughter, Tracie was also at my home looking after me for a few days and Dave took us both out for a wonderful Indian meal before he travelled all the way back to Nottingham a few hours later. He left saying, if there was anything he could do, just to let him know. A true friend indeed!

Other instructors from outside SSKI also offered their services whilst I was out of action and the four that immediately spring to mind are, Paul Herbert, Simon Staples, Darren Jumnoodoo and Graham Palmer. You don't forget these wonderful gestures. Genuine karateka who mean what they say. Their fine gestures

With my great friend Dave Hazard on a Hemel Hempstead Course in 2009

At Molineux with ex-Wolves player,
Andy Thompson celebrating a late birthday!

My trusty number two and good friend, Tony Bunting
(presenting him with his 6th Dan certificate)

reminded me of a quotation from Mahatma Gandhi: *'I shall pass through this world but once. Any good therefore that I can do or any kindness that I can show to any human being, let me do it now. Let me not defer or neglect it, for I shall not pass this way again'*

After I had been out of hospital for a short while, I was presented with a birthday present and a welcome back to the dojo gift. The club had arranged a collection and bought me and a guest a day out at Molineux Stadium, the home of my beloved Wolves. It turned out to be an absolutely brilliant day and my guest for the day was my great friend and colleague, Adam Cockfield, who I found out later, had arranged the whole deal through his work for the Football Association at Soho Square. We were taken around the stadium and shown all the wonderful history of the club. We had an excellent three course meal in, Billy's Boot Room, named after the legendary Wolves and England captain, Billy Wright and had many laughs with a few characters on our table who supported QPR, who were the opposition for Wolves on the day, and were also there as guests. I was then given a small birthday present and a birthday card signed by all the players and had my photo taken with a famous ex-player, Andy Thompson. We then had fabulous seats for the match, which was ironically against QPR, the team I used to go and watch when my good friend and karate student John Byrne played for them. The weather was great for the time of year and the match was so exciting with the final score of 3 – 3. Andy Keogh scored for Wolves in the 94th minute to equalize. What a lovely gesture from my wonderful students and dear friends.

I also remember my first lesson back in a gi and back in the dojo proper. I had watched every single lesson for four and a half months as Tony Bunting put the club through its paces. At last though, the time had arrived for me to don my karate suit again and get in front of my beloved club. It felt a little strange at first but at the end of the bowing session the club just let out a huge applause, which I have to say left me in tears. They were just happy for me and I was so pleased to be with them again as their sensei. I gave Tony a hug. He had been what I always envisaged a number two to be, honest and loyal in times of adversity. He is a wonderful friend and a great sensei. I treated him to a new black belt and a new heavyweight gi just to say thank you for all his hard work whilst I had been sidelined. As a famous advert on our television screens states:

New belt = X amount of pounds. New gi = X amount of pounds. What Tony had done for me = Priceless!

At the next grading in Hemel Hempstead I was presented with another beautiful present. This was a drawing of the photograph of me performing tobi-yoko-geri (jumping side-kick) that was on the cover of Shotokan Karate Magazine (Issue number 8.) The artist was a karate student in the Winnersh dojo in Reading and was an artist by profession. His name was Andrew Brooks. It is absolutely beautiful and underneath the drawing itself it has the famous calligraphy of

The superb drawing of my tobi-yoko-geri by Andrew Brooks

Gichin Funakoshi's, *Parting the Clouds, Seeking the Way*. This stunning drawing was also accompanied by a card that I think was just about signed by everyone in the Association.

But every person in this life, who is, or has been in a position of leadership, will eventually or indeed already have been betrayed. People who are envious and jealous of what you have achieved and think it is their God given right to have immediately, all that you have worked hard for over many years. All leaders will eventually have their Judas and the art of karate is no stranger to this appalling attitude. I call it the Brutus syndrome, a quick stab in the back when nobody is looking, (Et tu, Brute?). And so, when you are really down in the dumps for a myriad of different reasons, not only do you find out who your true friends are but quickly find out who are not your real friends at all. I have always been extremely suspicious of people who are all over you like a bloody rash. Men and women, who on the outset can't do enough for you and who call you their sensei, mentor and great friend, only to very quickly vanish and shit on you when the chips are down. How very sad! Everything the martial arts and life in general goes against. These people are only out for what they can get. Take, take, take! How small-minded and selfish can you be! Then of course you get the stream of lame excuses why they actually crapped on you. Get a life! All I can say is that excuses are like arseholes. Everyone's got'em, and they all fucking stink! I wouldn't even give them the satisfaction of seeing their names in this chapter of the book.

'What's in a name? That which we call a rose by any other name would smell as sweet' *Shakespeare*.

'What's in a name? That which we call an arsehole by any other name would smell as bad' *Phipps*.

Hey, this philosophy stuff's a piece of piss!

I can forgive what they did but I find it very hard to forget. I think it is very important to be able to forgive those who shit on you and I sincerely believe this is a strong point and not a weakness. Why spend your whole life being angry with these people, when they probably don't even know that you are angry, or for that matter, probably don't bloody care. This kind of person is out there thoroughly enjoying their life, while you are the one that is hurting and angry and yet you were the one who was crapped on in the first place. Doesn't make any sense. It's like taking an overdose of poison yourself and hoping your enemy will die! Anyway, I sincerely believe in the saying, what goes around, comes around, which is said so much better and more profoundly by the brilliant prophetic line attributed to *Sun Tzu* (544 – 496 BC) who wrote the magnificent book, *The Art of War*. If you wait by the river long enough, eventually you will see the bodies of all your enemies float by.

Grandson Chris and granddaughter Tiffany

Generally though, it is at times like these when life gets put into its true perspective. All of a sudden you figure out what is important in life such as your faith, your family, your friends and the more natural things of the world. I am very lucky to have a wonderful daughter, Tracie and three fabulous grandchildren, Christopher, Sarah and Tiffany, who all live in London and, in all truthfulness, who I should see a little bit more of. But you also quickly figure out what isn't quite so important. Mortgages, the poxy interest rates, your next bloody car and indeed anything of the material world spring to mind. I like nice things as much as the next person but I refuse to struggle to get them. If I can't afford them comfortably then so be it. This experience has left me totally believing in the four F's of life, faith, family, friends and fucking arseholes!

'There is no possession more valuable than a good and faithful friend' *Socrates*.

Karate comes extremely high on my personal positive list, as I believe it is one of the really good things in life, especially in the day and age we live in. It keeps us healthy, mentally and physically and it gives us many goals and is just one of life's more beneficial attributes generally. It has taught me respect and humility and has done absolute wonders for me in my

The three girls in my life (My daughter Tracie, and my two granddaughters Sarah and Tiffany)

personal life, giving me an existence I could only have dreamed of in my earlier years. It has calmed my temper. I was in many scrapes in my younger days both in Civvy Street and in the RN but karate has straightened me out and put me on the right path. My mum always said that I got my temper from my Irish blood father, Thomas Moran who I never met. Who knows? She said that my temper would get me into serious trouble one day but luckily enough this didn't come true. I am now a great believer in the saying: Let emotions subside, then decide! As opposed to the old days, which would've been more like: Fuck the emotion, let's have a commotion! This is what karate has done for me in my life but I know for sure that it was the good Lord who put it in my path in the very first place. I have taught some really wonderful people throughout my karate career and many of these have reached a very high standard in karate, winning world, European and many national titles and have achieved some very high dan grades. Some have gone on to become great instructors in their own right, running their own clubs and groups. This is absolutely wonderful but I just hope my teaching has improved the general life of all those who have trained with me though, whether competitors, instructors or just day to day students.

Before I sign off, I know that I have been lucky enough to have been twice put forward for an MBE. What the fuck for I'll never know, but when I see some of the prats in the pop world and acting profession who get national honours I'm not really surprised. I found all this out because the people that actually put me forward for an honour, later fell out with me and handed me all the documentation and correspondence with the Houses of Commons. I feel very flattered. There were some very wonderful letters put forward by friends and students and this alone was very touching. Sadly, I wasn't successful but this was probably because I hadn't

Yoko-geri kekomi with Allison

done enough to deserve it or didn't have enough money (cash for honours scandal) or I wasn't in a big boy's club (funny handshake brigade). Perhaps they had remembered with vengeance, my time in Her Majesty's Royal Navy. Who knows? Who fucking cares? Mind you I did receive the WBE (Wanker of the British Empire) which I richly deserved, as you can see by my colourful life story. Comically enough though, after my final prostate operation and for a short while, this actually and very sadly became the truth! I was told by my consultant urologist that it was a case of, use it or lose it, and he put me on a course of Viagra. The only good thing about this is that I don't fall out of bed anymore! Until this inconceivable moment of time in my life, I thought that Viagra was a waterfall somewhere between Canada and the USA and that Wanking was a bloody town in China! Just joking, but I am now a fully qualified black belt in *hand-to-gland combat*!

As I write this book, I have had cancer of the prostate gland. I have osteoarthritis in both big toes due to football and karate injuries and a very dodgy medial ligament in my right knee and at the end of every week I ache like crazy. But I tell you what. I wouldn't swap my life now or the life that I have had for anybody else's. I wouldn't want to be one of those folk, who just sit around doing nothing and waiting for the final curtain to come down. I personally believe we were put on this earth to be ourselves and to do something with our lives and not be a clone of anybody else. So enjoy life to the full if you can and if you are lucky enough to be

And finally, still flying high! Seriously thinking about collecting bloody air miles!

a karateka, keep training, therefore keeping mentally and physically fit and having a great direction in life itself. As we get older it is imperative to keep training, although there will probably be things that we cannot do anymore, that we could once do in our youth. We just have to swallow our egos and get on with life. It is better to be a living dog, than a dead tiger!

Reminds me of a story I once heard about a student that hadn't trained for a long time. On meeting a certain karate instructor in the street, the conversation went something like this.

'I train in Shotokan karate.'

'Really, what grade are you?' The instructor enquired.

'I'm a black belt but haven't actually trained for about twenty years.'

'Well, by that logic, I'm a fucking schoolboy!'

Sadly, there is much truth in this story though and I'm sure we all know of people who attained their black belts and others who even achieved phenomenal competition success but who eventually packed up training. What a waste of talent and indeed life! Karate is for life and not just for a period of your life. I remember Kanazawa sensei explaining once, that there were two trees in karate training. The first tree is the kyu grade tree and at the top of this tree is shodan (first degree black belt). Once this grade is achieved, you then go to the bottom of the second tree, the dan grade tree. This tree has no peak to it and eventually lands up in heaven!

If we are to get the true benefits from training in our remarkable art, it is extremely important that we train right through old age until our days on this earth are over, as did our admirable Shotokan grand masters, Gichin Funakoshi, Masatoshi Nakayama, Keinosuke Enoeda, Hidetaka Nishiyama, Tetsuhiko Asai, Taiji Kase and many, many others. Never lose your sense of humour and keep on smiling and remember, if you turn your face towards the sun, all your shadows will fall behind you! Personally, with my Christian beliefs I would probably spell the word sun a little differently. There have been times in my life that I would rather forget and also many wonderful times but please do not judge me by what you have read and remember, he without sin, cast the first stone!

As I plough through my sixtieth decade on this planet, sometimes I feel a bit like a has been but I believe it was Sir Ian Botham who once said, that it was better to have been a has been, than a never been!

One of the most prophetic few lines in a song that mean so much to me in my personal life these days and indeed are a good sign of getting older, are the wonderful words written by Mike Hugg of Manfred Mann and Ian La Frenais for the excellent television comedy series, *Whatever Happened to the The Likely Lads?*

Oh what happened to you, whatever happened to me?
What became of the people we used to be?
Tomorrow's almost over, today went by so fast,
*It's the only thing to look forward to, **THE PAST**!*

And always remember those wonderful, immortal words. The older I get, the better I was! Hope you enjoyed my life's story, as on the whole, I DID!
Boiiiing! And now it's time for bed, said Zebedee! Get a fucking life, said Dylan!

Now I lay me down to sleep, I pray the Lord my soul to keep;
Should I die before I wake, I pray the Lord my soul to take,
And if I never finish this darned book, I pray the Lord my soul has took!

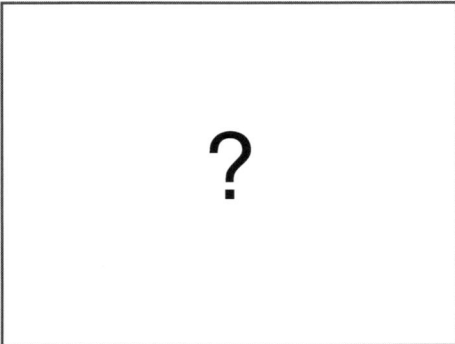

?

Wedding No. 4 - Any takers?

Must be female and have a pulse!

And still training...

SSKI-USA instructors with Sensei Hazard, Sensei Phipps and Sensei Banfield.
(L to R: Dave Hazard, Randy Bodey, Jan Meyer, Jeff Sanders, Malcolm Phipps, Dennis Huff, Shaun Banfield)

Bibliography of Malcolm Phipps

Wild Oats in Cornwall
Published by the Book Guild (ISBN 0-86332-690-0)
Phipps (Flip) and Grimble are two ex-sailors with a yearning for freedom. Leaving behind the Royal Navy as fast as their legs can carry them, they throw themselves headlong into a summer of madness by the sea. The likely lads are only after three things: drink, women and enough money to get them by. One dead-end job leads to another – usually at the point of a boot – and every one lands them in some hilarious adventure. Given a choice between behaving normally or getting a wicked laugh out of any situation, Flip and Grimble don't hesitate. Insult the public, egg on the innocent bystander, take revenge for any setback – anything goes in this bawdy and sometimes moving tale of two merciless practical jokers who just don't want to settle down.
The Book Guild

Uchi Deshi and the Master
Published by eMPi Publishing (ISBN 0-9519835-0-4)
Also published in Germany as Uchi Deshi und der Meister (ISBN 3-928975-12-9)
Uchi Deshi and the Master strikes me as one of those little gems on the art of karate-do. Sometimes serious, sometimes light-hearted but always entertaining, these stories of a wise, old Master and his young prodigy bring home the many complex philosophies of karate-do in a way that you will never forget them.
Terry O'Neill

The Conequest
Published by the St. Ives Printing and Publishing Co. (ISBN 0-948385-31-6)
The Conequest is a wonderful story for children of roadside cones that come to life during the middle of the night. They are fed up with their humdrum lives on the M4 motorway and so make a trek to Cornwall to search for the better life! Come and meet such characters as, Conefucius, The Conejuror, The Conestable, The Conel, Conefuse, Conetempt, Conedemn, Conen the Vulgarian and the rest of the gang!

The Ah So! Stories
Published by the St. Ives Printing and Publishing Co. (ISBN 0-948385-32-4)
The Ah So! Stories has turned out to be a karate bestseller. It is a similar book to Uchi Deshi and the Master in its content but this time the principal character is a young boy learning the art of karate and about life in general from his wise old Master. This book is a really superb read, for the young and not so young alike, and many instructors have actually used this book to read to their youngsters at the beginning or at the end of lessons. The philosophy of the book is very easy to read and to digest and is a superb learning tool for the martial arts and life in general.

The Little Book of Seishinkai
Published by eMPi Publishing
All a student needs to know about Seishinkai and indeed Shotokan karate as a whole. The book includes the syllabus, an in-depth glossary, explanations of Shotokan maxims, and a history of Shotokan karate and of SSKI in general. An extremely interesting book that is a good read for all Shotokan practitioners and not just for members of Seishinkai. The Little Book of Seishinkai is now in its fourth reprint.

Nunchaku

Published by eMPi Publishing

All you would ever need to know about this dynamic Okinawan weapon, including a history of the weapon, care of the weapon and nunchaku and the law. There is a glossary and in-depth explanations of the many striking, blocking, choking and swinging techniques. This book also contains a structured syllabus for the ETNA (English Traditional Nunchaku Association) belt system.

Wild Oats

Published by eMPi Publishing (ISBN 0-9519835-1-2)

This book incorporates the unexpurgated version of Wild Oats in Cornwall and the new book about Flip and the dreaded Grimble and their many new adventures in London, Wild Oats in Smoke.

'The many hilarious adventures of Grimble and Flip – a must read book for the lads! I enjoy a cracking story and this is nothing like a cracking story. It's better than that! Wild Oats kept me laughing. I read it in one afternoon!'

Richard La Plante

'I thoroughly enjoyed writing this book and all I hope is that it makes people laugh. I don't particularly want to be Shakespeare or Dickens. They're both dead!'

Malcolm Phipps